CW01497643

TALES OF THE SUBURBS

'From New Addington to New Malden, from Croydon to Crawley, from Torquay to Tunbridge Wells, John Grindrod's resourcefully assembled collection of very human stories – often inspiring, occasionally dark, never sentimental – breaks new ground and adds an invaluable dimension to our understanding of modern suburbia.' David Kynaston, author of *Austerity Britain*

'Grindrod is one of the best chroniclers of British life, his storytelling so subtly revealing, his observations astute and often laugh-out-loud funny. *Tales of the Suburbs* skilfully manages to be two wonderful things: an essential work of social history and a moving trek through the memories and minutiae of so many vital lives.' Jude Rogers, author of *The Sound of Being Human*

'The patchwork of captivating stories that make up *Tales of the Suburbs* show that it was no queer wasteland beyond Britain's urban centres. Stretching back more than a century, we see how suburban development was entangled with changing understanding and experiences of LGBTQ+ life. And we see too that whilst they might be by-words in convention and conformity, suburbs across the country in fact nurtured and accommodated queer difference. Indeed, it was perhaps the polite indifference and tacit knowledge that allowed it to flourish. Grindrod's expert storytelling reminds us of the diversity in our midst, and also how age, family, class, race, wealth and poverty matter to the ways queer lives are lived.' Professor Matt Cook, co-author of *Queer Beyond London*

Concretopia: A Journey Around the Rebuilding of Postwar Britain

Outskirts: Living Life on the Edge of the Green Belt

Iconicon: A Journey Around the Landmark Buildings of Contemporary Britain

TALES OF THE SUBURBS

LGBTQ+ Lives Behind Net Curtains

John Grindrod

faber

First published in 2026
by Faber & Faber Limited
The Bindery, 51 Hatton Garden
London EC1N 8HN

Typeset by Faber & Faber Limited
Printed and bound in the UK by CPI Group (UK) Ltd, Croydon, CR0 4YY

*Some names and details have been changed to
protect the privacy of individuals*

A CIP record for this book
is available from the British Library

ISBN 978–0–571–38286–6

Printed and bound in the UK on FSC® certified paper in line with our continuing
commitment to ethical business practices, sustainability and the environment.
For further information see faber.co.uk/environmental-policy

Our authorised representative in the EU for product safety is
Easy Access System Europe, Mustamäe tee 50, 10621 Tallinn, Estonia
gpsr.requests@easproject.com

2 4 6 8 10 9 7 5 3 1

For Lily and Daisy.

And for all LGBTQ+ suburbanites,
past or present. There's a place for us.

CONTENTS

LET'S TAKE A RIDE
AN INTRODUCTION

We have gaybours. In our close in Milton Keynes a young couple have moved in, all loafers and Breton shirts. I've been really cool about it though. The first time I met one of them I was putting the bins out, and introduced myself by my partner's name. *Hi, I'm Adam*, I said, with confidence and a smile. *Adam*, he replied, with a micro-hesitation. He'd already met my partner the day before, and so in that moment we both knew that I was very much not called Adam. *Lovely to meet you.* I never used to get flustered when I lived in Vauxhall, where *everyone* was gay. But this felt different, somehow. More unexpected. A signal that something had changed since I last lived in the suburbs, decades ago. *How very twentieth century of me*, I thought. Another neighbour tells me she identifies as bi. It's practically Barbary Lane, if Armistead Maupin had located *Tales of the City* in a cul-de-sac in Buckinghamshire built by Persimmon. But there is a reason his celebrated novel is set in San Francisco, and why the city is central to the title. It's a story of escape to a place of transformation and new beginnings. Suburbs like mine are the prisons his characters have fled. They're the battles fought, the conventions broken, the memories overcome.

There's a place for us, goes Stephen Sondheim's opening lyric from that evergreen LGBTQ+ anthem 'Somewhere'. But with the best will in the world, I don't think he meant Milton Keynes. Or Wilmslow, Ruislip, Surbiton or, for that matter, Croydon, where I grew up. For many of us, the narrative of Bronski Beat's beloved 'Smalltown Boy' tells us everything about the gay community's complicated relationship with suburbia. It's a place where hetero-sexuality rules unchallenged, where physical and social abuse has been endured; a place where any hint of difference will not be tolerated; somewhere you'll never find a soulmate. But in my research for this book, in the conversations I have had with LGBTQ+ people from around the country talking about the sub-urbs they live in now or knew back then, a different story has emerged: tales that are messy and moving, awkward and absurd, uplifting and extraordinary, dark and strange.

In Britain, both LGBTQ+ people and suburbia have endured endless stereotyping, while inspiring many of our richest and most cherished works of popular culture. Think of the haunted Croydon of *All of Us Strangers* or the frosty Isle of Wight of *It's a Sin*; the claustrophobic suburban Tyneside of *Blue Jean* or *Pride*, where Bromley features so prominently one of the central charac-ters is even named after it. These dramas are relatively recent, but all look back to earlier times, where suburbia equals the bad old days. The resulting collisions usually end in some sort of explo-sion, gay people fleeing, the suburbs left to fester. But things have not stood still for either the suburbs or LGBTQ+ life. In the modern day, the diverse cast of characters of *Heartstopper* are trying to make a go of it in the dreamy streets of Kent. It might signal a generational shift in attitude – or just that they're all too young to get much of a say in where they live.

It's not all heartstrings and angst, of course. Perhaps one of the most significant things suburbia has brought to LGBTQ+ people is an irrepressible sense of camp. Houses dragged up to be something they're not, occupants caught forever in aspir-ational class anxiety. Signifiers of pretension, from misguided home décor to misapplied euphemistic language, have fuelled many a queer cabaret act, sitcom character or novel. Spotting and subverting its norms has given many of us a lot of joy, helping to redress the sense of oppression those norms have created. Its sharpest observers, from Alan Bennett to Victoria Wood, Caroline Aherne to Jack Rooke, have found their work endlessly replayed by generations of LGBTQ+ people glad to find others who can celebrate the absurdity of the everyday. Queer writers and artists have a complicated and semi-detached relationship with this symbol of hyper-normality. As far back as 1785, William Cowper, composer of 'Amazing Grace', was throwing shade in his poem 'London Suburbs', where suburban villas 'Delight the citizen, who, gasping there, Breathes clouds of dust, and calls it country air', and later, 'There, prison'd in a parlour snug and small, Like bottled wasps upon a southern wall'. Cowper's celibacy has cast him today as a queer figure of his age, 'what the world calls an old bachelor' was how he described it. A century later, in 1891, the decidedly un-celibate Oscar Wilde was similarly scathing, writing of the 'hideous suburbs of our vile cities'. His way of dealing with them was to ignore them. Think of one of his most famous creations, Ernest Worthing, caught playing Ernest in town and Jack in the country. It's a game where London is propriety and country is playtime – and vice versa. His life will be revealed as fatefully entwined with the Brighton railway line, but the dormitory towns en route – Croydon; Redhill; Haywards Heath – are neither city nor country, and of no interest to him or Wilde. The game bypasses the middle and working classes in their new estates, removed as it is from the mundane world of Metroland and mortgages. And it's a trope that long endures in LGBTQ+ writing: a decade after Wilde's death, E. M. Forster's novel *Howards End* dismisses the suburbs too, as an affront to the romantic ideal of the country and the city. Forster's next novel, *Maurice*, remains unpublished until after his death due to its gay themes, and again is played out in country estates and city bachelor pads. I can't be the only reader disappointed that the Penge mentioned in *Maurice* is a mansion in the Home Counties and not the South London suburb.

For many of my generation, the safe space for gay people was not just the city, it was the gay pub, bar or club. Somewhere where the rules were different from the outside world, a place that acted as a magical barrier against the pressures of the world beyond. Now many of those spaces are closing, and much as we are now encouraged to feel at home anywhere (regardless of whether that actually *is* the case), those venues will forever be a hugely important haven for generations of queer people. Meanwhile, to read many histories of Britain's LGBTQ+ past, you'd think that, historically, gay life has taken place only in delicious city centre anonymity or pampered country house seclusion. There are reasons for this beyond snobbery, mainly a scarcity of good records and the kind of people whose legacy gets to tell the story of our times. Male homosexuality was illegal in England and Wales until 1967 (and in Scotland and Northern Ireland until the 1980s); and until the advent of second-wave feminism in the 1970s, women's history was often ignored by the establishment figures who acted as gatekeepers for our national heritage. Stories of bi, trans or non-binary people crop up in a vanishingly small number of official archives, despite such stories going back as long as there has been human life. It has created a gap in our understanding of LGBTQ+ history. This is why I hope the tales in this book will be valuable. Records of LGBTQ+ suburban history are also elusive, and that has been one of the inspirations behind this project: to record the lives of people, and of these strange places, before those memories are lost to us. In meeting with dozens of interviewees and hearing many and varied experiences, I've been privileged to encounter different times, places, genders and sexualities, and to find out what all of these have to say about our suburban queer experience. Some of us have yearned for escape; others have transformed both themselves and the situation around them within the confines of the suburbs; some tales are remarkably singular, others feel universal. The tales also reflect a straight culture that has kept evolving, and perhaps has never been quite as wholly heterosexual as it might like to imagine. What I hope we have here are different ways of looking at the suburbs – places that have proven very good at watching us, and less comfortable with being seen back – and observing them through the eyes of people for whom these Acacia Avenues in mock-Tudor drag were never intended. As any gay person can tell you, visibility is a double-edged sword. We may want to be seen, but it's not always a safe or desirable aspiration. Sometimes invisibility is your friend too.

Here we have tales of families of all sorts, some lost, some found, some built entirely anew. Then there's the friendships and lovers, the formative experiences at school and work, the strange encounters, the gossip, the bullying and violence. There are mid-week gay nights in straight clubs, and friendly mods, punks and goths – so many goths! – whose subcultures have intersected with our suburban stories. (In writing this book I have been surprised how much the Venn diagram of suburban, queer and goth has overlapped. I recall one of my classmates in the mid-eighties saying that with my colourful bat-winged jumpers, yellow baseball boots and stripy trousers I dressed like a European exchange student, and they weren't wrong. Certainly, I was the anti-goth. If only I'd realised this whole other subculture existed, I would have made more of an effort to wear the one colour I owned nothing of – black.) And most of all, there are the transformations: of us, as we negotiate our way through this complicated environment of codes and control; and of the restless suburbs themselves, forever evolving from privet hedges and flying ducks to gas barbies and wicker hearts.

There are many stories I have not been able to record for this book, and I apologise for not tracking down, for example, inter-sex, asexual or aromantic suburban tales to tell. I can only hope that the existence of this book will open up more conversations, and many more memories will come to light. After all, this is just the start of a story. Added to that, our complicated relationship with suburbia is changing all the time, affected by everything from apps and equal marriage to anti-trans legislation. And because of that, the suburbs feel altered from the place I experi-enced growing up. So much of it is down to what we expect to see: while there was undoubtedly queer life going on around me, and alternative sexuality hinted at in the pampas grass and the rumours of swingers' parties, I was determined to see a vanilla straight world in the suburbs – until one day, I was not. But the question remains – is it a place for us?

I'm drinking cider in the beer garden of the Bird in Hand, a straight-run gay pub in Selhurst, South London. It's a summer evening in 1993, and only the second Croydon Area Gay Society meeting I've attended. At the first I didn't speak, and ran away as quickly as possible. This time, I'm determined to make a better go of it. For the most part the members of CAGS are twice my age, men born in the middle of the twentieth century who've seen different worlds come and go. Here, they mingle, squab-bling over who said what in a restaurant five years ago, taking the piss affectionately and not-so-affectionately, laughing generously at the minor absurdities of their everyday lives.

I sit on the edge of the group like a nephew who's tagged along, reeking of Lynx Africa and anxiety, and dressed like a jumble sale. That evening I get chatting to one friendly face, a man perhaps a decade older than me, with shaven head and biker leathers. Ben is eloquent, kind and warm, but also a little shy, which suits me fine. We're joined by the only other younger guy present, a blokey dentist in a Ben Sherman polo shirt who introduces himself confidently as Asim. I can tell right away that Ben is keen on Asim, and that this is part of an ongoing flirtation. Although to my confusion, Asim seems interested in talking to me. *Have you thought of getting your teeth fixed?* is his opening gambit. My poor dentistry is something usually best avoided, especially as flirtation, but Asim tramples confidently wherever he wants, serving Muslim dentist Grant Mitchell. *I could do you a deal.* I just nod.

I can sense Ben's hurt now Asim has focused on me. *There's nothing I can do about it*, I think. Most of my life takes this pattern, of feeling out of control – not exactly trapped in a runaway train, more sitting in the back of a Vauxhall Astra with the handbrake off, rolling slowly into a low wall. Asim invites me back to his, and the questions keep on coming as he tries to work me out. Questions edged with a kind of bafflement: I was making short films and wrote scripts? How was I going to make any money out of that? *Oh God*, I think. *This all feels very grown-up.* I'd come out to my parents five years ago, during an ad break in *Taggart*, but I'd not yet acknowledged I was an adult. Not for the first time, I wonder why I'm so poorly prepared to do something vaguely normal.

We arrive at what seems to me an alien thing: a large detached half-timbered 1930s house behind high hedges, far removed from the small council semi I've come from. Not all suburbs are equal, it seems. The car, the house, the hedge: I was in no doubt that dentistry paid. *Let's go in quietly, they may still be up*, he says. So I creep in, focusing on the 'quietly' bit and not really thinking about the rest of that sentence. He shows me where to hang my jacket, and we make our way stealthily down the hallway and through a rusticated door. The dining room is large, high-ceilinged, heavily draped and patterned, with a huge brick inglenook fireplace cascading down the wall. It's quite the statement, but it's not the focus of my attention. There are three figures huddled around an armchair. An older woman stands, hands resting on the shoulders of a younger one, who sits with a small girl clasped close. It's a peculiarly posed tableau, just a kitten away from a mawkish Victorian painting. How long have they been here like this, I wonder? I feel panic. Asim lets out a big sigh and ushers me to a small sofa. *This is my wife and her mother*, he says. The girl, presumably his daughter, doesn't get an introduction. Perhaps that's stretching his cognitive dissonance too far. *This is John.* He doesn't add *the creature who has come to destroy your lives*, but that's implicit. Somehow, I've gone from flirting with a hot dad in the pub to becoming the mistress in some heavy domestic melodrama with someone who has turned out to be an actual dad, with none of the fun bits in between.

I sit on the edge of the sofa like I'm doing Ibsen. Asim tries to keep it breezy. *I said I might bring someone back. John is going to be staying tonight, as I explained. We'll go up shortly. Coffee?* I don't speak. Has he pulled this trick before, I wonder, or am I the first lucky guy? Asim busies himself in the kitchen, talking loudly with the same confidence he displayed in the pub as he boils the kettle. To hear him, you'd think he was chatting about a tradesman he'd brought in to fix the skirting or a stranded neighbour who was having trouble with their Daihatsu. As the chatter continues, I see it's a way of managing his nerves, bringing together these two sides of himself: his married self, and this – surely? – newly acknowledged gay or bi self. All the while his family are silently watching me, the home-wrecking homosexual invited into their house like some kind of learning tool. It's admirable that no one has chased me from the house with a Tiffany-style lamp. *This is my wife. This is John.* For some reason that eludes me all these years later, I do not bolt for the door and run down the street screaming. I'm scared. I hadn't paid much attention while we were driving and I'm not sure where we are. Even so, I should surely get out, hunt down a bus, make some kind of effort to get home and leave this family to their soap opera plot twists. But I don't take the initiative, and instead sit there, pretending I'm invisible, while never having felt more seen.

When Asim asks me if I'm coming up to bed, I shake my head. It seems to break the spell. The room is suddenly animated with something other than resentment. His daughter is led yawning up to her room by her grandmother, leaving husband and wife to have a hushed argument in the kitchen, the latest instalment of an ongoing row that sounds like it has plenty more mileage yet. Eventually, having reheated the leftovers of their marriage, they call it a day too, and I'm left alone in the room, facing the most awkward sleepover of my life. I get a couple of hours of neck-cricking sleep on the sofa, and as first light creeps through the leaded windows, I feel released from my paralysis. Quietly, I let myself out, taking a walk through the cold streets of enormous houses. I'm not sure what to think of Asim. I feel a little traumatised, not least for the anguish I must have caused his family just by being there. But presumably he's going through all sorts of turmoil too? It can't be easy, a successful dentist with a wife and kid and an inglenook fireplace, trying to come out in his thirties. What's clear is that he needs someone more together than me to navigate this with. I wonder what Ben is up to. One thing is for sure, I'm now giving up all attempts to be grown up. I look at these conventional homes with their conventional cars and their conventional gardens, all trying to pretend that everything is fine. But this night has opened my eyes that the suburbs are the heartland of affairs and divorces, of unorthodox set-ups and unhappy marriages, swingers and 'arrangements'. I hurry home, a part of me marvelling that even here, in what seems the most ostentatiously conservative street in Croydon, things aren't so straightforward – or straight – after all.

In the twentieth century there's something isolating about being stuck out here, on the edge of big towns and cities, among all the other hidden lives. As a teenager, the escape routes from my house are slow buses with their meandering paths, watching the different sorts of same smudged through misted windows. From our house it goes fifties estate, sixties estate, comprehensive school, playing field, A-road, twenties semis, woodland, technical college, thirties villas, private school, Edwardian mansion blocks, Victorian houses and finally town centre and railway station, by which time I'd usually need McNuggets and a fizzy drink before I had the energy to push on. The sprawl seems designed to slow everything down, to enforce a soporific torpor, to suck the marrow out of bones. But there's something exciting about this near stasis too, where the resistance, the pushing back, exposes something almost illicit. Where loitering and looking can reveal more than the streets will admit. On the fifties estate, the maisonette where I'd had my first kiss with another man. In the woodland beside my A-level college, the cruising ground. On the bus, unexpected flirtations and violent obscenities. In the shopping centre, nods of recognition and secret trysts. On the high street, books and records telling stories of different lives and experiences. At the railway station, furtive glances on late trains. The same places but different, to be experienced as a Cold War spy, alert for moments of transgression and the spilling of secrets.

I was obviously queer. Not queer in the modern sense, that liberated and transcendent term for a whole constellation of experiences and lives. No, I was queer in the boorish fag-smoke-belched holler of it, in the feeble light entertainment cliché of it, in the seedy secretive shame of it. Not one of those kids that managed to hide it, either. I'm not sure I ever wanted to. Such was my immediate feeling of not wanting to be like the others, being queer was an efficient – if brutal – way of separating myself. As a teenager in the 1980s, fourteen or so, impatient at the cruel boys following me from the gates asking 'Johnny, Are You Queer, Boy?' like the old punk song but with none of the music. *Yes*, I turned and snapped, *I am queer*. Usually, it was impossible to get a reaction from me. Now, here I was, a safe broken open. Their howling laughter grew louder and more delighted. A few minutes later, and I was swallowing the words back down, full of denial. After all, at that point the queerest thing I felt I was capable of was learning the words to Divine's 'You Think You're a Man' from *Smash Hits* or failing to catch a ball.

So many of my gay experiences have been in the suburbs. Dates from small ads that took me out to semi-detached Pinner or the Morrisons café in Bishop's Stortford, trekking to provincial discos and pubs for their weekday gay night, night bus rides back to the outskirts with some poor unfortunate. Around the millennium, I lived in the decaying Victorian sprawl of South Croydon. Queer friends I'd met at arty LGBTQ+ club Duckie would come to visit, and there we'd plan adventures. In the next flat lived a glamorous lorry driver in mid-transition and her partner, their place packed out with so many racks of astonishing clothes there was barely any room to walk. For a time I dated a Brazilian guy round the corner, who took me along to queer

Sunday morning breakfasts with friends in the mock-Tudor wilds of Addiscombe. Each encounter a glimpse of a different sort of hidden suburb out on the edge of my experience.

And so exploring the suburbs has long been an obsession of mine. One of the people I spoke to for this book, Jack, is a fellow traveller. He wants to walk every street in London. He's been doing it for a decade now, and has seen a lot of the city: how the landscape changes as you leave the tightly packed streets around the centre, and how loosely doodled the twentieth century's suburbs feel beyond. He grew up in south-east London, amid the mock-Tudor and steep roofs of Mottingham. 'I have fond feelings about suburbia,' he tells me, never having moved far from his birthplace. Jack is bisexual, and his relationship with London, feeling part of both the urban mass and the edgelands beyond, has echoes of his sexuality too. 'You fancy girls, right?' he says, of his awakening. 'And so you go through exactly the same experiences that your friends are going through, because you're reading *FHM* and all of that stuff. But then you're like, *Oh, actually, I don't just fancy girls, I fancy the blokes in the perfume adverts between the* FHM *images.*' And now he's on a queer odyssey through our ever-changing suburbs, sparking off the strangeness and enjoying the different lives and places it reveals.

Camp Christmas was Channel 4's queer effort in 1993, a spoof of wholesome seasonal specials more usually hosted by Bing Crosby or Val Doonican. Much like the Asim adventure a few months before, I'm not sure what possessed me, as a befuddled young gay man, to think watching this with my parents would be a good idea. Perhaps it was an attempt to include them in my other life, and to help make it feel slightly less 'other'. It featured turns from the big queer names of the day: Lily Savage, Julian Clary, Martina Navratilova, John Fashanu. Pam St Clement – Pat from *EastEnders* – sang 'Nobody Loves a Fairy When She's Forty'. I tried to rewatch it recently on YouTube, and what at the time seemed a bit chaotic now seems completely baffling, a snapshot of a moment when the AIDS crisis and Section 28 were at their height, before the advent of civil partnerships and equal marriage. A fierce sense of insecurity and defensiveness hangs over the proceedings, of wagons being circled. The hosts – singers Melissa Etheridge and Andy Bell – struggle awkwardly with the format, while in a corner of the set an emaciated Derek Jarman – then just a couple of months before his death – rocks on a chair under a blanket. I guess what I hadn't appreciated when I suggested watching this with my folks was that it wasn't just a TV format that was being subverted, but the whole 'big hetero-fest' of family Christmas. *Family? Pah!* harrumphs stand-up Lea DeLaria, at the thought of spending time with them. *Don't you know that at your parents' house no one can hear you scream?* I laughed along, not feeling it, acutely aware of my folks sitting across from me. Later, she declares triumphantly, *I am not going home for the holidays – I'm spending it with my friends!* I could sense my mum bristling, not with indignation, but hurt. It was a strange kind of turnaround from how I'd felt watching so much television with them up until that point, all the stereotypes, spite and cruelty served up as light entertainment. Not their fault, of course, and the comments in *Camp Christmas* that did them down weren't mine either. *I hope you don't feel like that?* she asked. I'm not sure she believed my genuine denial.

It's easy to think that the story of LGBTQ+ people only begins when we are apart from family, of which suburbia is merely an extension. But of course, we all have roots, and as the world has changed in my lifetime many of us are now more accepted within our families, and understood as families in our own right. Neither of these things I saw coming when sitting there in the early nineties, squirming with awkwardness, caught between two worlds I had failed to reconcile: family and sexuality. The way most twentieth-century suburbs were built assumed a neatly gendered heterosexual world, and that assumption largely remains. And so for queer people they pose a constant dilemma: to come out or not. For all the empowerment it brings, coming out in the suburbs can be a frustrating business, because it's rarely something you'll do just the once. Instead, rather like circling endless roundabouts or being stuck in a particularly large ASDA, you'll keep seeing the same signs over and over again. The tentative enquiries. The blunt mislabelling. The excruciating awkwardness. Although, more often than not, the suburbs' most abundant natural resource – gossip – gets there before you do.

The story of LGBTQ+ people in the suburbs can never be an official history, because it was never meant to happen here. According to lore, cities are the places that attract us, because only there can we find enough numbers to make any form of queer solidarity viable. But even a quick scan of Grindr or Bumble reveals that despite all of suburbia's best efforts, gay people are not simply being born and raised here, but are increasingly choosing to stay here too. As the interviews in this book show, for every historical certainty we have taken at face value, there are lived experiences that tell of something completely different: families more accepting; neighbours more supportive; subcultures more established; LGBTQ+ people more out. Of course, we must not assume that the progress of many is felt universally. For significant numbers of gay, lesbian, bisexual, transgender, queer, non-binary, intersex or asexual people, the suburbs are just one part of a world that doesn't yet feel safe or welcoming. Supreme Court rulings in 2025 have undermined the legal standing of trans and non-binary people, a blow for all LGBTQ+ folk, showing that progress is not a one-way process but must be fought for by each generation.

The twentieth century is when the rules for suburbia and modern LGBTQ+ culture were set. The twenty-first has completely rewritten them. Not just because of our interconnected world, the advent of civil partnerships and equal marriage, or the fight for trans rights, but also through circumstantial changes, from working from home to the decline of the queer venue. Now that work and leisure are no longer the preserve of the city, the suburbs feel closer to urban life, and so this book focuses more on the time before that change, capturing stories of LGBTQ+ people's lives before that already distant twentieth-century experience begins to fade in our memories.

The people I've spoken to for this book hail from around the country, and their extraordinary range of experiences illuminates what it has been like living in the suburbs: of navigating neighbourhoods meant to provide for one sort of experience, and often having lived counter to that. Some of these tales are celebrations of these places and lives, others are painful and hard to hear. Most are a mixture of both. All of them are a reminder of how, no matter the circumstances we find ourselves in, acknowledging our difference gives us a unique perspective on who we are and where we live. And honouring those perspectives is how we best navigate through these cul-de-sacs and avenues.

On the edge of the City of London, an enormous rainbow flag hangs above commuters pouring from Liverpool Street Station. It announces the Bishopsgate Institute, through whose ornate Arts and Crafts doorway I step one spring morning in 2022. Everything about this place feels a little magical, a secret survivor from another age, like encountering a suffragette chained to a Lime bike or a music hall drag artiste having a quick sherry outside the Tesco Express. Its long corridors, like the arteries of a Victorian hospital, lead to the sunken rear of the building, where sits an astonishing archive. For many years it was known for its peerless documentation of working-class life, but more recently another aspect of its work has helped sustain it. A vast assortment of queer material from personal libraries and private stashes, donated gradually over decades, has been collected by Stef Dickers, Special Collections and Archives Manager, and his team. The first thing I see is a massive pile of boxes and crates stacked just inside the door. Hundreds of books, letters, scrapbooks, journals, flyers and magazines – so many magazines – have just been delivered, to be sorted through, a donation of someone's cherished treasures to the archive, joining others on every flavour of LGBTQ+ life produced in the last century. Fresh ghosts for the shelves, a few more of the gaps in our history filled in.

I tell the smiling librarian on the desk I'm looking for material on LGBTQ+ lives in suburbia. That does for the smile, replaced by a momentary look of panic that says this isn't going to be straightforward. But they're patient and helpful, and I'm shown the database, given a pencil and some request slips, and left to explore. My initial searches don't get me very far. Anything relating to the words 'suburb' or 'suburbia' has a decidedly heterosexual hue. But it's when I type in my birthplace of Croydon that things start to look up. The database reveals a collection of newsletters from CAGS, the Croydon Area Gay Society, dating from the 1970s to the 1990s. Despite attending a couple of their events, I'd completely forgotten about its existence until this moment. I fill in my slip with the regulation pencil and go back to the desk. The librarian heads off, and I hear Stef's jovial voice from behind the scenes: *You see, I told you someone would ask for them eventually.*

Five minutes later, a box of A5 photocopied newsletters is plonked on my desk. Reading them is not just time travel, it's taking me to a different place too, away from the heart of the metropolis and out to the semi-detached streets of my childhood, taking me to moments I can't quite believe ever happened there. Some are serious, some trivial, but all are deeply Croydon and entirely gay. What catches my eye immediately are the lists of events. A newsletter from 1981 offers up *Coffee 'n' chat at Arthur's (Epsom) from 8pm.* Below that there's the group's monthly meeting at a Unitarian church hall, *Tea and Symphony – music tea and chat at Graham's.* 'Chat' is the word that binds these events, it seems. Next there's *Women-only coffee evening at Jane's from 8pm.* I pick up handfuls of newsletters, hunting out more of these listings. *Treasure Hunt in the Surrey Hills starting on Epsom Downs, with a picnic and 2 country houses en route.* A 1983 edition reveals, *We are now in contact with most of the other gay groups in the surrounding area . . . but we haven't managed to contact the Streatham Group yet (we think it's called SAGG).*

The curious details of a bygone suburbia that illuminate these newsletters help form the spine of this book. We'll keep returning to the world of CAGS, those pioneers creating their semi-detached network, one far removed from both the inter-war country house set, whose exploits are detailed in books such as Radclyffe Hall's *The Well of Loneliness* or Evelyn Waugh's *Brideshead Revisited*, and the connections formed today through social media and dating apps. Their lives and lifestyle do not, of course, represent a full picture of suburban LGBTQ+ life in the second half of the twentieth century, being largely white, male, middle-aged and middle-class. But they do offer some insights into an ephemeral aspect of social history, a lost world of typewritten trivia, optimistic explorations and enduring camaraderie. And I hope the interviews I have conducted help broaden that story out, to other lives and experiences far beyond the ones catalogued in these flimsy photocopied pamphlets.

The discovery of CAGS sets me off on other searches, new request slips, more boxes of typewritten news sheets. The Kingston and Richmond group sounds pretty active: *KRAGS announce that their regular pub evening is at the Royal Charter, Maple Road, Surbiton every Wednesday from 9pm*, and *Ice skating evening at Richmond Ice Rink*. And now the search is connecting up all around the capital. *Gay treasure hunt in Tunbridge Wells with prizes*; *Annual summer tea party in Farnham. Bring a bottle. Raffle, book and video stalls, tombola, barbecue, etc. Then off to the Jolly Sailor pub after*; *Surrey Area Gay Organisation's Bluebell Railway trip*; *Inter-group bowling at Tolworth*. Here is a cosy, gossipy, fun side of suburban LGBTQ+ life, one that runs parallel to the sitcoms of the day and yet – with a couple of not very notable exceptions – was totally absent from them. So when in a Croydon edition from 1983 I find an announcement – *Our apologies for the confusion in last month's newsletter about the date of the whist drive* – it's impossible to picture it without seeing someone dragged up as Margo from *The Good Life* in kaftan and turban, dictating down the telephone to some poor soul at the Pony Club or the Music Society. As I pack up for the day, I must look considerably cheerier than when I arrived. *See you again soon!* calls the librarian on the desk. *Don't worry*, I say. *There's no escape.*

This is it, I think. *We're off!*

THE SOUTHBOURNE IDENTITY

Granny Grimble and Granny Grunt are taking a walk to the sweet shop. In ancient heavy woollen coats that smell of mothballs they shuffle along, nodding and waving to smiling neighbours as they pass. A familiar sight in this seaside suburb in the late 1960s, they're stumbling in shoes that are too big and pushing back hats as they fall over their faces. The bell tinkles on the newsagent's door, and the shopkeeper catches sight of them, the two barely higher than the counter. He's been known to give them sherbet dips for free, and today is no exception. The grannies leave delighted, scoffing their sweets on the way back, hats askew. Junior-school boys John and his best friend Robert regularly dress up in frocks and coats found in a wardrobe at John's house. Granny Grimble and Granny Grunt have been cheering the street for the last few months. Everybody knows the grannies. One day, John's mum says, *Can you and Robert go and see Auntie Margaret?* Margaret is their neighbour, auntie in name only. John prepares to go and collect Robert, but his mum stops him. *No, no,* she says, *I want you to dress up, because Margaret loves seeing you as Granny Grimble and Granny Grunt.* Apparently, now they're taking requests. A few years hence, teenage John will spend four evenings a week round Auntie Margaret's watching *Crossroads* – a show, he suspects later, that no heterosexual male has ever expressed an interest in. These days, seaside suburbs in Dorset are heavily gentrified, the stucco and brick painted, pots of spiky yuccas in front of key safes. Once, this had been the piggeries of Tuckton Farm. Now it's Southbourne, a clifftop suburb of Bournemouth, briefly fashionable around the turn of the twentieth century as a health resort, and by the time of John's youth a hushed pedestrian world. Even in the stifling silence of those grey streets, John is not going to remain quiet. The grannies are just the beginning.

Granny Grunt and Granny Grimble's outfits are inherited from John's beloved grandmother, who has recently died. His family are clearing out her bungalow, the grey smudge of television news chattering away in a corner. He catches his dad saying to his mum, *Your mother wouldn't have approved of that.* John, who is seven years old, finds his ears pricking up. He knows, somehow, that whatever is on the television applies to him. The Sexual Offences Act 1967 has just been passed, legalising sex between men over the age of twenty-one. And much as John knows he's connected to this story in some indefinable way, he's also horrified that his grandmother would have disapproved. It's a first glimmering that he does not fit in. Even the people he loves may reject him. But there is no hiding it. John, the middle child of five, soon begins to realise he won't need to tell his family. 'I didn't have to come out,' John tells me. 'I was very lucky because it was bloody obvious to my mother when I was growing up. And my mother was someone who never said anything about important things, so you couldn't have a conversation with my mother about being gay or anything really. You never went to my mother with any problems. She was the last person you would. She wasn't able to love us. You know, she gave us food and values and standards. But she couldn't hug her children. But it was obvious without any words being spoken. I was accepted as a little gay boy.' His father is an Edwardian in spirit: shiny shoes, natty suits, tennis whites. John's parents split up when he's a teenager.

Not having to come out might seem a blessing, but for John it's just as stifling as if nobody knew. Because now it remains unspoken in a different way, impossible to broach because it's been decided it's unnecessary. Unnecessary for everyone else, that is. John longs to talk to somebody about his open secret, away from the bullies in class. There is a hairdresser's shop on the corner he passes every day on his walk to school. One of his sisters had gone to school with the hairdresser, and she tells John he's queer. *Queer* is the word for it then, away from the stuffiness of *homosexual*, and before *gay* has become a more widely recognised term thanks in part to the Gay Liberation Front and the first Gay Pride marches in the early 1970s. Each time John walks by the hairdresser's he longs to be acknowledged, just another lonely queer. One day, when he's fifteen, he plucks up the courage – or breaks, depending on how you look at it – and pens a note to the hairdresser. *Dear Stephen, I am queer too. I'm Jill's brother. You probably know me. I come by your shop every day. I'm really lonely. Please help me. John.* And he leaves a telephone number for Stephen to call. He puts the note through the letterbox in the hairdresser's and heads home, full of excitement and anxiety that he has finally done something, made contact with someone. And very quickly Stephen does call him up, but it's in a white-hot fury. *How DARE you write that note to me!* he shouts. *How DARE you insinuate that I am queer! I'm gonna tell your sister!* John begs him not to, pleading and pleading and pleading. The boy who is already out, but who is trapped by its unspoken consequences. 'It was awful,' says John. 'This poor shy fifteen-year-old boy reaching out for help.' He manages to calm Stephen down and the hairdresser doesn't tell his sister, and his unspoken open secret remains.

It's the *TV Times* that helps rescue John. It's 1974, and his classmates are shouting at him, *You queer bastard, you queer cunt, you bender.* And he says, *Yes,* makes faces, adopts a snooty attitude, turns away, superior. 'I wasn't just gay,' he explains. 'I was *weird.*' A sex education book, given to him by his father in lieu of The Talk, has furnished him with the bare facts of homosexuality. He reads it over and over, and finds it unexpectedly positive and non-judgemental. But this acceptance of his sexuality just causes more bullying. Most days he dashes home at the end of school so he can gulp down a glass of water, his throat cracked and dry because he hasn't spoken a single word all day. Today he picks up the *TV Times* and flicks to his favourite page, Katie Boyle's agony aunt column. He pores over tales of unhappy marriages, anxious parents, bereavements, secret affairs. This week, to his astonishment, she publishes a letter from a reader about their closeted homosexuality and feelings of isolation. And she responds with the number of Icebreakers, a new telephone service in the 1970s to help connect lonely LGBTQ+ people, as we absolutely were not called then, to groups locally. So John sneaks out to a nearby phone box and calls Icebreakers. And they give out the number of the local chapter of the Campaign for Homosexual Equality, or CHE. So he rings up and speaks to Tommy, the convener of the group, and they meet up, skinny schoolboy and sensible middle-aged man. Tommy is in his fifties, and he seems to get John's obsession with *Crossroads*, which is almost as much of a relief for the teenager as being able to talk about his sexuality. In a pause while John is sharing his troubles they discuss the possibility of having sex, but John politely declines, and the topic is never raised again. But Tommy does invite John to join the monthly CHE meetings. John is by far the youngest there, amazed by this secret world of gay adults, seven or so of them meeting at the B&B, chatting and feeling a little awkward. One man, a retired solicitor, is seventy-one and travels the thirty miles from Dorchester. To help aid the cause of homosexual equality, at the end of each meeting Tommy sets up a cine projector and shows a porn film. 'It fizzled into my brain like a drug at that age, and I can still remember the first film I saw,' says John.

Still, he has to keep the open secret quiet at home. His family house is pebbledashed, like an upturned beach. John, now sixteen, sneaks up the side alley from his domain – a caravan nestled in the back garden. It's getting dark. His dad's is the sole car parked on the entire road. John has only just started to explore more widely, to travel the three miles into Bournemouth, thanks to his regular CHE meetings. And then one of his sisters tells him of a club, Gigi's, in Bournemouth Triangle. He borrows her jewellery, a chain with a dangling silver teapot that bounces on his chest as he minces, projecting an ostentatiously camp walk in the hope it will send a signal to his neighbours, the world: here is a gay boy, without him yet being able to speak it. 'And I thought that's what you had to do,' he recalls, head in hands. 'I'm almost embarrassed now because that wasn't me. I wasn't naturally that camp, you know. I'm *fey*. I'm the first to admit that I'm not the most masculine, but I put on a persona for the neighbours.' Larry Grayson and John Inman, the gay icons of 1975, middle-aged men with grey hair and wide collars, eyes rolling, lips pursed, projected a joyful and silly but also somewhat dusty and domesticated version of theatrical camp from another era onto a new generation. It was like rock 'n' roll Bowie and pop art Hockney had never happened. The two acts were warm, beloved, and hugely visible features in living rooms across the nation. Both steadfastly refused to come out at the time. *Gay News* thought Grayson's appointment as the new host of the BBC's *Generation Game* 'the worst possible thing that could happen to gay rights on television'. Grayson, with his attachment to life in the suburbs of Nuneaton, embodied a kind of cosy camp that was politically inconvenient for the progressive politics of the seventies, a visibility that was thought by campaigner Peter

Tatchell to be confirming rather than challenging prejudice. But while Grayson was happy to embrace a rather prudish distaste for gay culture, Inman did move with the times, entering into a civil partnership in 2005 with Ron Lynch, the man who'd shared his life for thirty-three years – Mr Humphries no longer free.

John meets members of the CHE group at the Triangle, in the centre of the hotel district in Bournemouth, and they nervously look both ways, knock on the door of Gigi's and wait. The grille opens, eyes peer out, recognise the group and let them in. Someone signs John in, as he's underage. It's crowded and noisy, long hair, tight shirts and wide trousers, four-to-the-floor disco music thumping away, the hits of 1975: 'Love to Love You Baby'; 'Jive Talkin''; 'I Wanna Dance wit' Choo'. 'I can remember dancing the first time on the dance floor, and I'm gay. I'm alive. I'm happy.' He quickly realises there are only two of them in the club under thirty, him and a lad called Paul, who, it turns out, is already dating one of the older guys there, a rich businessman from Fordingbridge who everyone refers to as 'Lady Fordingbridge'. The word is he throws extravagant parties involving top politicians and famous pop stars, back at his large, secluded house. In John's time at Gigi's there will be numerous police raids, men hauled out for being drunk and disorderly – *in a club!* – or for wearing lipstick. When the police steam in, teenage John has to hide in the toilets. One time he bumps into Stephen, the hairdresser who had so angrily denied he was queer and shouted at him down the phone. *Oh, I'm here for the music,* says the hairdresser quickly. Even here, in a gay club, it's impossible for him to let his guard down. Later, leaving is, if anything, more hair-raising than entering. Who's going to see John coming out of a famous local gay club? Who will they tell? Is there someone lurking to attack him? He's glad to jump in a taxi and feel safe on his way back to the inert streets of Southbourne.

On his second visit to Gigi's, John meets Andrew – *poor boring Andrew*, as John calls him now – who is thirty-five. They remain a couple for five years. 'I longed for someone my own age to have sex with,' says John. 'I only really fancied people my age. But I was stuck with *An-drew* – *thiiirty-five*. He was kind and he protected me for five years. But he was the first man that ever looked at me. So I just went with him, it was like an automatic thing. When I look back, *totally* inappropriate. Totally wrong for me, Andrew was, but he kept me safe for five years, and I could have got picked up by some very unscrupulous people if I think about it. I'm aware that I'm talking as if I was this sort of vulnerable . . . Well, I was, wasn't I? I was a vulnerable young person in this world, mixed up with all sorts of nice people, dodgy people . . .' After all the unspoken bullying, the friendless years at school, his mother is delighted when he starts to receive phone calls. Soon after, she finds the two of them in his bed, and her reaction is immediate: she brings them tea and toast. 'She could have just called the police in shame, but she didn't. Her sixteen-year-old son in bed with a thirty-five-year-old man. I mean, amazing, in suburbia.'

By 1978, John is a healthcare auxiliary and lives in a bedsit behind Southbourne's only health food store. From his window he can see all manner of oddly dressed people sitting in circles, meditating or smoking something in the back room of the shop. And rather than the regulars at Gigi's or boring Andrew's boring friends, here people seem to be much more appealing. Hippies. Friends of the Earth. Southbourne's very own counter-culture, but another elderly one: the youngest members in their fifties, many a good thirty or more years older than that. And instead of the gay bars of the Triangle, John begins to hang out at the shop. They accept him straight away. He becomes a vegan, studies Rajneesh meditation, travels to India and returns, replacing the affected camp of his youth with a newly adopted identity: full yogic drag, if anything even more challenging on the quiet streets of Southbourne. One day he walks to work at Christchurch Hospital in bare feet. 'So I started to self-identify as an eccentric,' he says. 'I've lived like that ever since. I feel more comfortable as an eccentric than a conventional Southbourne boy.'

By the early 1980s, John is living with a new boyfriend in the centre of busy Bournemouth, where they practise noisy Rajneesh meditation – dancing, stomping and shouting – which infuriates the neighbours. Unlike Southbourne, here is a concentrated pocket of gay and bisexual men, increasingly out in the bars and clubs. It's here he develops a new obsession: cruising. The town's lushly planted gardens that run down almost to the sea are a well-known spot for it, and John finds himself there most nights, caught in yet another subculture he finds slightly ludicrous. Very soon he's cursing the same old faces week in week out, men familiar with every nook and cranny of the gardens, the different trees nicknamed *cubicles* by the clientele. *Oh, I just met this nice guy in cubicle seven.* Tired faces, until holiday season hits. Suddenly, the town is full of newcomers who have stumbled across the gardens, or have been recommended them by fellow travellers. The tide of tourists comes in and out, the men in the gardens teeming and thinned by the seasons and then, as the 1980s progress, by the devastating effect of AIDS on the gay population. Then finally, one day in 1994, John returns home after an unsuccessful night seeing the same men he has known for years, and realises he has become one of those old faces he used to mock. And so he decides this is the moment to move on.

While gay men are beginning to populate urban areas like Manchester, Brighton and Soho in ever greater numbers, John moves out to the country town of Dorchester, to retrain in horticulture. 'I went in the closet when I moved to Dorchester,' he tells me. The boy who'd never had to come out going in the opposite direction to traffic yet again. All these years he'd hoped to go back into education, but the bullying he'd encountered at school has given him a fear of young people. He isn't sure how accepting the students in this college would be if they knew. And so he spends a year keeping his sexuality quiet from his housemates and fellow students. 'But one guy apparently was telling another guy in the house, he was taking the piss out of my voice. He told me one day, and I didn't like that. And I thought, *Oh gosh, so there's that.* That felt like homophobia. He'd said to him' – and John adopts an exaggerated camp voice – '*Oh, John, he talks like this!* You know, I was shocked because I thought I was hiding it so well. So I don't think I did a very good job of being in the closet.' It is a lonely time, away from friends and trying not to be the eccentric he'd identified as long ago.

It's there that John is diagnosed HIV positive. It's the mid-nineties, years before breakthroughs in combination therapy, and there is little medical hope for those with HIV. He's in Dorchester, surrounded by people he barely knows and doesn't trust. He's assigned a social worker and a buddy from the charity Body Positive to help him through the shock of it, and to help him accept the bald facts. 'I was gonna die,' he says, matter-of-factly. 'There was no treatment. I was taken to see the hospice in Dorchester. And I was shown where – I mean, I agreed to this, I wasn't forced – they said, *Would you like to go?* I said, *Oh, yeah*, I said, *I used to work with terminally ill people.* So they showed me the actual room where my body would be laid out.' There is still soil beneath his nails from where he's been planting and cultivating. Now here he stands, facing the cold facts of his death, in the same way that he has faced those of his life. A stark fate for a thirty-five-year-old, in the prosaic reality of the hospice mortuary.

Even then, in the darkest moments, John feels no stigma about HIV. It is life, it is death. He has been practising transcendental meditation for years, and now it appears to have a purpose. But those higher states of consciousness do not appear to have lifted those around him. John tells a guy about his diagnosis, who jumps out of bed screaming. And so John throws him out, naked in the rain, hurling his clothes after him from the upstairs window. He has no time for this any more. The bad behaviour, the prejudice, the bullying, the secrets. But eventually medicine catches up with him, from trials of AZT in the 1990s to modern antiretroviral drugs. Now, three decades later, John is one of those rare survivors of the worst days. And he's still growing things. He's finding new communities to accept his eccentricities in ever smaller towns. And he's performing on stage with a drama group, dressing up as he did when he was a boy, when Granny Grimble and Granny Grunt walked the streets of Southbourne, fizzing with sherbet and hope.

The clock ticks slowly towards closing time, and Norman is day-dreaming. It's 1916, and he's a young man toiling in a shop in Upper Norwood, the South London suburb where Sherlock Holmes novels and the impressionist paintings of Camille Pissarro were created a generation or two before. The grand villas were built for folk who'd fled the city to new houses that were once on the fringes, near green fields and away from the factories and the smoke. Norman knows it wasn't built for people like him. Upper Norwood, once part of the Great North Wood, is now just another suburb pulled in by the tendrils of the city. His grandparents' generation would have cluttered these homes with fans and ferns, aspidistras and alabaster, in an attempt to project an artistic sensibility, creating instead the kind of camp extravagance so recognisable as a rich source of snark in the work of Oscar Wilde. But by 1916 that world is long gone. Many of the young men are away at war, some killed in action. These families are facing a new reality of uncertainty and grief.

At his counter on the high street Norman is thinking not of that conflict, but of homosexual sex. It's an awakening he's reached partly with the help of utopian socialist Edward Carpenter. A contemporary of Wilde, Carpenter lived through the hysteria of Wilde's trial, but rather than going underground continued publishing books on sexuality, as well as on his other obsessions, from vegetarianism to women's rights. Carpenter even built a liberated rural idyll at Millthorpe in Derbyshire, where he lives with his long-time partner George Merrill, one of a line of working-class men he's fetishised. In a world of reactionary homophobia, Carpenter's books, such as *Homogenic Love and Its Place in a Free Society*, from 1894, and *The Intermediate Sex*, written in 1908, have been a lifeline for many an educated queer. They've long piqued the interest of Norman, who once even met his hero, the memory a treasured one. As another day of South London shop work drags to a close and the anxieties of the age buzz away in the background, he decides, what the hell, he'll visit Carpenter again. And so Norman makes his pilgrimage, from the heart of respectable suburbia to a gay rural utopia. It thrills the young shopkeeper. 'It was in the garden that Merrill kissed me,' Norman tells the researcher Jeffrey Weeks in an interview decades later. 'I must have only been twenty-one. Not good looking. I was rather shocked, owing to my loveless early life. I didn't know anything about kissing.'[1] The year before, a similar situation with George Merrill and the novelist E. M. Forster would inspire *Maurice*, a gay love story that will remain unpublished for over five decades, thanks to its themes of homosexual love and hot gardeners. (It's interesting that both Forster and Norman seem to see Merrill as Carpenter's gardener first and his lover second, because alongside sexuality, class appears to be a love that dare not speak its name.)

Edward Carpenter's books on socialism, anarchy and sexuality influence a generation of writers and thinkers, and not always the obvious ones. There's Arts and Crafts architect Raymond Unwin for one, a frequent visitor to Millthorpe much taken by Carpenter's lifestyle, which collides class and upturns social conventions in an environment the writer characterises as 'the simple life'. It's something that illuminates Unwin's work, and when the opportunity comes for him to help plan the first Garden City at Letchworth, he recreates the writer's idyll on a grand scale. With its homely bricks and mortar, generous lawns and hedges, his design for the Garden City will in its turn be echoed in hundreds of suburban settlements around the country. The 1950s council house I grew up in, with its plain brick and gardens front and back, was a simplified version of Unwin's designs. Addington Garden City it had briefly been called, when work began in the 1930s. Stripped of Carpenter's radical ideology and sexuality, these new garden suburbs and their descendants offer not the revolutionary, classless way of life envisaged by Unwin, but rather a pervasive new kind of conformism and uniformity. Yet thanks to Unwin, the echo of Carpenter's words and Merrill's kisses are embedded in these places, just as symbols from pagan mythology were once built into country churches, linking our suburbs back to something more transgressive than en suites and Ocado.

LOSING CONTROL IN LITTLEOVER

The service is over. Cath watches from the back row as her mum and brother lead the mourners from the church. They don't catch her eye or that of her then wife as they walk past. As the elderly people begin to stand and file from their rows to follow, Cath has finally had enough. 'I was like, *Right, fuck this,*' she tells me. 'And as they came past, I went, *Hello, I'm John's daughter. This is my partner. I haven't seen him for twenty-six years, because he didn't approve of me, but I just want to introduce myself.*'

Even getting to be in the room at her father's funeral has been an ordeal. Given everything that has gone on with him, Cath is determined to be there. 'Even though I hadn't seen him for twenty-six years, I still wanted to go,' she says. 'He was still my dad.' She describes him as right-wing and dominant, her mum quietly submissive. He'd told her mum that if anyone finds out they have a lesbian daughter, their friends will spit and shout abuse, so she's terrified of having Cath there. Her uncle does all the negotiations on behalf of Cath, which go from *You can go but you've got to stand at the back* and *You can go but you can't say that you're John's daughter* to *You can't bring your wife* and finally *You can bring her, but you can't say she's your partner.* The funeral ends up being delayed because of all these conditions. 'It was a real surreal day,' she recalls. The church is filled with seventy-somethings, members of the social club where her dad played snooker and her mum bingo. As they pass Cath, they hear her introduce herself. The response is not the fire and brimstone her dad had threatened. 'I probably had two bad reactions,' she says.

There's one woman who harrumphs, another couple who defiantly reply, *Well, we liked your dad*, but the general response is a fairly low-key *Nice to meet you* and *We didn't know*. And rather than being ostracised, Cath ends up Facebook friends with two of her mum's mates. 'They're nice people,' she says.

The church is in Wroxham on the Norfolk Broads, where Cath's family move when she is eighteen. It's a large village of 1950s bungalows and deep verges, very different from the suburb of Derby where she's grown up. She's born in 1969 and initially lives in a 1930s semi in Littleover in Derby with her older brother and mum and dad. 'I knew there was something different,' she says. 'The girls at school, it was all Duran Duran. I *like* Duran Duran, but it was Bananarama for me, you know?' In their lounge, her dad has an armchair on which he places a wooden board. Stacked there are accounts for his self-employment – 'perish the thought if you actually touched them' – and he comes home at six each night to do his own books. Her mum does his typing, then rushes home to be there when the kids get in 'because what would the neighbours think?' Her mum has a spot on the settee where she knits or reads Agatha Christies. 'When I look at it now, it just looks so different,' says Cath. 'It's like that feeling that you were there but you weren't there. That you were living somebody else's life.'

As a teenager she sits in her room listening to The Smiths and Billy Bragg on the Walkman she saves up for, making her own necklaces and dressing like a hippie. Her parents are very over-protective, monitoring who she sees and what she does. But that doesn't stop Cath making friends with Julie, the school rebel. 'My parents didn't like her because she came from a broken home.' Cath wishes she were as cool as Julie, who graduates from doing forward rolls off the railings to getting a tattoo and riding motorbikes. One day they get the train together to Nottingham.

Oh, I like Carol Decker, says Julie, of the singer from T'Pau. *Yeah, I know you do,* says Cath. 'And she said, *No, I LIKE Carol Decker.* And of course, I'm like, *Oh, I don't know what she means . . .* And then she was like, *Okay! I FANCY CAROL DECKER!*' Cath knows she's attracted to women too, but can't admit it, even to her friend who is trying her best to come out. *Oh, yeah, yeah. Okay,* is all she can bring herself to say. *I'm bisexual,* says Julie. *Oh, are you?* returns Cath lightly. That evening, she mentions it to her mum. *Julie's bisexual.* Her mum is horrified. *Oh my God,* she says to Cath. *Don't tell your dad.* 'I can remember thinking to myself, as I was telling my mum and she's getting a bit horrified, *I'll never be able to tell her I feel a bit like that . . .*' Up until Julie comes out, Cath has never had any interactions with anyone she'd thought was gay. 'I don't know if it was just where I was; there was no evidence of it. So it must have been either very closeted or just didn't happen.' Back in 1984 she is watching the Wimbledon women's final, and Martina Navratilova wins. 'For one of her celebrations she went up and kissed [her partner] Judy,' recalls Cath. 'And I could feel my mum flinching.'

When they move from Derby to Wroxham, Cath gets her first job, working for the government's publisher HMSO. On her first day, sitting in reception, she's worried about being the only LGBTQ+ person in the office, anxious about who she's going to meet. *Hello, I'm Maaaartin!* trills the man sent to meet her, who, she soon learns, everyone calls Mary. 'And I remember thinking, *Phew, I'm never going to be the only gay here.*' She makes a friend in Wroxham who's married and having an affair with a man in Norwich. It's a curious lifeline for young Cath. Her friend frequently picks her up as cover and gives her a lift into the city, and while her mate's off 'having a bit of whatever', as Cath calls it, she can venture into The Roebuck, an LGBTQ+ pub, and have a drink away from the disapproving eyes of her parents. 'It was hardly a hive of activity,' she recalls, 'but you know you're not the only one.' She also visits Kings in Great Yarmouth, which has a gay disco out the back; she finds it a bit loud, never having been into clubbing. 'Blokes would be on the dance floor giving it the big 'un. And the women, I guess at the time people were a lot more stereotypical, but women propping up the bar, and I didn't fit into that world either really.' She remembers far more visibility for gay men than for women in those days. 'Older people such as me can remember the days of just not being visible in the same way,' she says. 'And whether you like it or not, we still live in a male-dominated world.'

Eventually, when Cath is twenty-three, she's determined to move away from the family home in Wroxham and into the suburbs of Norwich. But the only way her parents will let her leave is if she buys a house with her brother, *So that way I can keep an eye on you,* her dad says. Together they buy a Victorian terrace in the city, even though they don't really get on. At HMSO, one of the cleaners, Emma, catches Cath's eye, and she finds herself hanging around late at work to try to bump into her. One day she plucks up the courage and asks Emma, *Can we go for a drink or something when you finish?* That night, she ends up bringing her back to the house. 'And I remember I had a voucher for Delight, which was a margarine spread,' she tells me. 'And I was using it as a bookmark. And we were talking on the settee, and for some reason, I think I must have been sharing the book I was reading, and that fell out. And it had "Delight" on it. And I said to her, *You're a delight!*' She cringes and cracks up as she tells me this. '*So cheesy!* I was next to her on the settee, and she came up and kissed me. I was like, *Oh my God!*' Her smooth talking has paid off and they end up going out for eighteen months. When Emma stays over, Cath sometimes catches her brother out the window sneaking off to the phone box opposite to call their dad to tell him. By 1996, she's in a new relationship – one that will go on to last for thirteen years – when she goes back to Wroxham to celebrate her parents' wedding anniversary. It's then that all those calls catch up with her. *You either carry on with what you're doing,* her father threatens, *or you lose your family. You can't have both.* Cath tells him, *Look, I'm not prepared to give her up.* 'And he said, *Well, you can say goodbye to your family. You've got to decide what you want to do.* And I rang the following day to see how they were, and my dad said, *I told you no contact.* Put the phone down on me.' The next time she returns to her house, she discovers the locks have been changed. She's been kicked out. She can't even collect her clothes and belongings, and has to take a few days off because she has nothing to wear apart from the clothes she stands up in. About a week later, her family let her get her things. It's the last time she sees her dad.

All of these times feel so strange to Cath. Now she's finally back in touch with her mum, she finds little in the way of shared memories or experiences. Instead, the more she talks about it with her, the more she feels like she's watching someone else's version of her life. Her partner, Laura, gets Cath to talk about her feelings, all of those things she hasn't been able to properly express for years, all the things she was never able to say to her dad and her mum doesn't want to hear. It's painful and difficult, but also it's not what her life is now. 'We have a lot of fun in our relationship,' she tells me. 'I really hope that we can continue having that. We've got a dog together now. That's commitment.' Exorcising ghosts and moving on, now she has control of her life.

The commuters pour from the station, out into a suburb of a suburb. Serge coats, bowler hats, umbrellas, briefcases, evening papers rolled beneath arms or left in the carriage, leaves fluttering as the heavy doors slam. In the evening light stands a woman and her grown-up son: the Pratt family awaiting the return of the man of the house. 'As we stood there, a stream of men in dark suits and bowler hats went by us,' the son would later write. 'I thought, *I'll never be able to get into step with them.*'[2] Denis Pratt, then in his mid-twenties as the decade ticked over into the threadbare 1930s, is mourning his former life in Soho, Piccadilly and the West End, a life where he has reinvented himself as Quentin Crisp. The family has moved from a flat in Battersea out to Flackwell Heath, a Home Counties village on the outskirts of High Wycombe. For Quentin, it's 'like a desert on the edge of civilisation', where the only distraction is walking his mother's dog in the neighbouring fields. There, he's overcome by visions of his former life in the coffee houses of Old Compton Street, mirages shimmering beyond hedges of hawthorn and clouds of rosebay willowherb.

Seen backwards through the lens of the twenty-first century, Crisp – the celebrated Englishman in New York – is here an American in the Home Counties, a spirit adrift in a place he seems most alien. Yet it is also hard to imagine what other circumstances could have formed him, to have powered the battery of his lifelong opposition to convention. A brittle, waspish disdain for his contemporaries seems to amplify his desire for non-conformity, for self-expression. With his dyed hair, make-up, dandyish clothing and perfume, Crisp cuts an extraordinary figure in the city, let alone in the suburbs where he spends a surprisingly large portion of his life. For many years, people take his very being as a provocation, an excuse for pity or contempt, ridicule or disgust. Not just heterosexuals, of course, but many of his fellow gay men see his existence as a threat – advertising his sexuality in an era of secret codes and meeting places. He's constantly hassled by the police. That he weathers all of this so calmly is remarkable indeed.

A stellar second act beckons for Crisp, as his life – portrayed by John Hurt in the 1975 adaptation of his memoir *The Naked Civil Servant* – begins to be more widely appreciated and understood: embracing celebrity; moving to New York. Until then, he yo-yos uncomfortably between city and suburb. Firstly Sutton, then off to school in Staffordshire, then back to Sutton; off to a journalism course in London, then back to Sutton; a family move to Battersea, then back to the suburbs, only this time even further out, to High Wycombe. When he finally seems to have broken free for the city, he will still spend years as an artists' model, travelling back out to pose at art schools on the fringes of London, at Hornsey, Sidcup, Ealing, Richmond. Quentin Crisp may be a creation meant for the city, but he's forged from a long relationship with suburbia.

It begins on leafy Egmont Road, a street of large Edwardian villas and semis in Carshalton, built in a handsome muddle of tile hanging, red brick, render and half-timbering, Arts and Crafts style pursued with a manufacturer's relentlessness. Crisp likes to play down his family's circumstances, but when he's born the Pratt family has staff. He attributes their position to a reliance on debt, a precarious state that would alter his family's situation on numerous occasions. While his parents struggle to keep up with the Joneses, he famously quips that 'It was not until many years later when I lived alone that I realised how much cheaper it was to drag the Joneses down to my level.' Within the decade, they have moved to a smaller house across the road with no servants, such are the Pratt family's circumstances.

Quentin Crisp connects us back to an era very different from ours. Born on Christmas Day in 1908, he recalls seeing soldiers billeted to houses nearby during the First World War, suburbia as war zone. No matter how much he insists he's his own creation, he brings Edwardian flamboyance and the manners of those early years with him through his life. But he's quickly frustrated with the rules of gender and conformity, the men who seek to rid themselves of any trace of effeminacy, for whom suede shoes or anything longer than a short back and sides is suspicious. In stifling times, he's a rare reminder that there are other ways to live.

Yet it isn't the city that needs him. It's suburban art schools who keep him in business in the mid-century. Crisp recalls how the students relied heavily on the model turning up, because although there would be thousands of people living nearby, finding someone else to pose for them is an impossibility. 'In the suburbs, the non-arrival of a model was a disaster,' he wrote. 'A replacement could not possibly arrive until the middle of the day and by then the students, always on the boil, would have wrecked the place.' Crisp, it has to be said, is not an ideal model. He can't hold a pose, but instead improvises with increasing mania and abandon, hanging from the curtain rails or rolling across the floor. As the Second World War collides class and nationality in Britain, an edge of danger adds a spontaneity he has not seen before. On trains, men proposition him for sex. Suddenly, gay life is not just confined to Soho and Piccadilly. It's all around him, between stations. And Crisp isn't at all sure he likes it. Maybe he needs that suburban compartmentalisation as much as the rest of us after all.

Perhaps his greatest saviour is a love of absurdity. It's this that helps him explode the norms of the day and the conventions of his suburban upbringing. Given how long ago he came of age, you might have expected him to have been happy with being Quentin in town, Denis in the suburbs. But the beautiful thing is he felt able to be himself all of his long life, no matter how people treated him, and no matter the circumstances he found himself in. Not Denis, conforming to the quiet, paranoid norms of Egmont Road, but Quentin, transcending the mores and expectations of the day, and dragging his often ungrateful gay peers with him into the light.

HOME ALONE IN CARSHALTON

'Did you ever go to the Water Palace/TGI Friday that was supposedly sinking?' Elliot asks me. They're talking about the notorious nineties leisure park in Croydon, long since demolished. 'I remember going down that log flume after queueing for ages and just being, *Well, I'm gonna drown. This is it: this is death.* And I guess it's a bit like that. I can either sink or swim. You just have to go with the flow.' The story Elliot has been telling me, of their life in South London's outer suburbs and of struggling towards a non-binary identity, is filled with currents that have been slightly ahead of them, sweeping them along. *I'm not sure I'm quite ready for that*, Elliot is saying one moment, and the next, *Oh, I'm doing it now!*

Carshalton is where the journey begins for Elliot, at the other end of the century from Quentin Crisp. Their summary is brief but fair: 'You've got a big park, you've got a big road. That's the gist.' It's a place of high walls – some belonging to a vast girls' school, some to the park near the duck pond – which make the whole district feel oddly medieval. Back in the 1990s, the families in these big houses all seem the same to Elliot, the kids two years apart, the dads commuting up to London, the mums staying at home or working locally. But Elliot feels outside of all this from an early age. Their mother doesn't believe in gendered clothing or toys, which is handy as Elliot is always more drawn towards the ones aimed at boys. Elliot dresses up in boys' clothes, with their hair hidden, playing on the boys' football team. 'I was the only girl that they let play,' says Elliot. These are moments of joy shrouded by an overall discomfort of not belonging. That feeling is expressed as they walk around the playground at break-time, singing 'A Whole New World' from Disney's *Aladdin* to themselves, a song of escape and transformation, of love and friendship being sung by a lone child in a crowd.

Elliot's family move down the road to a slightly bigger semi, which is more than they can afford but a matter of status for their dad. At the end of the garden, Elliot and their sister dig up the bones of previous owners' pets, and indoors there are secrets buried too. Their dad has a drink problem, which he indulges in bouts with neighbours of an evening. 'So even though we presented as this sort of perfect, middle-class working family, actually, it was all very dark,' remembers Elliot. Their mum and dad would go out socialising, while Elliot and their sister would be left at home in the big suburban house, watching *Home Alone*. 'I never really thought of us as a unit,' says Elliot. 'It was always quite broken. But I knew I had to just pretend that everything was fine.'

What are you? a random kid asks Elliot one day as they're in the Whitgift Centre buying a bag. 'And I don't know,' says Elliot. 'And that feeling of shame . . . I think the shame weighed heavily right from the start. I knew I shouldn't feel this way.' Elliot has always felt like there is something nagging at them, lying just beyond their ability to express. Answers initially come from an unexpected source: Irish band Boyzone. *Oh, I love them all*, is Elliot's take. *They're all gorgeous, probably*. Best of all, they love cherubic Stephen Gately – almost as much as their collection of yo-yos. By putting a sticker of Gately on their favourite yo-yo, Elliot creates what might just be the most powerful talisman in the universe. But the power doesn't last long. When Gately is forced to come out by the *Sun*, Elliot feels acutely embarrassed by that sticker and stops using that yo-yo. It's their first brush with what being gay means, and it leaves its mark. Elliot knows they should be ashamed, but is not sure why.

The awakening, when it comes, arrives as a stab through the heart, courtesy of *Buffy the Vampire Slayer*. Elliot begins the series besotted with Angel, the brooding, handsome vampire, all long coats, cheekbones and fangs. By the third season, Elliot has started high school and is going through puberty, and suddenly Angel is old news. Elliot only has eyes for Eliza Dushku's kick-ass anti-hero, Faith. *She's fit. Why not? Who wouldn't?* None of those earlier feelings of negativity have attached themselves. And soon Elliot is meeting their first girlfriend, thanks to an online *Buffy* forum. They decide to meet away from the high walls of Carshalton and among the spiky latex cyber-bags and transgressive trousers of Camden Market. Elliot brings a couple of mates along in case their date is an actual vampire, or worse, boring, but it goes better than expected. The perfect first queer experience. Out here, away from their disintegrating family, Elliot briefly feels able to be themselves.

When Elliot's parents divorce, teenage hormones, together with the unguarded honesty of MSN Messenger, push things to a crisis. After a few heightened messages, Elliot and a volatile school friend get together. But when their friend mentions the relationship to an ex-boyfriend, in no time at all news travels round the frighteningly efficient teenage grapevine in the Croydon–Sutton borders. Brothers tell sisters, sisters tell friends, and suddenly everyone at Elliot's school knows. It doesn't go down well. One very Christian friend tells Elliot they're going to hell. Elliot's reaction is: *Cool, you're my friend, but okay.* Then, in an unexpected plot twist, Elliot's mum starts a relationship with the divorced man next door, and suddenly Elliot finds they have three cool new step-siblings. Their new goth stepsister introduces teenage Elliot to an alternative world hidden in the suburban landscape. The gateway is The Black Sheep in Croydon, a pub that Elliot remembers as 'this weird mix of lesbians and drug dealers and ska. I never really understood it. And I loved it.' At sixth form, new friendships develop and new worlds open. Elliot's first New Year's kiss is with a trans man. 'It was beautiful. I was so happy. We just talked about *Torchwood* and then snogged. I'd say before sixteen I didn't really know anybody who was gay or queer or anything. And then it was all just like *boom!*'

Back when they were fifteen, Elliot experimented with becoming hyper-feminised, wearing revealing tops and flirting with older men. But these precarious situations didn't make them feel any better or less confused. Back then, they even chose a more feminine version of their name. 'I changed it to Ellie. I was like, *No, it's Ellie. Everyone, call me that.* And then when I came out in 2020 as non-binary I was, *Can you call me Elliot? Because actually, I hate this.*' What bothers Elliot more than sexuality is their body. It's hard to say when those thoughts begin. 'I knew my chest really bothered me, but I didn't really know why. I just knew that it wasn't right.' It's only when they're in the second year of university in Brighton that they first encounter someone who is non-binary. Before that, the possibility has never occurred to them. 'I just remember being *Oh, but you're dating a man, how does that work?* I just didn't really get it. And I guess because I was just *Cool, you're non-binary, whatever*, I never really thought what that meant in terms of my own self, because I was so repressed that I just couldn't even look inside to see what was going on.' Though Elliot buys a chest binder at university, they struggle to understand where that impulse came from because there is so little about these feelings out there. 'I knew I wasn't a man. But I didn't know what I was.'

It's not until years later, when Elliot is in their thirties and furloughed for nine long months in the first Covid lockdown, that they finally have time to analyse what has been happening all their adult life. The catalyst comes in the form of that most 2020 of things, a podcast. One podcaster says they wish they'd get breast cancer so that they could have a mastectomy. *Oh my God, I've had that thought. What does that mean?* thinks Elliot. These are dark, desperate feelings. Three years later, Elliot has top surgery. With characteristic understatement, they describe the process as *quite tricky.* They didn't know anyone who'd had it, and they're not sure if it's the right thing. Having spent half their life trying to suppress their instincts, it's not easy now to trust them. People say, *Oh, you must feel really euphoric.* That's not Elliot's thing. The nurses have been expecting a bigger reaction. But Elliot can't hide how positive the transformation has been. They've been hunching for so long in an attempt to hide their body they're having to learn how to hold themselves differently, confidence growing from this transformation. Having spent so long not looking at themselves, it's a big deal to be able to say, *This is who I am.*

Coming out as non-binary to their work colleagues isn't easy, but they almost seem more keen and proactive than Elliot is. The liberal arts organisation they work for makes it easy. *Let's change your pronouns and your bio,* colleagues say enthusiastically. *We want to make sure you're okay!* It quickly becomes normalised, which Elliot appreciates, though they are hung up on the words, whereas for Elliot it was all about their body, and how it feels.

Elliot now lives in the regular streets of Beckenham, a place not unlike Carshalton: conventional, earnestly middle-class, achingly sensible. But Elliot finds it surprisingly queer too; maybe not Quentin Crisp's New York, but the Hebden Bridge of Bromley. They moved here because a lesbian friend introduced them to the area. *Yeah, there's loads of lesbians,* Elliot is assured. And sure enough, 'Yeah, there's loads of lesbians everywhere!'

These few streets, they've become a protective space, queer critical mass, which Elliot is adding to. 'I look quite queer, but I don't think I'm threatening,' says Elliot. 'I just blend into the background.' A new kind of suburban staple. 'I'm lucky in that I've had a lot of supportive people. And they're so keen to help that they've forced me to make decisions. Which is quite useful sometimes when you don't feel confident to do that yourself. So a little push along the way isn't always bad.' They have found here a positively assertive suburbia, a protective and nourishing one. Somewhere that can cope with change, can encourage and thrive on it. No longer the high walls and mystery of Carshalton, but just ever-adaptable streets of old houses constantly being altered to new ways of living. 'Or it's just it's cruel to be kind,' says Elliot, in typical deadpan style. '*Sort your life out! Deal with it!*'

The bay-fronted semi. It's the first thing most of us picture when we think of suburbia. Well, that and the Pet Shop Boys. Stained glass around the front door, box room above the stairs, clipped hedges and mown lawns, long back gardens with sheds and patios. The backdrop to a million family snapshots, childhood memories and chilly divorces, sitcom aspirations and commuter ennui. Perhaps the most famous commuter suburb of this type is Metroland, a construction of pure marketing by the Metropolitan Railway Company in West London, whose line stretches out of the city into the Buckinghamshire countryside. It built houses around its new stations – Ruislip! Chalfont & Latimer! Wendover! – tempting buyers from the crowded centre to something approaching the garden city ideal, a place not quite town and not quite country. Hundreds of other developers were to follow.

These mass-constructed Dunroamins are a curiosity. The design of the typical bay-fronted semi – those front-room windows bulging out into the garden as a reference to medieval or Tudor houses – draws from the work of those artisans and rebels of the Victorian Arts and Crafts movement, who detested mechanisation and mass production as much as they loved an inglenook and a barley-twist chimney. They might have had handcrafted magnificent faux medieval homes in which to show off their skills, but the romance of it all unexpectedly appealed to a broad section of Britain's aspiring middle class too, people who could never usually afford such grand designs. And so it was here that developers spotted a profitable niche. By nodding to heritage styles and discarding the wilful Arts and Crafts philosophy behind them, they conceived a variant specially designed for mass production. Each could be repetitively built along those new A- and B-roads snaking from every town. And so what had once been bespoke becomes instead a production line of cosy clones, brand-new houses evoking nostalgic dreams of Merrie England, to lessen the culture shock of whole estates being rushed into being where green fields and old woodlands had recently stood. These houses also collide with a vogue for the modern and streamlined, creating a peculiarly British suburban cocktail of the latest technology hidden beneath the veneer of the historic – drag by any other name. So successful are these new estates that soon market towns and villages across Britain amass micro-suburbs of their own, places that either link them physically to the sprawl of nearby cities or at the very least contain something in their DNA that connects them to the commuter-belt mentality of their distant relatives.

And with these houses come gardens. It's reckoned that 200,000 acres of suburban gardens were created across Britain between the world wars. Like home decoration and hairstyles, they allow people to express themselves in ways that can be joyful, liberating, baffling or appalling, sometimes all at once. One of the most influential figures in their evolution is Richard Sudell, whose story is told in Michael Gilson's book *Behind the Privet Hedge*. Sudell was born in 1892 near Preston, and it's his work on a London County Council 'cottage estate' in Roehampton in the 1920s that made his name. As the red-brick houses go up – a neat municipal version of those grand garden suburbs of the time – Sudell is determined to make sure that the landscaping is as important as the homes themselves. He's a Quaker socialist, a believer in communal good – his ideas distant relatives of Edward Carpenter's – but he also sees gardens as a place of escape, calming as well as practical. He champions allotments, rose beds and crazy paving, encouraging gardeners through columns in everything from *Ideal Home* magazine to the top-selling *Daily Herald* newspaper and a series of influential books. Here are hints and tips for creating flower beds and lawns, and also appeals for gardeners to express themselves – sometimes with gnomes. He even helps present gold medals – not for extravagant Chelsea Flower Show gardens, but for ordinary London plots – in his effort to popularise his love as a hobby for everyone. And so the classic suburban gardens we see springing up from the 1920s onwards have his green fingerprints all over them.

Many of the houses Sudell designs are thrown up in the 1920s as part of a patriotic 'Homes Fit for Heroes' campaign, which demands better housing for soldiers returning from the Great War and the families they are returning to. Some are built privately, and some by the council – then a relatively new phenomenon in Britain. But just as we see politicians today misrepresenting our many diverse lives as 'the silent majority', the personal politics of these heroes are not as simple as all that. For many at home and fighting abroad, and despite its horror and bloodshed, the war is also a time of liberation. It enables people to experience new ways of living, and to react against the closed and claustrophobic nature of many things, including the silence around sexuality. That significant numbers of First World War soldiers have same-sex sweethearts – men lost in battle or lovers subsequently separated in civvy street – is conveniently ignored by the people planning these homes. So too is the reality that many of the female partners and relatives at home have acknowledged same-sex attraction, attachments not easily brushed off in an era of suffrage and new-found female solidarity. But 'Homes Fit for Heroes' doesn't just fashionably wallpaper over these cracks, it actively asserts itself as a moral crusade – semi-detached houses built in expectation of mass 'normality'. Behind these fake beams and leaded lights the order of things cannot be questioned, the fixtures a vague gesture back to time immemorial, evoking storybook knights or princesses, characters so tightly encased in armour or corsets that self-expression was impossible. These houses are just as buttoned-up. There's seemingly no space built into these streets for alternative ways of life, the mixing of class and desire that the war has stirred. But still we find it.

Garden designer Richard Sudell dies in 1968, his life having influenced the way all our suburban streets look and feel, his afterlife entwined in suburbia like a rose in a trellis. Later, his wife, Ida, shares a secret with their daughter, Anne. *Your father was gay*, she tells her. They'd had a happy marriage, but he'd never been able to live his life openly as a gay man. 'He really was the kindest and gentlest man and was very much loved by us all,' Anne tells Gilson.[3] The father of the suburban garden something other than he had seemed all along. And what could be more suburban than that?

CHANGING HAIRDRESSERS
IN WILMSLOW

The almost-goth haunts the streets around the big houses of Carrwood Road in Wilmslow. It's 1985, and Jon is fifteen. He has a bleached flick, copying his androgynous hero David Sylvian, a long coat rummaged from Afflecks Palace in Manchester and black Doc Martens shoes – boots seeming a little too rebellious at this point. It's not the weekend, so he's not wearing the black nail varnish or white make-up of his expeditions to gigs or the big city. The houses sit back from the road here, moated off by large gardens, an estate built in the 1930s on the grounds of a big house, which is now a boys' school. Convenient as it is, Jon doesn't go to this school. Instead, he's seen as a bit posh in Wilmslow for going to school in Stockport, and a bit posh in Stockport because he's from Wilmslow, home to rich footballers. 'I always felt like a double outsider,' says Jon, 'even before realising that I might be different for being gay.' He knows these streets well. When he was half this age, he set out to the shop to buy some flour for his mum. Feeling the freedom of 1970s children, he sees a funfair, shoves his bike in a hedge and goes on a couple of rides with the 50p he has in his pocket. 'My family still talks about that,' says Jon, 'because it's such a weird thing to do.' While the kids play together around each other's houses, the adults remain largely aloof, two communities operating in this quiet street.

But that changes in the eighties when a local actress, a rare beacon of glamour, starts a Neighbourhood Watch group. Among the adults, the novelty is almost entirely eclipsed by anxiety: not of

Neighbourhood Watch itself, although that's paranoia-inducing enough, but of having to mingle in a semi-formal setting with the people they have mostly ignored. Having to reveal something of themselves, even if it is only whether they prefer tea or coffee or *something stronger*. Before long, Jon notices that the meetings have turned into summer picnics and Christmas meals, parents bonding over wine and cheese and repressed vigilantism. What must the Neighbourhood Watch think of the wraith-like semi-goths of Jon's social group lurking beyond the tall, neatly clipped hedges, most wearing pale make-up and dark eyeliner, some of whom are – *They're not, Norman!* – boys. Perhaps this is what Neighbourhood Watch does, it makes us all the object of suspicion. Everyone in the street is unknowable, a stranger. Neighbourhood, watch thyself.

It begins around puberty, this feeling that Jon is different. And it's a feeling that hasn't been entirely self-generated; it's also imposed upon him by the boys at school. 'I felt a bit like they would judge me,' he recalls. 'Man, *I* didn't think I was gay – but they were calling me "poof" and stuff by that point.' Aged twelve, all of his friends are girls, and any social activity is shrugged off. He's staying in, doing his homework, behaving. But this only makes it worse, the boys now singling him out for thinking he's better than they are, posh, a swot. But his transgression, when it comes, is devastating. 'It still makes me cringe a little bit,' says Jon. He's friends with Sue and Jane. 'Very 1980s names,' he says. In breaks and lunchtimes at school, Jon borrows their magazines and becomes an avid reader of the photo stories, problem pages and gossipy interviews. But after a while the boys spot this, and his secret shame is exposed. 'So they would just start shouting, *Jon reads* Just Seventeen, as if it was this massive slur.'

From nothing, this small detail gets swiftly out of hand. Jon has been happy and chatty with his little group of girl friends, but now begins to retreat inwards. He sits in the second row in lessons and crouches down in his seat so as to appear invisible, to avoid being asked a question or singled out. One day, in the school language lab, Jon is one of a class of kids separated into little booths with clunky tape recorders, strange zones both public and private, the pupils all in their own worlds with their earphones, the teacher monitoring them via their headsets. As he *écoutes et répètes*, Jon's teacher's voice comes through his headphones. *Jon, is something the matter?* Jon, momentarily safe in his cubicle, is startled by the intrusion. *No*, he replies. *You've been really, really quiet for the whole of this term . . . If there's anything you want to talk to me about, then you can.* But Jon doesn't want to at all. Only later does he appreciate how smart this had been, and how grateful he is for his teacher's stealthy show of concern. But he says nothing, and the bullying continues. They tease him because he has not removed the black nail varnish carefully enough from the previous night's gig or the weekend's revels. They tease him when at sixteen he gets his ear pierced. 'I was the only boy in my school to have had their ear pierced,' he recalls. The only boy in a thousand students. 'Word got around, and I remember standing in a break one morning and the bullies of my year came over and actually grabbed my earlobes to look for the hole, and they went, *Yeah, it's true, he's got his ear pierced.* Like, *Which ear is it, left for gay or right for gay?* and all that kind of stuff.' Meanwhile, the girls he hangs around with have boyfriends, inevitably older, 'six foot six tall with massive black crimped hair and all that, and very skinny and kind of attractive'. Even teenage semi-goths have hormones.

The David Sylvian flick has been encouraged by a change of hairdresser. Not from the sensible barbers he'd go to with his dad, but the salon his mum visits once a week to get her hair cut, or more often than not, just styled and blow-dried. 'It was very

Wilmslow,' says Jon, 'so it was very much ladies who had a regular appointment on a Friday. Like, you knew that my mum always had eleven o'clock on a Friday.' Big Michael owns the salon and cuts Jon's hair a couple of times. He's gay but taciturn, not much of a connection for a teenager seeking some sign of a wider world of hope and excitement. Then one day he gets Little Michael, 'super camp and really, really bubbly, chatty, and I really fucking liked him. I didn't fancy him, but I just *loved* him.' Almost immediately, they're bonding over *Victoria Wood: As Seen on TV* and re-enacting sketches during haircuts, those sharp-eyed satires of suburban snobbery and overlooked women set in department store cafeterias and shoe shops, Italian restaurants and blowsy front rooms. Their raucous laughter brings the salon to life. Soon, like some dealer pushing suburban camp, Little Michael is lending Jon VHS tapes of more obscure Victoria Wood shows and Mike Leigh's *Abigail's Party*. 'So I watched *Abigail's Party* on a slightly scratchy video from my mum's hairdresser,' says Jon. 'And still, nothing at all. I never felt like I wanted to say, *I think I might be gay, Michael*, or whatever. Just because maybe that's what you can't do in a half-an-hour haircut.'

It's 1988, and Jon is in the sixth-form common room with his friends Janet, Mark and Phil. 'I suppose everyone thinks a little bit that they're in the misfits clan, don't they?' says Jon. 'But we really were, and I think we were quite cool.' They have endured the endless parade of middle-of-the-road music played by the mainstream sporty boys and girls: Dire Straits, Chris Rea, U2. There is an art to getting your music on the stereo, and they have to be forceful, to stand up to the wall of dadrock being played to them. One of the gang has brought in *Life's Too Good* by the Sugarcubes, and the strange Icelandic wonky pop fills the room, disturbing the sensible music for budding Volvo owners. Janet is Jon's best friend and gig buddy, while Mark and Jon are the biggest fans of Dead or

Alive in the world and travel to record shops in Birmingham and Manchester to track down obscure 12-inch remixes. This group of arty misfits is as close to a Gay Soc as there is in Jon's school. When they finish their A-levels, Mark and Jon come out to each other. It's ten years before Phil joins them and comes out too. All that time they had been a group of young gay friends at school, but in the age when Section 28 of the Local Government Act is just being enacted, prohibiting the 'promotion' of homosexuality in schools, and the TV is showing the 'AIDS: Don't Die of Ignorance' public information campaign, the idea that school is a place where they could be open about their sexuality is laughable.

At home, Jon is smuggling gay literature into the house: the inevitable copy of *A Boy's Own Story* by Edmund White; *Sucking Sherbert Lemons* by Michael Carson; copies of a monthly listings magazine, which he hides in the bottom of his wardrobe. The cover shows adult film star Leo Ford in a jockstrap, the headline reading *All I Want for Christmas Is Leo Ford*. Attached to the front with a paper clip is a note from the local indie bookshop, saying, *The staff believe this cover is sensationalist and exploitative, but we've decided to allow it to be sold this month in recognition of lesbian and gay freedom of speech.*

Jon has come out to a group of friends on a trip to London and, emboldened, tells his mum. His parents are loving and liberal, but she doesn't take it too well. Not badly – she doesn't throw him out – but there is talk of phases, and an implicit suggestion that he should not tell his father. And so he doesn't. In fact, it's six years before he comes out to his dad. He does it over the phone, and his dad replies with a light *Oh yeah, your mum told me when you were nineteen*. 'He said all the right things, like *You'll always be my son*,' recalls Jon. *Thanks for making the effort to let me know*, he thinks. And also, how funny it is that he has not considered that his folks talk about their children. Yet coming out to friends and family doesn't transfer to being out in Wilmslow. Instead, Jon goes to London and Manchester to be gay. Once, he invites a lad back to his family's house when they're away, and they sleep in the spare room because his bedroom still has a single bed. Afterwards, his main anxiety is that his parents will notice that the spare-room bedding has been changed. And so it takes time to be himself in Wilmslow. 'You know, I think that the first time that I felt comfortable was in about 2005,' he says. He and his partner, Nick, go out on a Saturday night with his family to Bar Med, one of those chains that sprang up in the nineties. 'And we walked from Mum and Dad's house, and I was walking down Water Lane, one of the main roads in Wilmslow, and holding Nick's hand, and it was really amazing.' He finds it bizarre that it took until his mid-thirties to be able to do this in his hometown.

Instead, it's a ghost from Wilmslow that will make the connection between that place and his wider world. It's 1989, and Jon is at Heaven in London with a group of pals. They have arrived early, and the big nightclub, with its amazing lights and sound system, is yet to fill up. Across the sparsely populated dance floor, beneath the lasers and rotating spots and glitterballs, he spies a figure from his past. It's Little Michael from the salon, there on his own. The wizard of VHS, the uninhibited voice of *Two Soups* and *Demis Roussos*. Jon has not seen him for five years. It's a test of who Jon is at this moment: the shy, bullied goth or the liberated city clubber. 'I just went up to him and went, *Hi, I'm Jon from Wilmslow, do you remember me?* And he's like, *I've been waiting to bump into you in here.*' He pauses as he's telling me this. 'That's not exactly *Heartstopper*, is it? But that feels quite a cinematic moment, you know, where we then met, and he could say things like, *Of course I knew when you were fifteen or whatever, but I wasn't gonna say anything.*' Little Michael, the gay hero we all needed when we were teenagers.

Back from work, Gerald starts the dinner, peeling spuds and opening a can of bully beef. Phil will be home soon, covered in plaster from the building site, full of aches and stories. Sometimes it's Phil who cooks, depending on who gets home first. It's a comfortable arrangement. Gerald's flat in Ilford isn't big, but it suits them well. Two men in domestic harmony. It's 1921, and Gerald and Phil have been together since meeting on a crowded boat back from Le Havre at the end of the Great War. Two servicemen amid the thousands, they would start a heroic new life as a same-sex couple in a world where that is illegal.

They share the chores, and it never gets too cramped because Gerald's army job regularly takes him away to Germany. 'We had quite a happy life together,' he tells Jeffrey Weeks over half a century later.[4] 'We done the housework between us. We shared everything fifty–fifty. If I saw the stove wanted cleaning I'd clean the stove. If he saw the chest of drawers [wanted] polishing he'd polish the chest of drawers.' They don't live in a place where other LGBTQ+ people are visible, but here, fifty years before the first Pride march in London, their neighbours don't seem to mind two men living together. While they never talk about their relationship to their families and straight friends, Gerald suspects they all know the situation. It's a far cry from E. M. Forster's country house set or the rapscallions of Piccadilly. The everyday suburban lives of working- and middle-class gay men and women were seldom recorded in this period, and to hear of Gerald and Phil co-existing so peacefully with their families and neighbours is a bright outlier in the existing records.

They are living through a great shift in British life, a culture shocked from its Edwardian restraints by the horrors of war and clouded by a mood of sombre reflection and memorialising. Suffrage finally gets women over twenty-one the vote by 1928, while inventions from the car and plane to the telephone and the gas oven transform life – at least, for the most privileged. Meanwhile, there are more curious cultural changes at work too. In Rebecca Jennings's book *Tomboys and Bachelor Girls*, she talks of how the city is increasingly seen as a masculine place and the home of deviant sexuality, while the growth of the suburbs creates a powerful new figure: the suburban housewife. But they are not the only new identities being expressed. For many women, their first exposure to a codified lesbian is in Radclyffe Hall's 1928 novel *The Well of Loneliness*. Soon, some are searching for an inner 'Stephen', her inimitable protagonist – well, as many as can get their hands on a copy before it is banned for the next twenty years.

Then there's the extraordinary central character of Virginia Woolf's novel of the same year, *Orlando*, who effortlessly gender-hops. And in real life, transgender pioneers follow soon after. Mark Weston of Oreston, a suburb of Plymouth, is born intersex and raised as Mary, until a series of operations in 1936. 'I was born and reared in Oreston,' he tells a newspaper in the US. 'I think without undue vanity, I showed pluck by continuing to live here, where everybody knows my story. But my old neighbours are very kind and want the rest of the world to let me alone.' A community not unlike that in Ilford. And later there's Roberta Cowell from Croydon, who distinguishes herself as a Spitfire pilot and racing driver, before having gender reassignment surgery in 1951. She becomes the first trans woman to have her name changed on her birth certificate. Lives transformed in the midst of the suburban landscape.

Back in Ilford, all is settled between Gerald and Phil for seven years, until one night they venture into town. They are headed to the Quebec Club in Piccadilly, a venue that, by the mid-1920s, is operating as a gay nightspot. Immediately, a man comes up to Phil, and they kiss 'and all that sort of business', according, years later, to a still bristling Gerald. Their conversation and canoodling excludes Gerald, and after a while he finds himself losing his cool. 'Good gracious alive!' Phil's friend says to him, with all the dismissive condescension he can muster. 'Gerald darling, don't you know I knew Phil long before you knew her?' Well, it's all too much for Gerald, who sees red – 'Bang, bang, bang!' as he puts it – and suddenly it's all over. Not just the night out, but the relationship. 'That was it,' he says. 'I left the flat. I left the flat to him.' Goodbye Ilford, farewell domestic bliss. The turbulent 1920s are at work again.

LOVE AND HATE IN SURBITON

Seena's family are hurriedly leaving Iran. The clock has been ticking ever since news of the Islamic Revolution became known. Seena is just three years old in 1979. Members of his mother's religion are being thrown into jail or killed; and while his father is Muslim, he's also a Marxist academic, and left-wingers are suffering a similar fate. As if all of that's not pressing enough, his newly born sister has been diagnosed with a serious illness, and they need to find somewhere that can treat her. Seena was born in Manchester, and so after a few hastily arranged months in Brazil the traumatised family decide to return to Britain. They arrive back in a cloud of anxiety, the confetti still settling the day after the wedding of Charles and Di. They start out in the bow-fronted streets of Warrington, which for young Seena is an idyllic time, playing outside with the neighbours' kids. Only later does his mum tell him about the racism she suffered there. 'That was always quite a difficult thing in the eighties,' he says, 'being foreigners.' After a year they move down to the outskirts of London, to Tolworth, one of the less affluent areas of Surbiton, in Surrey. And Surbiton does its Surbiton thing, dispersing their sense of imminent danger among the loft extensions, estate cars and plane trees.

Behind the stucco, the whole place feels very white. Seena's aware of a few Indian families, but his are the only Iranians around. Mostly, he sits at home, drawing. When he ventures out to the small park on his street, shooing his adventurous cat back home, he has to avoid the bullies who make fun of him as he picks his way along the avenue. But there's also the weird imaginativeness of childhood, where the trees in the middle of the park are a fort or a secret spy HQ or somewhere to bury treasure. Their neighbours are casually xenophobic and homophobic, 'Not to me directly,' says Seena, 'but you remember how people would talk in the eighties.' Their house is often filled with family friends who have escaped Iran, and intellectuals – after all, his mum is a psychologist and his dad an academic at Kingston Polytechnic. This is a sophisticated, intelligent and analytical suburbia, the adults questioning everything. Young Seena grows up, at home in such rarefied company, but at school is bullied terribly, adding to the instability and anxiety that swept in with him from Iran. It's while he's at school that he realises he's gay, and with a head full of romantic notions from reading artists' biographies, he decides he's going to come out to his parents. At first, he tries it through dropping rather opaque hints, but when they're not followed up it just adds to a feeling of unbearable suspense. But his strange behaviour hasn't gone unnoticed. One day, his dad, giving him a lift to school, says, *Your mum's really worried. Whatever it is going on, just tell her.* So Seena decides to go for a slightly less indirect approach, writes her a letter and puts it in her handbag. That evening when she comes home, she gives her anxious son a hug, and they talk. 'They were much more accepting than I thought they would be,' he tells me, 'and they were really hurt that I thought they wouldn't be accepting. But it was still quite new and strange to them. They were quite emotional about it. My dad got really depressed for about six months, I later found out, because he thought I wouldn't have any friends.' All this time he's feared he'll be thrown out, used to hearing of the bad reactions that so many LGBTQ+ people get. Instead, home becomes even more of a sanctuary. 'People thought I was really sophisticated to have come out at sixteen,' says Seena. 'I think I was in some ways, but in other ways I think I was very naive.'

Seena has been really close to his dad growing up. When he decides he wants to attend a meeting of a coming-out group, held on the other side of London in King's Cross, his dad says he'll drive him. 'This is pretty amazing of him,' says Seena admiringly. The group meets in a room above Central Station, one of the city's most established gay pubs. While Seena's up there talking through problems and hopes and fears with fellow travellers, his dad waits outside in the car for a couple of hours, watching the guys entering and leaving the pub (*They just look like ordinary people*, he tells Seena). On one occasion, he has to forcibly eject a prostitute from his passenger seat when she climbs in, not taking no for an answer. After all, this is King's Cross in the nineties. Over time, Seena becomes good friends with the couple who run the group, and, eventually, so do his parents. 'When I think about it, it is quite strange,' Seena says of the whole situation. 'But also lovely. It's *really* lovely.' He pauses. 'But it's quite strange.'

It's about this time that the family embark on another one of those epic moves. Now it's to an entirely different part of Surbiton. Berrylands is the epitome of 1930s suburbia, whose bay windows and leaded lights, low garden walls and decorative black-beamed gables speak of well-ordered and affluent middle-class life, a comfortable commuter-belt existence. From this sturdy base, Seena can begin to explore the world as a young gay man. He reads in listings magazine *Time Out* that there's a gay night in nearby Kingston, 'in the Bacchus Wine Bar', he tells me. 'I think it was called Erotic City or something like that. After that Prince song. But I never went to that because I was sixteen and I thought, *That sounds scary . . .*' Which, to be fair, sounds terrifying even now. He realises that much of gay life seems to revolve around bars and clubs, but these are alien environments for him. Neither of his parents drink, and so they've never frequented pubs nor understood their codes and traditions.

But LGBTQ+ life can be glimpsed in other places too. At his A-level college there's an openly gay lad in his drama class who goes to indie clubs, which intrigues Seena because that's the music he's into as well. 'I tried really hard to make friends with him,' he says. 'Probably too hard because I'd had such a tough time with being bullied, but he sort of wasn't all that friendly to me. I felt like he just about tolerated me being in his friends group, but really he didn't like me being there, because I think he thought he should be the only gay boy in the college and he felt threatened.' Later, he hears that one of the other gay students thinks Seena fancies him, 'but really I just was being friendly because I wanted gay friends'. Sometimes, finding other LGBTQ+ people is not the relief you hope it might be, all of us struggling to work ourselves out after years of hiding or confusion.

Instead, Seena begins to find friends through his other love: comics. Hanging out in a comic shop in Putney leads him into the world of queer zines, which is just beginning to explode in Britain in the mid-1990s. While his peers might have been out experimenting with drink, drugs or sex, Seena is geeking out with other comic artists and nerds. 'We'd be really quite gay about comics,' he recalls, 'in the way people have gay idols in music or in movies, but we'd be gay or camp about comic characters and writers and artists.'

Can Surbiton give Seena all he needs? 'There was a sense of wanting to escape all the time,' he tells me. 'I wanted to live in London and be artistic and gay.' So to give it a go, he gets a place at Goldsmiths College and moves to Deptford. He's immersed himself in the writings of Derek Jarman and imagines hanging out in a bohemian scene like Jarman's, although by the time he moves he's pretty sure it doesn't exist, and even if it does, he'll never have access to it. What starts as a great artistic adventure soon falls apart. Away from his family and the familiar comforts of Surbiton, Seena begins to feel anxious and depressed, and spends increasing amounts of time back at home. 'I was dealing with a lot of mental health issues,' he recalls. 'It just felt a lot safer to be there and be with them.' After eighteen months he drops out of the course, moves back to Berrylands and ends up working in a call centre in Kingston.

'I was reading Sylvia Plath,' he says. '*Really!* And then I noticed Alex.' He's an arty-seeming boy of around the same age who Seena thinks is probably gay too, but they don't work in the same team, so it's not easy to get to know him. The call centre is a very heterosexual environment, and after the bullying of school and the queer chaos of Goldsmiths it feels intimidating. Eventually, he manages to strike up conversation with Alex, and they discover they have loads in common: comics, books, art – and being gay in Kingston. 'We did hang out a bit outside of work,' he recalls. 'But in a very suburban way – we'd go for cups of tea in cafés, and stuff like that.' They also head into the city together, exploring alternative clubs and pubs like Duckie and the Retro Bar, trying to acclimatise. But Seena finds his old anxieties hard to dispel. 'I would arrange my shifts so that I would be working on weekends,' he recalls, 'and I think it was a self-protecting thing so I couldn't go out and feel vulnerable, even though I partly wanted to.' Bohemian London begins to slide away to the horizon once again as he studies for an art foundation course near home.

He ends up at Kingston University, where the shy boy from down the road becomes the president of what is then the Lesbian and Gay Society. At last he is at the heart of his local scene. Or is he? 'Even though I was the president of it, I felt quite out of it,' he says, 'quite excluded from what a lot of people in it were doing. There were just some bitches in the group. I mean, there are always gay bitches, right? And cliques.' The cliques are all keen on clubbing and London and escaping the places Seena is just beginning to suspect he might feel most comfortable in. Still, he gives a new local gay club a whirl ('The Reflex could have been really good,' he says, 'because it had this amazing light-up rainbow dance floor, but it was really horrible remixes of stuff') and a short-lived gay pub, The Lamb. 'I half enjoyed going to them,' he says, 'but I still found them quite weird and alienating.'

While he's at university he gets a job in Ryman's in Kingston, a place where the wonder of stationery has gone to be slowly hole-punched to death. Still, at least the budding illustrator can get a staff discount on sketch pads and inks. As with the call centre, he doesn't feel he can be out at work, despite still being president of the university's Lesbian and Gay Society. 'The boss would say jokey homophobic things,' he recalls, 'but I'm sure some of them would probably have been all right with it.' On the shop floor, Destiny's Child songs play on the radio, and he sings along behind the till with his colleague Fatima to 'Independent Women' and 'Bootylicious'. When Seena mentions this to Alex, he replies, *Are you sure she doesn't know?* So he takes the plunge. 'I was a bit like, *I want to tell you something.* She was like, *I think I already know.*' For his next job, in a DVD rental shop, he makes sure this time to come out at the start, the straight film geeks perhaps more comfortable with displays of emotional honesty if delivered by Morgan Freeman or Jodie Foster to a soundtrack by John Williams. All around him, the suburbs feel like they're gradually becoming more open. 'When I was a twink, I got cruised so much on trains going to Surbiton or Kingston,' he recalls. 'Usually it really freaked me out, even when I quite liked the guy.' But one day he sees a man he likes the look of, and makes an effort to actively cruise him back. They end up chatting. The guy is French and staying in Surbiton – on holiday, no less. Now that really does show commitment to exploring another country's culture. It's a flirtatious conversation, but at the end they say their goodbyes, and Seena forgets about it, until a week later in Ryman's, when the guy reappears. The Frenchman has come to find him. 'We hung out a few times. Stuff happened . . .' He grins. There are some sparks of joy even Ryman's can't stifle.

For a time, Seena moves back to London and lives in Limehouse. 'I started hanging out in Shoreditch and places like that,' he says, 'and I mean, talk about pointless and empty.' These days, he lives with his partner in Hastings, which although not suburban has a similar pace of life to Surbiton. 'I maybe didn't realise how much I actually really liked living in the suburbs until later,' he thinks. 'The smallness of a suburban town, just the sweetness of it.' But he looks back to how much he hated it in the eighties and nineties, and how he wanted to escape. 'But *did* I hate it?' he ponders. 'That's the question.' Perhaps it's because he had such a miserable time at school, or because of all the people he met there who were casually racist or homophobic. 'I think a lot of those people probably wouldn't be now,' he says, 'because I think so much has changed . . . But back then, you just felt everything was against you. It was very stifling and oppressive.'

These days, he still stays with his parents a couple of nights a week so he can commute to his job at the London College of Fashion. Friends ask him to go for meals or a drink after work, but mostly Seena just wants to leave the city and get home, be it the suburbs or the coast. After a lifetime of creating zines and comics and running queer club nights, the appeal of suburbia for him isn't that it's edgy and cool, but that it's not trying to impress anyone. 'When you're in suburbia,' he tells me, 'it just feels you can just do quite ordinary things and be quite satisfied by them.' And now, after all those years of anxiety, he feels like he can be out here, creating his extraordinary subversive queer art, and it's okay. 'It feels a bit miraculous.' And he's noticed how it's not just him that's changed, Surbiton has too – the shops during Pride month with their rainbows in the window, the pubs with their drag bingo nights, the Mardi Gras-style outfits on mannequins in the Princess Alice Hospice charity shop. 'It's been, like, two or three attempts to leave, but it always pulls me back in,' he says, the geeks of the DVD rental shop no doubt nodding earnestly at the reference. 'But then I guess it's really because it's about people. It's about me, it's about my family and being close to my family.' And that includes his partner. 'They love him. He loves them.' His partner is from Chingford, and before his mother died a couple of years ago he spent a lot of time there caring for her. Seena would find himself being put off if he ever showed an interest in visiting: *Chingford's not a destination* was the narrative. 'He didn't think I would be that impressed with it,' says Seena. 'Then when I went there, and we started hanging out there a bit, I was like, *This reminds me of Surbiton. I really like it. It's the suburbs!*' And finally that feels like home.

The police are pulling Gregory's room apart. They are in search of – what? Codes from a hidden life they barely understand. Evidence that even here, in the heart of Cheshire, deviants are at large. Back in 1936, a moral panic is gripping Altrincham: twenty-nine men investigated by the police for *serious offences* and *indecent conduct*. Here, in Gregory's room, they find what they're looking for: a powder puff, a jar of theatrical greasepaint and, most incriminating of all, a copy of André Tellier's melodramatic novel of homosexuality, *Twilight Men*. It's signs like these that implicate the men, at a time when having consensual gay sex in private is illegal. Most are in their twenties and thirties, with low-paid jobs: shop assistants, waiters, bar staff and the like. With no real evidence of their private behaviour, it's only under exhaustive police interrogation that the men begin to crack. Slowly, painfully, they start to incriminate each other with admissions of contact, teased out with the promise that the law will go easy on them if they shop the others.

At Chester Crown Court, five are sent to prison to serve between three and seven years; six more are sentenced to hard labour; twelve are bound over for five years; the rest acquitted. Lives casually ruined, for what? To bolster a boorish distaste for difference. But although the coppers of Altrincham might have thought they were exorcising the taint of homosexuality from the town, instead they find they've made the place synonymous with it, one long dirty joke that endures for decades. 'The vision was of a town populated entirely by predatory sodomites,' wrote Allan

Horsfall, founder of the Campaign for Homosexual Equality.[5] '*If you should happen to drop a half-crown in Altrincham*, people were solemnly warned, *don't ever pick it up*. I have heard this warning repeated when the half-crown had given way to the fifty-pence piece, and there may be areas where it lives on still.' He was writing fifty years after those men were sentenced, the echoes of their misery still producing a rictus of amusement, the vindictiveness of the law succeeding only in taking the reputation of the town down with it.

Some of these men are still in prison when war is declared in 1939. The conflict will have even more far-reaching social implications than the First World War. Young men and women serving in the forces will be thrown together in vast numbers, often in same-sex environments. At home, amid the blackouts and emergency regulations, a new counter-culture emerges, emboldened by a spirit of living for the moment in dangerous times. When all of these displaced people come back and are expected to carry on as if nothing has changed, cracks in the old ways of living begin to appear. And suburbia's codes of control will serve only to magnify those changes, its rules ripe for subversion by those who have experienced the strange new world the war has created and a new generation who would follow: the baby boomers.

NEIGHBOURHOOD WATCH
IN PENSNETT

It's gone closing time, two weeks before Christmas 1991. Eighteen-year-old Daniel is in the passenger seat of his boy-friend's BMW as they drive through the outskirts of Dudley. The couple have been out drinking, and now they're dawdling along through the last few metres of the journey to the cul-de-sac in Pensnett where Daniel lives with his family. Lee points to a turn-ing that would take them down to the old church. *Shall we go and have a bit of fun?* he asks. Daniel is keen, so Lee turns the car down the drive and into the car park beside the graveyard. In the quiet dark there's a fumbling, and Daniel is giving Lee head. A few minutes have passed when suddenly they're interrupted. It's the police: not just a copper, but two cars, a riot van and dogs.

The lads panic, but there's not much they can do, other than try to make themselves decent. Daniel guesses a resident of the new estate behind the church has seen them parked there and called the cops, Neighbourhood Watch in action. A copper bangs on the driver's window, and blokey Lee climbs out, still button-ing his fly. It's clearly just a couple of lovers; all the cops can see of Daniel is his fashionably long indie-kid hair, so they assume he's a young woman. 'They're like, *Wey-hey!*' recalls Daniel. 'And then they come over to the car, and I turn around.' The atmos-phere changes at once. '*Oh. Right.* Then the next minute we're frog-marched off to the police station in Dudley in separate cars and put into cells for six hours.' Daniel, at college, has gone a bit political – 'a tiny bit', he says. *You shouldn't be doing this*, he tells the police, to little avail, because they very much are. The two lads are interviewed and taken back to their cells. 'Then the major bombshell dropped,' says Daniel. 'Lee wasn't twenty-one, as he had told me, he was twenty-nine. I only found that out in the police station that night. So that's roughly a ten-year difference in age. Because of that they went up to the head of their station, [and] he made the decision to charge us both with gross indecency. Lee got gross indecency with a minor because he was twenty-nine. It was a total shock to me.'

It's 5 a.m., and Daniel is finally released from custody and driven home in a police car. He sneaks indoors and creeps upstairs, sitting on the edge of his bed wondering what to do now and who to tell. His dad is a lorry driver and gets up early; his mum works as an administrator for the local court, the very thought of which sends him into a tailspin, but he tries to push that down for a moment. He makes his decision, quietly wakes up his dad and asks to meet him downstairs. *I've got something to tell you*, says Daniel. *I'm gay*. His dad is taken aback. *What about your girlfriend?* he asks. *Well, we sort of finished*, explains Daniel, *and I'm seeing Lee, who's come to the house*. His dad pauses a moment to take that in. But Daniel isn't finished. And it all comes out in a rush. *We've just been arrested in the local churchyard and charged with gross indecency. Lee's been charged with gross indecency with a minor. We have to go to Mum's court. The court case is in Mum's court on Christmas Eve*. His dad, with admirable restraint, says, *I'm going to go back to bed for a little bit because I've got a big drive*. And then he adds, *You're going to have to tell your mum*. 'That was the longest day,' Daniel tells me, 'waiting for her to come back from work.' Her job is to type the lists of cases that are circulated to four courts in the local area. They have a very recognisable surname; everyone will know they're related. 'Mum comes home from work, and I tell her,' says Daniel. 'I got a slap on the face – of course, she was in deep shock. She then went and swept the drive for about forty-five minutes. A very, very long time.' But not as long as the wait till Christmas Eve.

Pensnett is a suburb of Dudley, and that's where Daniel grows up, with his brother Tom, his twin, born five minutes after him in 1973. Daniel thinks he always knew he was gay, and suspected his brother was too from an early age. 'We looked so similar, at school we had to wear badges,' says Daniel. 'I think people saw us as a bit of a novelty act.' Not helped when they later both go to Manchester University ('We were still seen as the gay twins') and work at the same Tesco, in East Didsbury ('Then, of course, it was the gay Tesco twins'). 'I've got photos of him in his *Ghostbusters* sweatshirt, pointing to his Boy George and Culture Club posters on one wall, the other one was Pete Burns and Dead or Alive,' says Daniel. Boy George is a touchy subject at home, because the pop star's last name, O'Dowd, is the same as his mother's maiden name, and she would tell the boys, *Don't ever tell people my surname.* The kinds of anxieties that don't stop them spending their pocket money on the picture disc of 'I Feel Love' by Bronski Beat and Marc Almond, on which they were dressed in chaps. *Are you sure you want this, boys?* their mum asks. *Yeah, we want it!* chorus the boys.

The cul-de-sac is made up of red-brick 1950s semis, and the residents are closely entangled in each other's lives, in and out of each other's houses. 'Growing up was lovely,' Daniel remembers. He might have had gay heroes in pop, but less so in Dudley, other than one boy at school, who on his last day turns up in massive high heels and a big billowing dress, full hair and make-up, as both a fuck-you to the others and a fabulous declaration of his new adult life beyond the confines of a Dudley comprehensive.

A-levels, that's when Daniel begins to suspect his brother is gay too, what with his camp new best mate and the guy with the moustache he spots dropping him off in his car. But at seventeen, Daniel himself is not out. In fact, he has a girlfriend, who he still describes as one of the loves of his life. It's not until New Year's Eve when he's seventeen that things suddenly change. He's in an indie club, and they're playing James's hit 'Sit Down', and so that's what the entire room does, backsides in the dirty beer and alcopop slops on the dance floor, as is traditional. A guy sits down next to Daniel, a worldly university student, and before they know it they're getting off with each other. *Here we go*, he thinks. He tells his girlfriend. 'She was really upset but supportive, she accepted it. She was amazing.' *You're going to have to tell your brother*, she says. Daniel ties himself in knots about it, but before he gets a chance to say anything, Tom breezes into the changing room in Tesco and declares, *Oh, by the way, I'm gay. Joel's my boyfriend. We go to a gay club in Birmingham called Tin Tins. If you and your girlfriend want to come, you can. If not, that's up to you.* 'I was open-mouthed,' says Daniel, 'but only because I was trying to think how to tell him, when he just dropped it casually. Typical of my brother.' For a time, Tom might have been relying on the thought that *at least one of us is straight*, but on a night out soon after Daniel finally manages to disabuse him of that, and a burden is lifted. A couple of weeks later, they're at Tin Tins in Birmingham, and it's there that Daniel meets Lee. 'He was a real working-class lad,' says Daniel, 'straight-acting, or whatever people used to say back then.' Lee works for a printing company in Telford. They start seeing each other, and he even stays over in the cul-de-sac one night, Daniel's parents none the wiser, still imagining he has a girlfriend. As working-class northern Catholics, they might not take the news that both of their sons are gay too well, the brothers think. The thing is to come out in a calm and gentle way.

It's Christmas 1991, and both of Daniel's parents now know he's gay, but not in the way he'd hoped. 'I remember during those two weeks that darkness had descended on the house,' he says. But in the background, wheels are in motion. His mum has to go to her boss in the court and explain what's happened, and they arrange a solicitor. 'I walked in and he said, *Right, Daniel, you better tell me what's going on. Don't worry at all, tell me all the details. It doesn't matter. Whatever you tell me, believe me, I've heard a lot, lot worse. Don't worry.* I explained everything. And he said, *I just don't understand why this wasn't just a caution at the car. It should have been a caution.*' After all of the dread, this feels like something to cling to.

'So Christmas Eve comes, and we go to court,' says Daniel. 'Lee's decided to represent himself. The solicitor wants to get us in first, hoping that the press wouldn't attend till later. Mum and Dad, by this stage, had cancelled all their Christmas activities. My dad was well known in the local Labour club, you know, a working men's club, and obviously it's a cul-de-sac. Basically, if it had gotten into the papers, it would have been front page.' Then, just before they file in, the press arrive, and Daniel's heart sinks. He stands up and says his name, and Lee says his, at which point something quite unexpected happens: the Crown Prosecution Service announces it's dropping all charges due to lack of evidence. There is confusion. Has the solicitor made this happen? They never really find out. Daniel leaves court in a daze. The wider world of the cul-de-sac may be none the wiser, but to Daniel everything has changed utterly. 'Christmas Day was pretty much a wash-out,' he says. There are few tidings of comfort and joy. All socialising has been cancelled; presents opened in a vacuum of unexpressed feelings; the turkey and trimmings dispatched in silence. And then to top it all, on Boxing Day, after repeated denials his brother finally comes out to their parents too. 'It was the worst Christmas ever.'

For a while, despite all the trauma, Daniel continues to see Lee. They meet in the car park of a pub in the cul-de-sac, before heading off in the old BMW. One day his mum asks, *Are you seeing him tonight?* She finds out their meeting place and goes in place of Daniel. Lee can't believe it when she comes round the corner and climbs into his car. 'To this day, I still don't know what was discussed,' says Daniel. But whatever it is, it takes a long time. And their relationship doesn't last much longer. Daniel sees a possessive and controlling side of Lee he doesn't like, and gets out. And what he gains from his parents is acceptance. Life gradually becomes less traumatic for Daniel. And now he is out, he can finally begin to be more open with his family.

His next boyfriends are Brazilian, South African and Italian, and Daniel enjoys bringing them to Dudley, to his parents' sofa. Samuel, the South African, meets Daniel's dad, who by that time is dying of cancer. 'I remember him coming into the living room on all fours, he was in that much pain, to meet Samuel. He said, *I'm sorry, son, that I can't spend much time with you,* to Samuel. *I'm just not very well.*' His Catholic mum goes with him to Pride in London and Mardi Gras in Sydney. 'She was saying, *Is he gay? Are they gay?* I was like, *They're all bloody gay, it's Mardi Gras.*' His relationship with her becomes very close. 'I did say to her before she died, *Is there anything that's been left unspoken? Is there anything that we haven't talked about?* She said, *I'm so proud of you. I love you both, I'm really, really proud of you. There's nothing to discuss or anything. You've never let me down.*' Words he really needs to hear after events he now tells as an anecdote, but which still have power to sting after all these years. How love can be strengthened by the discarding of secrets, and how, if you're lucky, nasty surprises sometimes lead to much happier ones further down the line.

In the drab austerity of 1948, the once pristine mock-Tudor houses look defeated, the leaded windows dark, the black beams peeling on the crumbling render. They surround Raphael Park in Romford, a place that has taken a worse hit: playing fields dug up; air-raid shelters rusting; the whole place mutilated in the cause of war. George Lucas has been here most of the evening, circling the bandstand. 'After dinner to Raphael Park,' he records in his diary on 2 May, 'where I met judgment in the form of a police constable, who took my name and address and demanded my identity card.' When he fails to produce it, the policeman tells him to take it along to the police station in Chadwell Heath, the suburb he's escaped for the evening.

Many years later, his diary and many like it are recovered by Hugo Greenhalgh, after he interviews Lucas with the intention of asking him about his experience with rent boys for a TV documentary. A book, *The Diaries of Mr Lucas*, results from their friendship and gives a vivid portrait of a gay life from mid-twentieth-century Britain, one that touches on gangsters, prostitution and London's underground gay scene in the 1960s.

Lucas is born in 1926 in Chadwell Heath, on the edge of northeast London, and his early gay experiences occur while living with his homophobic parents, before he throws himself wholeheartedly into the city's gay scene proper.

On that May day in 1948, he presents his identity card – a hangover from wartime rationing – at the police station, where he is told to expect a call in due course. It's over a month before he hears anything, so long that he's hoping it's all been forgotten. 'I received today a very terrible shock,' he writes in his diary, 'being informed by my mother that Mrs Strutt, the fat woman next door that is a clerk in the police station, had seen my name on the charge sheet.' But what happens after that, Greenhalgh cannot say. Lucas's diaries do not record it, and much as he has been anticipating his life being ruined by this event, instead things seem to continue in their old suburban way: the hopeless friendships with repressed men, the cruising and dreaming. Circumstances – a kindly policeman, inept admin, an intervention? – seem to have saved Lucas from the fate of those Altrincham men in the 1930s.

What remains are his diaries, which are astonishing. They are fragments that bring to light a life almost forgotten and experiences so rarely captured in their time. We should all keep diaries. Although you're definitely not reading mine.

THE EYES OF BEARSDEN

A girl stands in the doorway between living room and hall. Her eyes move from the patterned mustard wallpaper to the brown vortices of the carpet and back again. Suddenly, she's falling into those vortices, headlong into those patterns that make the house feel so modish, so 1970s. Rose's migraine brings with it vertigo, and everywhere she looks the decoration is pulling at her, sweeping her off her feet and down, down into its never-ending spiral.

But soon those migraine-inducing patterns are gone, swept away by fashion and her parents' restlessness, as they run from lower-middle-class origins to securely middle-class signifiers. 'When I think about the décor of our house, it's often quite inextricable from adverts for the products with which the house was decorated. I think probably my parents were looking for that life that says, *You've arrived, you're secure here, you are a part of this class*, and so they were always trying to manifest that in our house.' The Sunday supplements, the aspirational TV dramas, the symbols of 1980s affluence and consumer culture endlessly remoulded the home around her as she grew. 'My parents' class consciousness really manifested in that obsession with *that's common, that's trashy*,' she recalls. 'But then, an obsessive deference and conformity to your betters. And I think that did manifest in a restless redecoration of our home in a way that was very eighties and Major's nineties.' The house represents the impression they want to give to the world, and they constantly trade up inside in a desperate rush to keep their hard-won status, to outrun the spectre of disrepute. 'There's no avoiding the fact that my parents were snobs,' says Rose, 'the absolute soul of suburban snobbery.'

It's the early 1980s. Rose stands in the hallway, hands idly tracing the patterns of the blown vinyl wallpaper. A fingernail catches the soft tissue of a ridge and her fingertip works its way underneath, burrowing into the expanded plasticised membrane. In the lounge, fleshy shapeless peach sofas and chairs await, which in retrospect, thinks Rose, 'look like obscene soft sculpture'. Floral borders have appeared halfway up the wall, a pseudo-countrified kitchen, the tasteful pastels of Dulux's Whispers of White.

Her family live in Bearsden, a suburb of Glasgow. 'There were beautiful, big, huge deco houses with Crittall windows right next to a strip of the most George Shaw seventies harling on the edge of a playing field with a mouldering football goal,' says Rose. She grows up on a long, quiet road of 1920s bungalows. Their big, generous gardens remind her of the ideals promulgated by Dr D. G. Hessayon, the author of the Plant Expert books of the 1970s and '80s. These days, the bungalows are mostly white-washed and have dormer windows poking out from the long, low sloping roofs, part of the home improvement boom of her youth. 'I remember it both physically and emotionally as a space of constantly seeing and feeling seen, because despite these great large gardens you could see into all the houses all around you, from most angles out of most windows.' Everything is seen and nothing is overlooked.

It's from one of these dormer windows that young Rose observes the world. Her attic bedroom is as restlessly redecorated as the rest of the house, Care Bears wallpaper one year, Strawberry Shortcake the next, then the Miami pastels of the 1980s. 'Just a vague, slightly tropical jazziness,' she recalls, 'but not Wham!, because they're benders.' Nothing too camp, too ostentatious, just a quietly anxious palette of blandly good taste.

As she becomes a teenager, Rose starts to inherit beautiful mid-century furniture from obscure relatives. 'My early childhood was surrounded by these slightly baffling eccentric older people that you weren't quite sure who they belonged to. And some of them were really fun, and some of them are quite frightening. They're essentially Victorians, when you think about it, and they were disapproving. And they smelled weird, and you had to be tediously on your best behaviour, but our house had a fairly constant throughput as they all went like dominoes, they all snuffed it one after the other in the eighties and nineties.' And so Rose becomes the custodian of their G-plan tables and cupboards, which she immediately covers with collages cut from pages of *The Face* and *NME*. Where once Care Bears and Strawberry Shortcake smiled down, now darkly painted murals glower.

'Suburbia is a shifting place for me,' says Rose. 'Growing up in suburbia feels like a space of seeing and being seen all the time. It feels like a surveillant space.' Her mum, who she describes as a 'real clacket-tongued gossip', introduces Rose to a whole different way of looking at her neighbours. Some of that's unconscionable, but to Rose it's also life-saving, seeing a different grown-up way of looking at this place that seems so private and yet so exposed at the same time. Even as a child Rose is taught that there is what you see, and there's a different world of things pulsing beneath. She spends a lot of time in the garden, making up stories of sapphic boarding schools. But as she becomes a teenager that dream world dissolves. Instead, she finds herself a subject of suspicion. On Bearsden's high street she feels excluded from all the places she most wants to explore. 'All the shops had signs where they said, *No schoolchildren! No teenagers! Back off! Go away! Don't touch anything!*' There, in a place she describes as *the most tantalising shop in the world*, she's captivated by stickers and trinkets, rubbers and dangly earrings. They openly stare as she pokes about earnestly in the shop, and one day the shopkeeper pounces: *You're shoplifting!* 'I couldn't have been a squarer child,' says Rose. But this was all just a numbers game – some of the teenagers undoubtedly were shoplifting, just not bookish, awkward, four foot eleven, vividly ginger Rose in her big thick glasses. She begins to yearn for the city, just twenty minutes away, but it's somewhere she's not allowed on her own. 'I remember that period as all these intricate layers of longing, and overwhelming tedium,' she says, 'and I suppose that's the point at which you're starting to reject things about your parents. You're starting to observe things about them as people, perhaps you're starting to develop your own politics and aesthetics, and suddenly this place that is the same size it's always been feels like it narrows in around you.'

That constriction is pulled tighter by Mrs McGregor, her neighbour, who stares from her window at all the people walking by, and who runs to her front door if she suspects any of the neighbourhood kids of doing anything transgressive. And while Mrs McGregor might think she's the soul of respectability, Rose's mum has decided she's a bit common because she has a sauna, 'and probably assumed that they were a bit pervy, as saunas are fundamentally a space of nudity, and dirty as a dog's arse'. So while her mum didn't like or trust Mrs McGregor, she was happy to have her as an informant. One day, Rose is reading *On the Road* and feeling rebellious, so walks home in bare feet on the scalding tarmac, gravel and pebbledash, a choice she immediately regrets. Mrs McGregor tells her mum, *I just saw Rose walking about with no shoes on!* Nothing goes unnoticed or unremarked. These days, Rose wonders whether her neighbour might have been bored, lonely or depressed. But back then she just added to her uneasy feeling of oppressive surveillance.

The best time of the year comes when the nights begin to draw in and people leave their curtains open and their lights on, so that

Rose can look in at their furnishings and décor, the accumulated symbols of their lives. She's begun to hope for transformative encounters, to stumble across Bearsden's own Derek Jarman and be taken away from the boredom of her daily life into a queer bohemian utopia. With little evidence, she becomes convinced this will actually happen. 'I remember having this experience with a very camp straight woman, who again was the subject of gossip,' recalls Rose. 'She was one of those people who, when she was mentioned, everyone did the drinky-drinky hand – and she did smell quite extravagantly of Gordon's.' One day as she trails around the streets, Rose encounters Drinky-Drinky, who is at her front door as she's passing. Before she can really explain it, she's inside this woman's house, being shown into her groovy parlour, full of the swinging remains of its last redecoration in the 1960s. Paintings of crying boys hang on wallpaper whose optical illusions are like a Cold War brainwashing technique, or are covered in extravagant florals. They explore the rooms together, Rose cooing and admiring all of this kitsch glory in its natural habitat, its owner an extension of its lurid stylings. But now she has stayed out too long, and her mum has come looking for her. A knock at the door, a curt thank you to Drinky-Drinky, and then back home amid a torrent of disapproval and incredulousness. 'Nothing happened. But I think specifically things like that made me go, *What if one day someone else that lives just around the corner will invite me in, and they'll be* the person. And they never were.'

She's not a joiner-in at school, unlike her contemporary Brandon Lee, who is in the football team and stars in a production of *South Pacific*. It's only after he leaves that it's uncovered that Brandon is actually Brian MacKinnon, a thirty-two-year-old who has faked his way into the school by pretending to have an ageing disorder. 'If you want to know how much that school valued conformity above all else,' she says, 'it had no problem with the thirty-year-old man that was there pretending to be fifteen, because he joined in and he excelled at exams and all of that. And actually, genuinely, they were far too busy pursuing kids like me for having a pierced nose or dyed hair, or having rolled up the sleeves on your blazer or whatever.'

Every day feels like a firefight or relentless bar brawl to teenage Rose. Unlike John Hughes movies, where teenagers find their tribes or common ground, here the pupils engage in constant warfare. 'Anything was an insult, particularly all the sorts of terms for queer people, as you're starting to suspect you are. It's the language of brokenness and accidents, all that *benders* and *whoopsies* – and those are the not-so-horrible ones. If girls cut their hair short, they were *a big lezzie*, said as if it's a terrible thing to be.' And all the girls find their sexuality policed viciously. Who is doing what to whom? What she quickly learns is whatever they do, it's all equally a mistake. 'It was terrible not to have got off with anyone and let them finger you behind Spar; and you were a fucking whore if you'd got off with someone and let them finger you behind Spar.' She's careful not to misremember her own behaviour as somehow above all of this. 'I have no sense that I was a nice or a kind person. I was just desperate.' Trapped in a cycle of living defensively and being bullied, Rose feels as if she is having a panic attack that lasts six years.

Here in Bearsden, there aren't many signs of other queer kids or adults. But with the rigorous policing of norms by all the other teens, any slightly subversive tell alerts Rose to other possibilities. 'It's unfortunate really,' she says. 'The only gay grown-ups conformed to spiteful heterosexual stereotypes of them.' *The one lesbian-coded teacher must hate coming in every day*, she thinks, *as must her camp colleague*, who 'was the saddest, angriest man in the world, again with adult empathy, because he knew everyone gossiped about him'. The kids all do flappy wrists around him, and thinking back, Rose suspects she may have too, in her desperation to deflect from herself for a moment. Every encounter with otherness feels like a chance to claw her way to a fleeting moment of acceptability, or at least to distract from her own.

Meanwhile, Rose is beginning to find the furtiveness of suburbia alluring in its own way too, 'all that sneaking down desire lines, or just having a sleepover and watching a video'. On the one hand, all of this clandestine activity is poisonous; on the other, it's 'really achingly fucking sexy'. One thing she particularly associates with her queer experience as a teenager is 'feeling like no amount of you is the right amount – you're either insufficient or excessive by turns, sometimes bafflingly simultaneously. But certainly, the amount of you that exists in the world is always wrong.' *You're too emotional*, she's told, or is asked, *Why do you have to be so strange?* She becomes a goth, which she now dismisses as *heteronormative vampires and heaving tits being bitten by pallid men.* She begins to recognise the bi and pansexual sides of herself – not that she has a language for that, but she is experiencing the desire. 'It wasn't that I had no desire for men or boys, it was that I had desire for women as well, and trans or non-binary people if I'd known any at the time, but I didn't.' As the AIDS crisis grows, she's seeing gayness being conflated with disease and contamination. As a young bisexual woman, Rose thinks for a while, '*I might be able to tap out of this! Might just be able to find a way to be mad for cock, and I don't have to think about this ever again, and that's fine.* And who could blame that little version of me, in that world, in that atmosphere?' Meanwhile, she has been inspired by Drinky-Drinky's camp and kitsch aesthetic, which takes her beyond goth and in a much less heterosexual direction. She's a telly addict, a voracious watcher of suburban sitcoms and Channel Four pink triangle movies, in which she sees the contents of her head reflected back at her in often warped and unhelpful ways. 'The portrayals of queerness, the camp that's instrumental to my aesthetic, a lot of it was laughing at, not laughing with. I am – and, in retrospect, always have been, and probably always will be – an incredibly camp person, both aesthetically and socially. I just have very glittery bones.'

Rose leaves Bearsden at seventeen, goes to art college in her mid-twenties, and now in her forties finds so many of those ideas of conformity, insufficiency and excess from her days in suburbia still shaping her life. All the books, art, music and film have inspired her, urged her onward. And this is something positive she has taken from her parents, their engagement in culture: reading her mum's racy pot-boilers when she was much too young; the newspapers and magazines at home; the escape that her local library gave her, to experience other worlds and other ideas. 'Although my parents were snobs and they policed my behaviour, they never policed what I read and watched. They did have an idea that all art and literature was in some way worthwhile.'

These days, when she revisits her old neighbourhood of Bearsden it's the ubiquity of CCTV and Ring doorbells that strikes her. All of that rubbernecking and neighbourhood watching has been outsourced to tech and security companies. Rose is glad she had the opportunities that arose from going off-grid, 'that life-saving furtiveness, the ability to be invisible to your parents the second you walk around the corner from the house'. No matter how much she felt observed back then, and how much she strove to stand out, she was occasionally able to melt into the shadows and explore an alternative to the life she was being trained to accept. 'All the best things that happened to me during that period of my life were to do with my parents not having a fucking clue where I was. And never being able to find out – as long as you didn't do it anywhere near Mrs McGregor.'

Away from prying eyes, the schoolgirls are in bed, kissing. Here, in a flat in Hendon in the early 1950s, Gilli and Ann know what they're doing is forbidden, but it's also too good to stop. Clothes have been shed, and Gilli feels like she might faint with the excitement of it all. And then, when there is a sudden knock on her bedroom door, she feels like she might faint for a quite different reason. Unexpectedly, her mum is home from work. She's been taken ill. At that moment Gilli is glad she locked the bedroom door, but now her mum is becoming distressed because her daughter won't let her in. To Gilli's horror, her mum heads out to find the caretaker so she can break into her daughter's room, where she is convinced she's trapped. In a panic, Gilli pushes a terrified and half-naked Ann through her bedroom window onto the fire escape. Then, door magically unlocked, Gilli makes up a story for her mum about being sent home from school because she's also been feeling ill. There's a lot of it about. To escape the inevitable questioning and fuss, Gilli then stages a sudden recovery and announces she's off back to school again. Her mum, worried by her daughter's erratic behaviour, waves her off at the front door and, much to Gilli's frustration, watches her walk all the way down the street. Once finally out of sight she has to double back, like a heroine in a French resistance film, and stealthily re-enters the flats. As quietly as she can, she makes her way to the roof, where she finds a freaked-out and sobbing Ann. Calming her down and trying to make an adventure of it all, she helps her down from the roof and into the street.

Tales of the Suburbs I 91

After the promise of freedom and fluidity that the war has brought, the 1950s sees the dead hand of conventional morality reassert itself. Male homosexuality is still illegal, of course, and arrest figures for men having consensual sex with other men creeps ever higher throughout the decade. Lesbianism remains largely culturally invisible, while few women are encouraged into further education and work, their primary focus expected to be on home and family life. These attitudes are policed by age-old control mechanisms, ones at which these new suburbs excel: gossip and innuendo, enough to make the most semi-detached of neighbours' curtains twitch.

For a young LGBTQ+ person arriving into this culture, it must have been bewildering. Gilli Salvat's family arrived in Tilbury from Calcutta in 1947, just after the national trauma of Partition. Around the Hendon flat her parents try to keep Indian culture alive, speaking Hindi, but Gilli is soon swept away by Elvis and Ann. She and Ann have already been warned off seeing each other, after Ann's mother finds her daughter's diary, filled as it is with declarations of her love for Gilli. 'I was absolutely astounded,' Gilli later tells Allegra Damji of the Lesbian Oral History Group, 'because it was what I felt as well, but she'd actually articulated it.'[6] Ann is the prettiest girl in Gilli's class, and although they're banned from seeing each other all summer they manage to carry on their intense teenage affair, even though it's something they can't yet sing – or even sob – from the rooftops. Visibility will have to wait.

BEING SEEN IN RUISLIP

'I thought I was non-binary for a little while,' Jim tells me, 'because I was just *I actually have never felt a woman*. There's certain aspects of femininity that I think are lovely. And I really love all of my women friends and stuff, and I respect them. Obviously, I want to dismantle the patriarchy. But I just have never really felt aligned with it, you know?' This all begins to happen during lockdown in 2021, when Jim, like so many of us, is sitting around at home with time to think. The overriding feeling is that if this happens again, he wants to be in a better place, no longer yearning to be someone else. And so begins a slow and logical chain of thoughts. '*I actually love binding my chest. I actually love the idea of having a beard, and I love the idea of my voice being deeper*. And then I was, *I don't think this is non-binary any more. I think we're leaning straightforwardly into wanting to be a man*.' And with that realisation comes defiance, not to people-please but to push back against those who might not support his decision. 'I realised you get one life,' says Jim. 'As soon as you realise what makes you happy, you start to live it. As long as you're not hurting actively other people, then you should live that way.'

Jim starts out life in the 1990s in the least suburban place imaginable, brutalist Trellick Tower in Notting Hill, but pretty soon his family have moved out to a semi in Ruislip, on the edge of north-west London. In the garden Jim's dad, a carpenter, will build a pond and a treehouse, creating the perfect family environment. On the day they move, Jim and his little brother,

Michael, are playing in the street and notice another kid their age watching. The next day there's a knock at the door: it's one of the neighbouring dads, asking, *Can my son come and play with your kids?* 'His name is Paul,' says Jim, 'and he's still my best friend now.' With a video camera they make mini movies together, create a snail farm and go and explore the woods nearby. 'Found a bag of porno mags,' he recalls. 'It was the funniest day ever. I think every single person who grew up in suburbia and lived near a park has found a bag of porno mags.' All these years later, Jim has transitioned and Paul is gay. 'I do find that queer kids find each other,' he says. 'It just happens.'

Back before thoughts of transitioning, there are the awakenings of sexuality. On the TV, Madonna is performing the video to 'Beautiful Stranger'. It's not that unusual to have a dad who fancies Madonna. What's more unusual are the feelings of attraction Jim is experiencing too. 'I feel I'm watching this in the same way that my dad is watching this,' recalls Jim, 'which doesn't feel right.' In time, Jim might have been able to talk to his dad about this, but time is something they don't have. When Jim is fourteen, his dad has a heart attack and dies, quite unexpectedly. 'I think if my dad hadn't died, I probably would have had an easier time figuring all of this out,' he says. 'I changed after that. I had to become a different person.' No longer a child, with a mum who has had to go back into work to support him and Michael, who Jim ends up caring for on the days when she's out.

Clothes begin to change, from the skirts and dresses chosen by his mum to the baggy black garb he's choosing for himself. At school, he's now part of a group. 'I dated a boy who ended up being gay. My first girlfriend dated a boy; he turned out gay. This is what I mean about queer people – the freaks and geeks – we find each other.' He describes them as a marginal group, 'a queer little group without even knowing it . . . I was called a dyke and lesbo and stuff,' he recalls. 'And I think it's really interesting how kids know before you even do. In a way, is your identity already there? And do you just have to step into it? And do other people see it before you see it?' The group open their arms to all the others on the margins too, the first stop for anyone who doesn't really fit. 'We were always just very open,' he says. 'And I think that is a benefit of being different. Especially now, I think being trans, you almost sit above society. You can see stuff with more clarity, because I think from a young age you're forced to think, *I'm different. And I need to think differently about this in order to survive.*' Aged fifteen, he tells one school friend, Jess, *I want to go to Gay Pride.* He's not sure why, he just wants to go along, show support, wave a rainbow flag. *Yeah, I want to go to Gay Pride too*, she says. *I think that'd be funny.* And so they do, travelling from Ruislip into the centre of London and being part of all the colour and fun. They like it so much they go back the next year too, after which Jess's mum says, *I don't want you to go to Gay Pride, because they are predators. Those lesbians, they'll come after you.* 'I was gobsmacked,' recalls Jim. 'I remember telling my mum, and my mum was like, *Well, that's just stupid, isn't it? What a ridiculous thing to say.*' He's grateful to his mum for the support, but it opens his eyes to what Ruislip might be like more widely, a suburb with small-town views.

It's only when Jim escapes Ruislip for university in Bristol that the strength comes to assert his identity. He gets his first proper girlfriend and decides, '*I'm gonna tell people about her*, which was, I think, a mistake, because I ended up regretting the whole thing, and it was awful.' He starts to come out to his brother, whose immediate reaction is to say, *Oh God, are you pregnant?* – to which Jim replies, *No, it's kind of the opposite.* His mum says she has suspected. *Do you like boys and girls?* she asks, and gets a tentative *I guess?* in return, Jim not having written off men completely at this point. *So you're kind of like Jessie J then*, she says. Later, she sends a text: *I think Angelina Jolie likes women as well.* He has a moment imagining Jessie J and Angelina Jolie walking through Ruislip holding hands. 'I'd be, *Fair play*,' says Jim. At Bristol, he has a big fringe, piercings, skinny jeans and lots of black eyeliner, at which no one bats an eye. 'You go home for the weekend and you're a spectacle,' he says. 'You are not what the people of Ruislip expect to see when they go into the post office.' The staring becomes something he has to get used to, something he's more alert to since wanting to transition. 'There's almost no malice behind it,' he says. 'It's just a stare of *You're different. Right?* Just a stare of confusion or curiosity. The same thing you have if you hold hands with someone of the same sex. You get looks. And often they're not *Oh, that's disgusting.* It's just *Oh, that's a strange-looking person.*' Bristol starts to feel more like home. 'A home that you make yourself,' he says. 'I think that's what queer communities do, you make a home with the people you like. Chosen families and stuff.'

The city and the country might afford room for anonymity or escape, but in suburbia we are known, and our identities often feel set by others, by the culture of the streets we live in. To take control of those narratives, to change them and pass back into that world with its codes of control, is not easy. And while superficially you'd think suburbia would embrace change, given how fluid its own physicality has proven to be, that's seldom the case. In some ways, suburbia's evolution has been a never-ending series of transitions, from leafy edgelands to in-between places, houses remodelled and transformed over generations, each gradually blossoming in different ways, our modifications creating in what were once uniform streets a patchwork of individual colour and personality. It should love change: it *is* change.

But one thing that has helped Jim become more comfortable in Ruislip is a realisation that often other people don't care about you as much as you think they do. And also, that he doesn't really care what they think either. 'The more I medically transitioned, the more I became comfortable with myself, the more I passed – and I know that's a really bad thing for a trans person to want, because the idea isn't that you pass as a cis person, because trans people, no matter what they look like, should be accepted everywhere.' If Jim and his girlfriend were out and about, he would sometimes avoid getting too close to her to avoid drawing attention to himself. Since the transition, it feels less of an issue. Being gendered correctly has made a huge difference to Jim's life. 'That makes me happy,' he tells me, 'because I'm being perceived as the person I want to be.' Able to live on his own terms, a life he's now in control of, moving forward with a confidence he never used to have. Feeling love and support, feeling strong. Holding hands.

Philip Baker kick-starts his Lambretta and begins following his best mate as they set out on a ride from Crawley to Brighton. He's in an Italian suit with cloth buttons, bum-freezer jacket and winkle-pickers. He hides these clothes from his foster parents and has to get changed at his friend's house. There isn't much they know or understand about what Philip gets up to with his Mod friends, off catching gigs by jazz bands and, later, the Spencer Davis Group and Steve Winwood, Manfred Mann and Ginger Baker. As he speeds along, a flashier flock of Mods, on their faster and more stylish Vespas, jeer as they pass Philip and his mate.

Philip is the son of a Black American saxophonist, who his mother met in wartime on a night out at the Café de Paris. He's born in Croydon in 1942, and eventually is fostered out to a white couple in the new town of Crawley. By 1957, he's working there at a plastics factory. 'There were four other gay men at the factory where I worked,' he tells Paul Marshall of the Gay Men's Oral History Group some thirty years later.[7] Most importantly, one is his manager, who teaches Philip about culture, from books to theatre. Everyone knows his manager is gay, and no one is bothered. Philip has a fling with one of the other guys there. 'We'd do it when we could, in lunch breaks or we'd stay behind late or go into the grounds.' While on the one hand it sounds like quite a liberated life for the time, it's a strangely invisible world, even to the other LGBTQ+ people he meets. He shares a flat with a guy who he doesn't realise is gay until many years later. You have to be careful deciding who you can trust.

Crawley, his hometown, is a rational new settlement, looking to the future rather than the past. By the 1950s, scientific methods are employed to help design homes; functional kitchens and ergonomics might have been pioneered in Germany in the 1920s, but it takes decades for those lessons to be applied in Britain. Cities lose many of their urban residents to these overspill outposts throughout the mid-twentieth century, hollowing out centres and spreading beyond the fringe. The critic Ian Nairn dubs these new landscapes 'subtopia', distinguished by a lack of vitality, diversity or authenticity. These fears have underpinned many LGBTQ+ people's suspicion of suburbia too, as somewhere that stifles individuality. Here, among the sputnik-legged tables and brightly abstract soft furnishings, the nuclear family rules. Everyone is assumed to be living by supposedly wholesome heterosexual convention in these planned spaces, the people designing these estates not factoring in the variety of lives that will be lived here. Queerness, often glimpsed in unexpected corners of old towns, is either designed out of these new settlements or conveniently ignored. The 1950s is a decade in denial, with gay life scratched from the public record, unless in the salacious proceedings of local courts. But things are changing. A post-war generation are creating diverse new youth cultures, their refusal to be seen but not heard bringing generations into conflict.

Philip is one of those pushing at the boundaries of the day. Eventually, he leaves the plastics factory and trains as a dancer, auditioning for big London shows like *Sweet Charity* and *Carmen Jones*. 'There were only about ten coloured dancers in London,' he recalls in the language of the time, 'five women and five men.' As for the barriers he meets in his dancing career, he says he isn't aware of prejudice straight away. His Black identity, like his sexuality, is something he becomes more engaged with as he gets older. It flourishes when he moves away from his adopted family and the modern suburb that created a Mod, and he begins to understand just how the world at that time saw a young Black gay man.

AVANT GARDE IN CRAWLEY

'In Crawley, gay didn't really happen,' Owen assures me. Crawley in West Sussex has a muted take on mid-century modern style, a new town as if designed in a *Blue Peter* competition. When Owen is growing up in the 1970s and '80s, little has changed there since the days when Philip was riding his scooter. The working-class respectability of the place has stuck with Owen. His parents had been born early on in this modern town's life and became childhood sweethearts. By the time Owen came along at the start of the seventies, a sense of aspiration characterised its second generation. 'I think the new-town story was written in straight couples, families or families-to-be – a strong element of social engineering,' he tells me. 'Those houses were offered to couples – married couples. You got the keys to three or four houses, got to look at them to choose the one you want.' Growing up there, Owen aspires too, but not to the organised heterosexuality of the post-war dream. He aspires to escape, to find somewhere to be himself.

There are few hints in Crawley of the exciting LGBTQ+ world Owen glimpses in the pop videos or arty films that so captivate him. Even what might be the most tangible evidence of gay life in his neighbourhood is resolutely uninspiring. A few doors down from him, two men are living together. 'They were two joyless older men,' says Owen. 'Absolutely joyless. I never saw them smile. When I delivered their newspaper, I never got anything from them, nothing. But my dad used to call them *the nurses*.' He pauses. 'They weren't nurses. But in my dad's eye, that was a categorisation of what these two blokes must be.' Even explaining them away as cabin crew seems to lack sufficient respectability, so nurses it is. Not that Owen is ready to be identified as gay himself at this point. It's the early 1980s, and Owen is watching the television with his aunt. Boy George is on the screen, flamboyant, remarkably dressed, extraordinarily made-up. 'I never liked Culture Club,' he tells me. That day, his aunt asks, *When you grow up, do you think you'll be like him?* Owen, only just a teenager, is mortified. He knows what she has seen in him, but he does not know how, and he's not ready for it. 'I said, *No, I'll never be like that.* And so I hated him as a result.'

If Crawley has little in the way of queer joy for young Owen, the nearby towns of Brighton and Horsham make up for it. 'They had an aura of decadence,' he says. Aged eleven, he begins drama classes in Horsham. (Crawley doesn't get a theatre until the 1990s. 'There was a Portakabin on stilts that was called Art Centre 80,' Owen explains. 'That centre was run by an ageing thespian who just stood out a country mile. My dad would say, *You don't go near there.*') Walking round the streets of that old town, with its jumble of architectural styles and the accretion of centuries rather than decades, what fascinates him most is the lack of net curtains, allowing him to look right into these suburban homes, these different lives. These were houses 'with pine shelves and spice racks, books they actually used – houses full of books, pianos in the room. Whereas in Crawley none of that happened. What you really needed was your three-piece suite and your television in the corner.' He hesitates to describe Horsham people as louche, but they were certainly more flamboyant than his immediate new-town neighbours. 'When I went there, you could definitely be a bit more Horsham,' he says. 'My theatre school people used to call me Ollie, so I even sort of had a different name when I was there, inhabiting a completely different person. In the theatre school, teachers would say amazing things that no one would ever say in Crawley, like *Get into bijou groupettes.*' It's run by an actress called Esmée Alexander, who wears huge scarves and surrounds herself with a coterie of younger gay male admirers. 'And all she did was sit on the door and collect the money,' he says, 'and tell them, *This year's* Bugsy Malone. *Give me* Bugsy Malone!'

Owen describes his parents as avant garde in the 1970s. Athena prints of Lowrys on the walls, Ercol chairs, clean-lined Habitat furnishings, shagpile carpets and, most significantly, no net curtains. They prop the TV up on bricks rather than getting a unit for it. His grandparents are horrified. *What are you doing? Are you not waiting for the furniture to come?* But Owen's friends think it's really cool. By the 1980s, Laura Ashley has begun her relentless war on that hipper and hippier age. His mum starts embracing soft furnishings in a muted Victorian-style tile pattern called Mr Jones, chintz cropping up everywhere like mould in a damp basement. The furniture too begins to change. 'My parents invested in, as they would say, *some really nice "pine pieces"* for the house, stripped pine, so that it looked really, really smart.' When Owen is eleven, he chooses new décor for his bedroom too, from Marks & Spencer. 'It was a pink patchwork bedspread, pink patchwork cushions, everything was pink. It was something to behold. I mean, whether or not it's entirely right for an eleven- or twelve-year-old boy, you have to wonder, but eventually it got changed.'

Owen's best friend at school is a boy called Andrew. They're inseparable. Years later, in their late teens, they will come out as gay to each other. They agree there's no sign of gay life there for them to latch on to – which, given the proximity of Gatwick Airport and the sheer number of cabin crew living there, does feel almost wilful on their part, but also gives an idea of how compartmentalised and private life in the suburbs could be. 'You couldn't say that Crawley had any pubs, or even parks,' he says, 'all the places that you might, in your mind's eye, somehow think we're associated with. That slightly repressed atmosphere.' Instead, the best they can find is their biology teacher, who lives in sophisticated Haywards Heath and listens to opera. 'We didn't know why we liked him,' says Owen, 'but we quite liked hanging around chatting to him.' Owen hides his sexuality and difference behind a shield of bookishness and academic achievement. He also has a smokescreen that works for a while: he's great at getting on with girls, if not getting off with them, and is happy for his parents to assume that he has a lot of girlfriends. One tells him later how he *slowly quenched the flame*. He and Andrew become pals with Steven and Claire, both of whom, he's pretty sure, came out later too. They spend a lot of time re-enacting *French and Saunders* sketches. 'We would sit together in class or hang out together at lunchtime, eat our packed lunches together. And I don't think that was us protecting each other, bullies weren't going to come and see. We just loved each other's company, we would just absolutely rock ourselves laughing at things and people.' As far as coming out is concerned, he knows that's something for tomorrow. 'You know when you think when you're about sixteen, *Oh, really I just yearn to be a grown-up, to be myself?*' he says. 'I lived that. I love being a grown-up.'

After university he gets a job teaching in north-west London, and ends up living in Radlett, near Watford. For all of his desire to leave Crawley for a more cosmopolitan life, he has landed in another vast and seemingly straight suburb, this one on the straggling edge of Metroland. He's in his early twenties, feeling lonely, convincing himself he's never going to meet anyone. One slow weekend, Owen is making his way dutifully through the *Independent on Sunday*, and in the classifieds section he reads a lonely-hearts ad that catches his eye. Another young guy like him, at a loss as to how to find someone. He throws the paper away and gets on with his day. Later, he tells his old school friend Andrew, who says, *Get that newspaper out of the bin. You need to look at it. What have you got to lose?* And so he fishes it out, replies to the ad and ends up on a date with Paul – who, it turns out, lives just seven miles away in St Albans. And so rather than the customary trek into central London for a date, they meet in a nearby pub. The only gay one in the area at the time is on a lonely road between St Albans and Harpenden, whose sole attraction seems to be that there are no people around to see you go in. The one time he goes there, a row of old men on bar stools look him up and down like a piece of meat. So they don't go there, where all hope dies in the car park of broken dreams. Instead, they meet in a rusticated straight pub in St Albans, and through a haze of Simply Red and spicy Nik Naks there is an immediate spark.

Back when he came out, aged twenty-one, his grandparents sat him down at their kitchen table a few days later with a pot of tea. 'You always knew when something serious was going on with my grandma, because she turned the radio down,' he says. His grandmother told him, *Now we've heard, you know, and we want you to know that we love you.* His grandpa added, *I think it would be best if you joined the theatre.* 'It was that sense of, *You'll be safe there. Because you'll find people like yourself.* And I knew instantly what they were trying to do and be caring. But I knew in that moment that I needed to be gay in whatever I wanted to do, I didn't need to be back in another space that was closeted.' All these years later here he is, married to Paul from that date; he's a headteacher, the height of respectability. Perhaps after all of that yearning and desire to be free of Crawley, it's not Owen who has escaped the suburbs, but the suburbs that have escaped themselves.

It's the love letters that seal their fate. Vince is twenty-four and John nineteen. It's 1963 – that supposedly enlightened era of The Beatles and the recent overturning of the ban on D. H. Lawrence's *Lady Chatterley's Lover* (like E. M. Forster's *Maurice*, another novel about a randy gardener that is influenced by George Merrill and Edward Carpenter). Well, it doesn't look very liberated to Vince and John and the other eight men arrested in Bolton. It all begins because Vince wants to leave the army to be with John, so to be discharged he informs his superiors that he's gay. What happens instead is the police search his belongings, find John's letters and trace them back to an organisation called the Popular Pen Pals' Club. By pulling John and Vince in for questioning they find the names of other gay men in the area, and arrest them too. Soon, ten are standing trial at Bolton Magistrates Court. 'In this case, there was no public sex, no underage sex, no multiple sex. Yet they were all dragged to court,' says Allan Horsfall, then a local Labour councillor.[8] The usual way of these proceedings is that the defendants are cowed into shame and humiliation by the law. Not so Vince and John. The younger man tells the court, 'You don't understand. I am in love with Vince. I don't think we did anything wrong.'[9] Yet Vince is charged with being the 'ringleader' of this disparate group of gay men, five of whom work at the local hospital. He's sentenced to twenty-one months in prison. Outraged, Horsfall writes to the local paper, and he's not alone in penning letters of support for the men.

Together with Colin Harvey, Horsfall founds the North Western Homosexual Law Reform Committee the following year, soon renamed the Campaign for Homosexual Equality, or CHE. 'The trendsetters may well have been in London, but the blokes overwhelmingly were not,' he tells Helene Curtis and Mimi Sanderson for their book The Unsung Sixties.[10] 'We happened to be located in Manchester, but it wouldn't have mattered if it had been Bristol or Newcastle; it just had to be somewhere away from London so people could see that we could push homosexual law reform forward in the provinces without the sky falling in.' There is certainly a lot of evidence in towns big and small across the region that gay subcultures are flourishing. 'It always seemed to happen in the best hotels,' he recalls.[11] There was the Thorn Hotel, Burnley, for example, or the gents' bar of the Nelson Hotel. 'It was never in a scruffy pub, because in the best hotels it was presumed you'd get a certain amount of tolerance.' The society they set up might be based in Manchester, but Horsfall is not. He's working for the National Coal Board and lives initially in the small town of Nelson, before moving to a pretty terraced house in Atherton, a mining village in south Lancashire; his partner, Harold Pollard, is a teacher, and he says they cannot live together because of the rules that come with the Atherton house, which is tied to Allan's job.

Just a few years before Horsfall wrote to the local paper to defend the ten Bolton men, such public action would have been unthinkable. Back in early September 1957, Allan is sitting in the Sunbeck Café in Nelson, working his way through a stack of newspapers. The Wolfenden Committee's report on Homosexual Offences and Prostitution has just been published. 'I was delighted to see what the committee had recommended, rather less pleased to see some of the editorial reception, which was mixed,' he recalls.[12] He tries to order a copy of the report itself from HMSO, but all 5,000 copies sell out on the first day. The government has severely underestimated the interest in the subject. When he's campaigning to become a Labour councillor, he pens a letter about homosexual law reform to a Labour paper of the day. 'I dropped it rather merrily into the post-box and then felt sickness in the pit of my stomach.' His worst fear is that he'll be hounded by the local press. After a couple of miserable days he heads off to London in a state of anxiety, to see if he can speak to Peter Wildeblood, a man caught up in one of the biggest gay scandals of the day. Wildeblood, Lord Montagu of Beaulieu and Michael Pitt-Rivers had all been sent to prison in 1954 for 'conspiracy to incite certain male persons to commit serious offences with male persons' – by which they meant having sex with a couple of perfectly willing RAF men. Wildeblood, a journalist, emerges from the ordeal fighting, writing a bestselling book, *Against the Law*, which helps spur the Wolfenden Committee's formation. Horsfall tracks Wildeblood down and knocks on his door. 'He was good enough to ask me in, sit me down and give me a drink and talk me down from this state of high anxiety by saying that things seldom turned out quite as black as one anticipated.'[13]

When in 1958 the Homosexual Law Reform Society get their first campaigning leaflets printed, it's Allan's address they put on them, and the local paper runs a front-page story. He's a Labour councillor, and although his local branch supports him in private, they're too anxious to speak up publicly, which frustrates him no end. He expects a hideous backlash from neighbours and the community more widely, but apart from a bit of disgruntlement at work there is nothing. So, next, he tries to set up a gay social club called Esquire, based in an assembly room in nearby Burnley. 'The church were after us; even the local doctors formed a committee to oppose it,' he recalls. 'We held a public meeting to try to explain our plans in Burnley public library in the town centre, and it was packed, priests getting up and bringing down hell fire on us, councillors, everyone.' Teddy Boys are asked by the police to remove their boots outside to try to minimise the threat of violence, and a line of bovver boots steams along the pavement outside like a threat.

What Wildeblood gives to Horsfall is the certainty that this is the right thing to do. What Horsfall gives to the rest of us is a campaigning organisation across the country that brings people together both in and outside of the big cities. His legacy is seen throughout this book, in the CHE groups formed, the lasting friendships made and the outposts of hope springing up in the most unlikely of places.

THE TRIALS OF THORNGUMBALD

Her sixteenth year is a big one for Allison. It's 1985; choices beckon. She has her heart set on joining the RAF, aces the aptitude test and is called in for an interview. 'The sergeant major or whatever he was – bear in mind I'm a sixteen-year-old girl who has not seen a lot of life – actually asked me in an interview if I was one of those lesbians,' she tells me. 'Well, it was illegal, wasn't it? So obviously, I said no.' But that one off-colour comment changes Allison's life. She really wants to be in the forces, but now that doesn't feel possible. She may be young but she knows she doesn't want to live a lie. She's had enough of those already. And so she walks away from it, and instead she joins a Youth Training Scheme in Debenhams in Hull, earning £27.50 a week. After all, for all of its shortcomings, at least it's not illegal to be a lesbian in Debenhams.

The department store is packed with the fashionable items of the day: pastel waffle cardigans, sun loungers, Transformers. But Allison's head has been turned by something else: one of the other young women on the YTS, who is pretty and ostensibly straight. Not that Allison expects anything to come of it – she's much too used to hiding her feelings. But on a night out the girl unexpectedly says to her, *Do you want to stay at ours?* This has never happened before, something so direct. Allison's immediate thought is to run away. But instead of her usual defensive *No, don't come near me!* she finds herself instead saying yes, and going back with her. It's the start, not of a relationship, but a secret affair that continues for some months, both of them careful not to say anything and to make sure that no one suspects. After a while, Allison doesn't quite understand why they're still creeping around. None of her straight friends are having to do that with their relationships. They're making a big deal of them, with all the dates and plans and general fuss that comes with young heterosexual love. Instead, Allison feels pressure not to talk about hers. But, like the secrecy in the RAF, she doesn't want that either. 'It big time messes with your head,' Allison tells me. And it's a pattern she finds repeating over and over, seemingly straight girls enjoying Allison as a bit on the side. 'I used to do the deed, shall we say, they'd kick me out and go and get their boyfriends and do whatever. So I had a lot of that sort of thing going on. Bloody awful.'

The suburbs of Hull have always felt this way to Allison. It's 1979, and she is eleven. At school, she's popular: funny, good at sports, always first picked by the boys at football, hanging out with the best-looking girls. But on the inside she's very different. She knows she's attracted to other girls, has known for years, back in infants' school chasing them round the playground, not noticing she's the only girl doing it. 'I always had that guilt, I think, that I wasn't the "normal" child.' And so Allison begins self-harming, 'just because I didn't like myself', she says. The pain is a punishment, it's what she deserves, she thinks. And then, as she hits puberty, she begins to drink. 'I probably started drinking when I was thirteen to cover stuff up,' she tells me. 'And that carried on. I just drank when I could. It's weird living a lie, isn't it?' Around her, the pressure increases. She gets called 'butch' a few times while she's playing sport. She gets asked out by boys, and she dates a few to keep everyone else happy. 'And then as soon as they got a bit frisky, I got rid of them.' She has hankerings for some of the girls but never does anything about it. One day, a couple of them she regards as good friends sit down either side of her, and under the table she feels their hands on her legs. 'I don't know what it was, but it made me feel horrendous. I think they were saying, *What will you do?*, wondering whether they were pushing me to do anything or admit something.' Like the crows, watching for any sign of weakness. And so the drink, the self-harm, they're different ways to obliterate the feelings she's having. And they add a burden of further secrets, so that the whole mechanism keeping her sexuality hidden is now tangled up with other lies and anxieties, her life a complex dance over trip wires that, if she stumbles, might trigger alarms all around her, might set off an explosion.

And so, when Allison reaches the fateful age of sixteen and her mum and dad ask her if she's gay, she's already on maximum alert. 'So obviously they had an inkling,' she tells me. 'I mean, everybody does, but they don't say anything.' The curiousness of keeping a secret that everyone already knows, a feeling LGBTQ+ people have lived with down the ages. But instead of leaning into it and finally being able to be who she is, defusing the bomb, Allison retreats in fear; she lies and denies it. 'It was just getting too much,' she says. At sixteen, she's finding herself relying on drink more and more to get her through the day. And so her solution is to go out and immediately find a guy. 'Literally thought, *Right, I'd better get a boyfriend.*' She finds a likely lad, but can't go through with it. Years later she will bump into him again in Silhouette, a nightclub in Hull. He's there with his wife. 'And his wife came over to me and said, *Will you please tell him that he didn't turn you gay?* Because all these years he'd convinced himself that that one experience with him had turned me into a lesbian. So I have to go over and say, *No, definitely not.* Bless him.'

This is the era when straight pubs and clubs have gay nights 'where we all came out and felt safe', remembers Allison. 'And it was never a *good* night, never on a Friday or Saturday. It was a Monday evening where they let the gays go out in the club.' And Mondays in Hull were Romeo and Juliet's, where she'd see all the boys voguing. She calls it 'my nearly coming-out phase'. Finally, she hears of Silhouette, an actual gay venue, 'And that was like, oh my God, the Mecca, when you finally realise there's other people.' In 1987, a friend wins a competition to go to the Hippodrome in London, and Allison goes with her. They're put up by her friend's gay uncle, who takes them out to the gay bars of the city. 'Oh my God,' she says, 'it's like a new world! People like me everywhere!' They hunt out places marked with a pink triangle, then still the symbol of gay venues before the rainbow flag becomes ubiquitous. The trip opens her eyes. She has yet to experience life in the wider world as an out gay woman, hasn't really seen other women together. At this point, she's much less coded as a lesbian; a few months later Allison will radically change her look, taking inspiration from Annie Lennox and cutting her hair daringly short. Even so, when the duo head to Soho, a big transvestite stops them in one of the side streets with a practised *Ooh, we've even got something for you in here.* 'We were like, *How do you know?!* It's bizarre when you think about it, how the worlds are so different. I was like, *That's it. I'm moving to London.*'

But she doesn't. Instead, back in the suburbs of Hull with her parents, she finds the old anxieties returning. She cannot be herself in these streets where the crows watch everything, where everyone wants to know her business. She goes out one night and doesn't come home, sleeping rough in the city centre, overwhelmed by it all. The next day she returns home, her parents worried about where she's been. 'I came in, looking bedraggled, and I just said, *Do you ever wonder why I do things like this?*' she recalls. '*It's because I'm gay!* Real dramatic.' The trip wire has been caught, and the explosion catches them all off guard, Allison included. 'It was all a bit shouty, shall we say.' She thinks they might say, *Yeah, we knew, because we asked you,* but it's not like that at all. 'And my mum's crying, and my dad came home from work and he was crying. And I don't know whether it's because they wished I'd have told them or what.' The trip wire seems to have set off a chain reaction. The amount of emotion pouring from them is a big shock, her parents not usually ones for showing their feelings. 'But I know they love me,' explains Allison. And the sense of relief is enormous. *That's it,* she thinks, *I've done it. I'm all right now.* So next weekend she brings a girlfriend home. But her dad puts a stop to that. *No, that's not happening,* he tells her. *Just cos you come out, you're not doing that.* 'So that was that,' she says. 'It was the talk round the village. *Poor lady –* my mum. Not *Poor Allison, going through all those years living a lie.* It was always about the parents. *What will they think?* So I got out the village fairly quickly after.'

Later that year, Allison's round the house of a mate at an Ann Summers party. She meets a woman, a young mother of two, who is there six weeks after giving birth, and there's an immediate connection. In no time at all she has moved in with her, from her family's beautiful bungalow on the edge of the country to a council house with holes in the roof and no carpet. 'It was pretty shocking,' she says. But there is more to it than that. 'It was one of those rescuing each other things. I think she'd had a really crappy upbringing in foster homes.' Allison's family don't really know what has happened, who she's with or why. But at eighteen here she is, 'this father figure, mother figure, other mother for these two kids', she recalls. 'And I used to take it in turns to take one of the kids back to my mum and dad's on a Sunday. It was never asked what was going on.' Allison surprises herself that she can do this, that she can persevere. 'I became a parent and brought money in to furnish the house, and grafted almost like some sort of thirty-plus man who'd just got married and had two kids and felt a responsibility.'

The Preston Road Estate in Hull has a reputation for being tough, rows of plain local authority semis tightly packed together, crowding the streets. Overwhelmed by responsibility, Allison is standing on the doorstep, the older of her partner's kids calling for her, and her next-door neighbour is there. *You'll be all right*, the neighbour tells the little boy. *You've just got two mummies now*. 'It's the first time somebody's been okay with it,' she recalls, wonderingly. All the things she's been told, about how if you live in a poor area you'll be treated like shit and beaten up, and now she finds the total opposite.

When that relationship ends, she moves back with her parents to the creeping suburbia on the edge of the city. Then, at twenty-one, she gets her own place in Hull, working in a factory and living a more urban life. She remembers the man who runs the works, a huge guy who leers through windows at the women working there, hounding them. Allison gets off with a couple of female colleagues, and ends up in a relationship with one of them. Somehow her boss finds out, and sacks her because of it. If this is civilian life, she might as well have stuck with the RAF. It's not the last time a man will come along and take brutal exception to her sexuality. On a night out in Scarborough, a drunk guy pulls a plank from a skip and smashes her across the head with it because, he says, he doesn't like lesbians. When she reports it at the police station she tells the coppers what the man has said, 'and this policewoman said, *Well, are you?* I was like, *Well, what do I say now?* Why did that matter? A six-foot-four guy had just lamped me, and she asked if I was a lesbian, because obviously I'd deserve it if I was.' And she gets beaten up in a pub by the landlord, who says he isn't keen on her type. He attacks her and she falls, smashes her head on a wrought-iron table and is knocked unconscious. 'So I was blue-lighted to the Hull Royal Infirmary,' she recalls. 'And again, the attitude of the staff then, because of, I'm guessing, the way I looked – I was, as I said, quite butch-looking – and they just assumed I'd been fighting and pretty much treated me like shit.' Even now, when she's out with her partner, Tina, she will stop holding hands if she sees a group of men coming towards her. 'It does stay with you.'

After being sacked for being lesbian and with her confidence knocked, Allison ends up unemployed for a while, getting the odd gig working in various chippies. Still drinking and smoking, she decides she would like to get fit, rediscovering the sporty side that had so sustained her childhood. She starts swimming at the leisure centre in Ennerdale. Every time she's in the pool, the manageress seems to appear from nowhere. 'I thought, *Yeah, you bat for my side, love*,' says Allison, 'but she was pregnant.' One day, they get chatting. *What do you do?* the manageress asks. *You're here a lot.* Allison tells her she's unemployed. *Do you want to do some lifeguarding?* Allison often swims there with her girlfriend, so she's quite obviously out. And soon after she starts working there, another female lifeguard comes out. Then a couple of the other women staff. Soon, even the manageress has come out. 'It got nicknamed Ennerdyke,' she recalls. 'Because all the leisure centre girls came out!' To be a pioneer empowering a whole group of women is a significant moment for Allison, told for so long to hide her sexuality by women who didn't want to admit it, or men who didn't like it. After the secrets and gossip, the sacking and the injuries, this feels like a new chapter. 'I felt a not very brave person a lot of the time,' she says, but 'once I was out and accepted it a little bit more, it was nice that it led to these young girls being able to say it.'

These days, Allison lives with her partner in Beverley, an old market town not far from Hull. They've been together for seventeen years. Her mum and dad live in Hedon, near where she grew up. She thinks she subconsciously avoids the suburban centre there in case she bumps into people she knew from school. 'I'd like to gauge their reactions to me,' she says. 'I see the odd one who is obviously absolutely fine with me, but you still get that thing, *What are they thinking? Why didn't they say something at school? Why didn't they ask me*, you know?' And when she does meet them, it would be great to say that all of those ghosts have been exorcised, but it's always more complicated than that. 'I did bump into a girl from school once in town, and even though I knew she knew about me, and even though I was well into my forties then, I still had that thing, that almost shame. Bizarre, isn't it?' Sometimes she will go for a drive around the old haunts, where she'd once played cricket or football in the street. They bring back nostalgic memories of 'when you were happy, before you realised what the hell was going on', she says. It was probably difficult for her parents, she thinks, and they have been support-ive over the years. And of suburbia itself, she tells me: 'I still have nice memories of it.' Despite all the turmoil. The bungalows, seemingly so low-wattage, instead carry the most extraordinary supercharge of emotion. Allison thinks about it for a moment. 'Whether I'd go back there,' she says, 'I don't think I would.' She might live less than twenty miles from where she grew up, but it's a lifetime away. A world where it's now safe to be herself.

Hester Caulton closes the door to her office at the end of a long school day and sits there for a moment. It's 1968, and she's surrounded by the dreary paraphernalia of the school office: cardboard folders in all shades of drab; olive filing cabinets; a long desk with few personal touches; empty chairs for those difficult chats. She thinks of the school she runs, the kids bright or struggling, parents engaged or detached, and wonders what they see. A successful head teacher, someone in control, not a fully rounded character to them, just an authority figure. She wonders what they might think of her if they knew about her life outside school. 'If the parents of the children of my school learned that I am a lesbian, and happy to be, their immediate reaction would be one of disgust.'[14]

In the days before the internet, isolation is one of the most difficult things for LGBTQ+ people to deal with, especially if they live away from any of the big cities. But by the 1960s, culture is slowly beginning to represent a broader spectrum of lives. Social change has begun to be glimpsed in the kitchen sink dramas and new wave films of the late 1950s and '60s, with LGBTQ+ characters including Geoffrey in the 1958 play *A Taste of Honey*, Melville in the 1961 film *Victim* and June in *The Killing of Sister George* (1964) all providing valuable touchstones. It's in this atmosphere that April Ashley becomes Britain's most well-known transgender figurehead after being outed in the *Sunday People* in 1961; lesbian magazine *Arena Three* is launched in 1964; and the partial decriminalisation of sex between consenting men over the age of twenty-one in private becomes law in England and Wales three years later.

It's *Arena Three* that succeeds in reaching Hester in her school in Staffordshire. But the experiences she shares are painful. 'In fairly small communities such as this, scandal runs like a flame through straw,' she writes in that magazine. 'Despite my sincere efforts to give all that is best to my pupils, parents would believe that I would "contaminate" their children, or teach them "dirty habits", or educate them to be "not nice".' Instead, Hester maintains an inscrutable front, her blankness the reassuring backdrop to student dramas and parental anxieties, while beyond a whole other world is beckoning.

ROUGH LANDING IN WORCESTER

Up where the Atlantic Ocean meets the North Sea, an aircraft is turning for home. On board is Kevin, navigator of this RAF Nimrod out on submarine-hunting duties. Something is nagging at him, but it might be all right, he thinks, it might be all right. As the lumbering jet touches down at the Air Force base at Kinloss, up near the northernmost tip of the Scottish mainland, the crew have an unusual welcome party out to greet them. The wing commander meets them from the plane and makes his way straight for Kevin. In a confused few moments, the navigator finds himself taken away by his superior – very publicly, in front of all his colleagues and crewmates – and driven to the military police. Kevin will spend, in his words, 'a few hours under happy interrogation. Very personal and intrusive. Then pretty much immediately suspended and then kicked out.' One moment he's out hunting submarines, the next he's the submarine being hunted.

In 1994, a ban on homosexual personnel in the UK forces is still in place, as it has been since 1967, and will remain so for another six years. 'It was still a court martial offence,' Kevin recalls. 'You were undercover, deep cover. And that's where people stayed.' He's not aware of any gay networks within the RAF at the time. And so Kevin feels very alone with what has been a slow revelation to him. The RAF has been his obsession since childhood. And because he knows that being gay isn't allowed there, he buries the thought of any sort of sexual relationship for years. He joins up in the late 1980s. 'I perhaps had some inkling that something wasn't quite right in the early days of being in the Air Force, where perhaps I was questioning my sexuality. But I didn't act on them.' Instead, he channels all of that frustration and confusion into his training, and slides deeper into denial.

He meets a woman, and they start a relationship and get married. Here begins an experiment in heterosexual family life in the forces, in Carterton, a suburb purpose-built for RAF officers at Brize Norton, an air transport base in Oxfordshire. 'In a lot of respects it felt just like any other housing estate,' he says. Streets of prefabricated houses covered in pebbledash. 'Very basic design, but they were quite solid. Lots of space, lots of room. The ones that the junior ranks had were not so pleasant.'

Although the estate is not gated off from the rest of the town, everybody here belongs to the military. It's a strange male-officer-dominated version of a suburb, a very social environment, full of parties and get-togethers in a modern garrison town. Kevin's wife soon falls pregnant, and they bring their first child up in the married quarters of the air base. Like many of the other officers, he's off on long flights for days or weeks at a time. The women and children left behind in Carterton form a community apart from the men, a gendered suburban picture more 1950s than 1990s.

But under the surface, Kevin's awakening is slow but insistent. On an extended trip to Hamburg he explores the Reeperbahn, the red-light district, and it's there he sees things that help awaken his sexuality. They're expecting a second child and have moved up to Scotland to be with his wife's family, but by then he knows the game is up. 'Things cemented within me and I realised that, actually, the relationship I was in wasn't the right one for me. And I came out to myself as being gay.' Kevin is twenty-five. 'I was quite a late developer.' None of this is easy, but after he and his wife separate Kevin moves into an officers' mess in RAF Kinloss, becoming one of the lads in a much less suburban environment, a few rooms near a communal dining room, lounge and bar. As far as the Air Force knows, he lives here for two years as a single man. But manoeuvres have been launched. Kevin has met a man. It's not straightforward. Because of his job, and the time, it can't be.

Just meeting guys isn't straightforward. 'It was 0898 chat lines and things like that,' he recalls, of nineties gay dating. He doesn't make calls from the base. Instead, he drives to a nearby town to stand in a phone box, ramming down coins and talking to random guys from around the country. 'And I met someone.' In a story not short of surprising elements, this might be the most unexpected. After all, it's probably fair to say that owners of 0898 chat lines didn't really envisage them being a successful matchmaking tool for their users. They were simply a scam, like pyramid selling or having your drive re-tarmacked. But in this instance, successful it is. Tony is a farm manager and lives miles from his nearest town. And so for a gay RAF officer breaking the rules, it's the perfect hideout for weekends. There, Kevin finally feels like he can relax and be himself. 'But then you'd go home and it's *Right, pack all that in, pack it down.* You can't say, *Oh, I was away with him* or anything like that. You can't use names, can't use locations. Just, *Oh yeah. Just went home to see family. And it was fine.* And you just couldn't relax. Because any hint . . . Every few weeks, there was some sort of *Oh, so-and-so on such an RAF base has been thrown out,* or whatever. So there were lots of indications that you couldn't let things slip.'

Eventually, he and Tony start to venture to clubs, and even in the early 1990s many of them still require membership cards. One night out, Kevin loses his wallet. What for most of us would be an inconvenience, for Kevin is potentially disastrous. In the days and weeks that follow, he wakes up full of anxiety in case someone has handed it in, the cards connecting him to those gay clubs. But time passes. 'The longer it went on, you start to think, *Oh yeah, great, I must have lost it in town, and nobody's noticed it.*' But six weeks later, it finally makes its way through the system. And waiting for him as he climbs down the stairs of the RAF Nimrod stands his commanding officer, and the start of an ordeal that still carries echoes today.

Kevin is born in 1967 and grows up on housing estates in Banbury in Oxfordshire. Remarkably, his dad actually builds their first house. In this suburb, all the homes are different, giving Kevin an unconventional edge from the off. It's on the outskirts of town, where the boy and his friends can cycle off for hours. They don't have a car, but life is walkable, small scale, domestic. 'A very compact life,' he calls it. But then they move to a much more straightforward suburb, and his dad gets a car. Kevin's progress goes push bike, family car, subsonic jet aircraft. He's flying-mad as a kid, watching the planes from nearby bases rumble over his house, the sky some kind of astonishing world of adventure that the ground just can't live up to. He's surrounded by endless propaganda for the RAF; less so for being gay. No friends or family, no teachers or neighbours, there's no one he even suspects is any flavour of LGBTQ+. Whereas the Air Force is everywhere. He sets his heart on the RAF at an early age, and joins up when he hits eighteen. But by the time he's twenty-seven, the lifelong career he has signed up for is all over. And he's having to start again.

The 1960s house he lives in now sits on the edge of a suburb of Worcester, where newbuilds and thirties semis have joined much older farmhouses and inns to turn a village into an out-crop of the cathedral city. Kevin and Tony move here in the mid-1990s after Kevin's 'administrative discharge' from the RAF and when Tony is made redundant from his farming job. They get a bad feeling from the first place they see. Something about it just doesn't seem gay-friendly at all, so they pass on it. But here on the outskirts of Worcester, things feel right from the off. Neighbours drop by, all smiles, saying, *We're Bob and Jilly from number six*, or apologising for their cats. They meet Rita, the elderly woman next door, with a cheery *Hi, we're Kevin and Tony.* 'I don't recall explicitly saying we are a couple,' says Kevin. They hit it off straight away, popping round to do bits of DIY and IT support. One time they ask Rita to keep an eye on the house because they're going on holiday; she's there with her sister. *Oh, so if we hear any strange noises we should call for help?* says the sister. Quick as a flash, Rita replies, *Oh, I'm used to strange noises!* 'But not in a malicious way,' says Kevin hastily. Dog walkers stop to chat on their way past, and Kevin and Tony usually make sure they have treats to keep the pets happy. After the enforced conformity of the RAF and its hetero-only suburb, the gentle routines of the estate feel soothing. 'It's been a very good experience for us,' says Kevin. 'We're not flamboyant. We haven't got pride flags flying from the front of the house and all this sort of stuff. So we're not in your face. But at the same time, we don't hide the fact any more that we are a couple. We were never ones for significant public displays of affection anywhere. And I don't know whether that's just a generation thing or whatever. But at the same time it's quite obvious in our interactions that we are a couple. It seems quite obvious to me.'

They have a civil partnership in 2009, with a reception at the pub a hundred yards away – nice buffet – to which they invite the neighbours. 'It was all very uneventful,' he says, sounding relieved. They've not had any negative reaction at all, until recently when out walking the dog and a kid whizzing by on a scooter makes a snarky comment about the mildly gay slogan

on one of their T-shirts. 'It is a sign perhaps of different generations, and the fact that kids these days still potentially haven't
learned lessons about inclusivity and so on,' he says. They used
to have a group of gay friends in Worcester they'd meet up with,
for swimming or dinners, but as time has gone on, some have
died, some have moved away, so these days their social circle is
a bit broader than the local suburb. Just when I think he can't
get any more *Top Gun*, Kevin turns out to be a biker too. 'I'm
actually currently the chairman of the Gay Bikers Motorcycle
Club,' he explains. 'I wasn't really into biking, it was something
that sort of developed at the same time I was coming out. Partly
because my partner is a biker.' He also works with the charity
Fighting With Pride, which supports LGBTQ+ veterans. 'We
had the apology from Rishi Sunak in the middle of July,' he tells
me when we speak in 2023, 'following the publication of Lord
Etherton's report, and now we're in that phase of making sure
that the recommendations are followed through.'[15] Kevin sees it
as their responsibility to hold the politicians to their promises.
'Of course, with politics, just because they've said they're going
to do something, we haven't necessarily agreed exactly how they
will deliver it.'

Kevin hasn't kept in touch with many of his former RAF
workmates, but through his work he's meeting a lot of LGBTQ+
veterans. 'My experience, as bad as it is, is fairly lightweight compared to some of the people who were imprisoned, who were
given prison sentences and names put on sex offenders registers,
and they were bullied and abused by doctors who forced examin-
ations on them and things like that. So all of our experiences are
valid. We've all been abused by the state. But for some there are
degrees of abuse, aren't there?' He was preparing to march with
Fighting With Pride for Remembrance Sunday. 'So that's going
to be quite an important and emotional day.'

When he first introduces Tony to his parents, his partner is pretty anxious about it. Particularly meeting Kevin's dad: *He's a bricklayer, he's a bloke, he's going to be really difficult, he's going to punch me.* 'But my dad was one of the most laid-back people you could ever meet,' says Kevin. In fact, he was extremely supportive of Kevin, the golden child, former RAF navigator, father of his grandchildren, and now out and proud. Tony's dad, not so much. He refuses to acknowledge the couple. But their mums have been brilliant, and after the death of Kevin's dad often stay with each other, as well as with Kevin and Tony. The couple still occasionally head off to visit friends in London, Birmingham or Manchester. 'And every time I go, I think, *I couldn't live here. It's nice enough to visit but I couldn't live here.* It just doesn't shut off. Too much. It's just overload. And yeah, okay, it's nice that at four in the morning, if I fancy a doner kebab I know exactly where to go, and I can get a bagel here, and we can do this. And you think, *Okay, yeah, there are times when that will be nice.* But personally, I couldn't cope with that for life.' The former RAF navigator cooling his jets. Instead, pottering about with their bikes and the dog in their house on the edge of the estate is where they want to be, feeling grounded – this time through choice.

Trevor Thomas has lived in London, Paris and New York. Now he's in Bedford. It's 1965, Thomas is fifty-eight, and after an eventful life he finds himself working for an art greetings card manufacturer, deeply depressed and lonely. 'I found I wasn't very happy in what struck me as a dull town,' he tells sociologist Ken Plummer.[16] 'I didn't see anyone even out on the streets who looked like they might be even remotely interesting or fun to know.' He lives through the late sixties and early seventies in a small terraced house in what he calls 'this philistine town'. In the end, he's treated for depression in a psychiatric hospital. 'I went again into the desert in Bedford of all places. Just going to work in the morning, coming home, getting a meal, sometimes not bothering with a meal, being utterly lonely.'

Thomas has long been an aesthetic rebel. In the 1940s he is curator of the Leicester Museum and Art Gallery, where he acquires a collection of German expressionist art that disgruntles the city's more establishment figures, as does his dandyish attire and queer attitude. One evening on his way home from work he's arrested in a public lavatory on the edge of Victoria Park while talking to one of his brother's friends. He goes to court, spends a weekend in custody, and endures his name being dragged through the local press. He gets a tough judge, who rants about protecting society from creatures like Thomas. But the curator is well connected and knows the prison governor, who makes sure he gets proper meals, although he spends most of the weekend alternately distressed or sedated. On the Monday, the judge tells him it will be no good sending him to prison because *You'd corrupt the others*, and Thomas's response is, *I should be so lucky.* While Leicester's establishment go for him, old friends come and stand by him, including Kenneth Clark, art critic and chairman of the Arts Council of England. Career and life in ruins, it's the Arts Council who help keep him afloat in the aftermath.

He's fined £100 and made to attend a Freudian psychiatrist for a year, who tells Thomas he can be cured of his homosexuality. As a result he marries Kay, a much younger woman who he has warned that he's gay. But by this time they both believe what the psychiatrist has said – that he can be a changed man. So they are married and have two sons, initially living in Paris while Thomas works for UNESCO. But soon Kay has an affair and leaves him to look after their sons. Back in London, he's the last person to see his upstairs neighbour alive, the poet Sylvia Plath, narrowly escaping being gassed himself that night thanks to their shared chimney.

When he moves to Bedford, his sons are almost grown up, and very soon he's alone. Distanced for so long from his sexuality, he fails to notice the change in the law around homosexual sex. But then, through a chance meeting with a friend of one of his sons, he hears of the existence of the Campaign for Homosexual Equality, and writes to their HQ in Manchester. 'One day this young man was at the door,' he says. '*I'm the secretary of the Bedford CHE group and we've had a letter from Manchester to say to get in touch with you. Will you come along to a meeting?* I liked him, he was from Canada . . . I went to a meeting, and it was quite fun.' It's a lifeline. By 1975, Thomas, now disabled and walking with the aid of a stick, attends a national CHE conference in Sheffield. What began as a harmonious organisation is beginning to fracture amid the political turmoil of the 1970s. In the hotel, he wanders upstairs and finds the CHE disco, where they're playing 'Rock Your Baby'; 'The Hustle'; 'Shame, Shame, Shame'. Two lads from Brixton come and sit beside him as he watches the men dancing with men, the women with women, the lights whirling. *Come on, throw your stick away and let's dance*, they urge. Thomas tries to resist, but moments later they have him on his feet, supporting him and pulling him to the dance floor. 'Well, I used to dance a lot,' says Thomas, 'and I thought, *Well, I'd better do something*, and I liked it a lot. I came out then, in effect.'

The *Yorkshire Post* interviews him as the oldest delegate there. He tells them 'three days in Sheffield did more for me than three years on Valium'.[17] At first, all this attention makes him anxious, especially after his experience in Leicester. What if there are bricks through his windows? Instead, for the first time since the 1940s, he feels liberated. *It's amazing meeting you*, young people tell him, *you lived through it all, the thirties, the forties, the fifties. And here you are out on the other side.* He lives out his final years in Bedford as an embodiment of Sondheim's valedictory song 'I'm Still Here'.

POLARI ON THE PAPER ROUND IN SOUTHSEA

Terry has travelled up to London on a school trip. June 1981 has been a drab kind of summer so far, a moment when urban decay, racist policing and unemployment have resulted in riots across the country. The capital seems impossibly exciting to a fifteen-year-old from Southsea, a dense Victorian suburb of Portsmouth. But Terry isn't intimidated by the city, far from it. He's on a school trip to watch the tennis at Wimbledon – but as soon as they arrive he jumps from the coach, evades his school-mates and teachers, sells his ticket to one of the people queueing to get in, and sets off to Oxford Street. His aim is to blow the rest of the ticket money buying records at the giant HMV. Two hours later, and mission accomplished, he contemplates, *What next?* And he thinks of The Stranglers' song 'Hanging Around', which has lodged, nagging, in his brain, with its verse about men in leather at a pub, The Coleherne. He's heard someone say the pub is in Earl's Court, so on a whim he heads there next. He asks a guy at the Underground station, *Where's The Coleherne?* The guy chuckles and points him on his way. And so he turns up with his bag of records. 'I was in school uniform. They didn't look at me twice.' He can just about afford a Coke. 'I got chatting to somebody, and they lived in Wimbledon. And so I went back with him.' Later, the guy drops Terry off by the school bus. 'I got in so much trouble,' he grins. 'So much trouble. I think I was banned from future school trips. And everyone was like, *Where have you been, where have you been?* And I was like, *Never you mind!* So yeah, I had about three albums and some 12-inch singles and I was just smiling all the way home.'

Terry starts life in a two-up two-down with no bathroom, no running hot water, no heating and a toilet at the bottom of the garden. There are wrought-iron boot scrapers by the front door of this old millworker's cottage. Southsea is a muddle, a seaside town but also a suburb built to house workers from the naval dockyard and the mills. 'During the summer, it was amazing,' he recalls. 'To be able to go to the beach every day.' He'd leave the house at eight o'clock with some sandwiches and squash, trunks rolled up in a towel, and return home at six, starving. He'd go cycling for miles, watching the storms form out at sea, far from the safety of the shore. Yet something about family life lights in him a desire to escape. Terry's mum is a care worker, his dad a docker. 'We weren't very close,' he says. 'Even when I was at home, they put up with me.' But soon it's family life that escapes Terry rather than the other way round.

It doesn't take long for the storms to reach him. When he's twelve, both of his parents die, at which point he's put into a children's home. 'Maybe some people would consider that traumatic,' says Terry, 'but when you're young you just cope. You just do what you can do to survive. And that's what I did, really. I was really quiet. Nothing really bothered me.' He takes on a paper round to be able to afford things, and to escape. The children's home is not an improvement. When he arrives there, it feels like a land of broken toys. The other kids look so damaged and hurt. Terry vows that is not going to happen to him. But school is not the escape he needs either. If you were expelled from every other one in the town, you ended up here. The day he returns to school after his mother dies, he's greeted by a chorus from his classmates. *Where's your mama gone?* they sing. *Where's your mama gone?* When the teacher arrives, he's baffled by the pandemonium. *Because Terry's mum died,* the kids inform him. 'And the teacher actually laughed,' says Terry.

He realises he's gay at thirteen, and comes out at school when he's fifteen. He tells his best friend first, with a nervous *I think you're going to get really upset.* His mate says, *Just bloody tell me,* and so Terry does: he's gay. *Fuck, I thought you were going to say you had cancer,* his mate says. *Thank fuck for that. Well, so what?* That reaction stays with him, helping him through dark days in the times ahead. He comes out because there are already constant threats of queer-bashing from his classmates. 'And I remember thinking, *Well, they obviously know something, they're obviously aware, and I'm not hiding it very well.*' When he does come out, it scares the life out of them. 'Why would anyone do that? It actually made them question my sanity and whether I was safe to pick on.' But still the insults are relentless. 'I always said I thought my surname was You Poof,' he tells me, 'because they'd call, *Terry, you poof!* The teachers as well.'

Yet near the children's home is the Kings Theatre, the local rep, and it's there teenage Terry begins to pull away from his school friends and make some older ones. He starts by hanging out with them socially, and graduates to going behind the scenes and doing odd jobs. He watches the shows from the gods, then dives backstage for the gossip and the thrill of the secret world of theatricals. The heyday of repertory theatre is long gone, and the Kings Theatre survives thanks to some touring erotic revues bringing in what Terry calls 'the raincoat brigade', and some more legit shows bought in from other theatres. But it's not the shows that captivate Terry, it's the people who run the place. 'I've been very lucky. A lot of the time there are older people who have been like real mentors to me. I've never felt exploited, never felt unsafe with them, but they are people who have come into my life and said, *This is the way this works. Watch out for this, don't* do that, *this person's horrible, be careful who you're seen with,* and that sort of thing.' He's dressing 'a bit Marc Almond': studded belts and wristbands, spiky hair and eyeliner, occasionally nail polish. A local group of punks show him how to make his hair stick up into a mohican with soap. So he's not inconspicuous on the streets of Southsea. But even so, Terry feels like the theatre opens a secret world for him. There are parties like speakeasies, where he'd walk down an alleyway, knock on a door, a hatch would open and he'd give a code – *Joseph sent me!* – before being let in. 'It actually made me realise just how undercover every-thing was. It was so secretive and so fear based.' He recalls the theatre staff and older gay men using Polari. 'It was like being part of a shadow society, that we existed in both planes.' A gay subculture hidden from view.

While some parties took place in these subterranean venues, others were in the respectable bay-fronted Victorian terraces of the town. One such, beautifully renovated, is the home of Michael and David, a couple in their early forties with extremely coiffured hair, one grey, one blond. 'If you wanted to annoy them, you'd say, *Oh, what's that bald patch?* and they suddenly ran screaming to a mirror.' What is remarkable to Terry is their kind-ness, collecting waifs and strays and bringing people around to their house for meals. 'And there was nothing seedy about it,' says Terry. 'And then they'd sing songs around the piano and I'd think, *See, if my parents had done this, I'd have hated this, but I quite like it . . .*' The songs would be camp music hall and cabaret numbers, 'The Boy I Love Is Up in the Gallery' or 'Burlington Bertie from Bow'. 'They wore what I considered far too much jewellery,' says Terry. 'Everybody seemed to be dripping in gold and dripping in silver.' He can hear them rattle as they walk.

Then there is the young man who looks about fifty, does drag and plays pantomime dame. And a shady geezer 'a bit Del Boy before Del Boy – he was from Central Casting if you wanted mockney geezer who worked on the market', who gets 12-inch singles from America from a friend who is cabin crew on the transatlantic jumbos. To his surprise, one of the first people he meets at the parties is Wilf, who runs the newsagent's where he's still doing his paper round. They spot each other, and both react with a little shout of fear and surprise. *You know what kind of party this is?* says Wilf. *You know you could get into trouble?* To which Terry, ever the pragmatist, says, *No, I wouldn't, because I'm under twenty-one.* He's more concerned to know if he's still got a job. *Yes, don't worry about that,* Wilf assures him. He becomes one of Terry's mentors, telling him: *Don't do this; don't go there; he's dodgy. And come around and have a meal tonight.* There, they'd chat for a couple of hours before the teenager toddled off back to the children's home, where there was a curfew. Wilf allows him to do his homework there too, all part of Terry's mixed-up life, where school, children's home, paper round, theatre and secret gay parties all swirl around.

He moves out of the children's home when he's sixteen, and lives down by the docks in a 1930s flat with a mate and their friend, a prostitute. 'A couple of times we just had to go in and jump on somebody who was beating her up,' recalls Terry. 'We also had a neighbour who had a very big Alsatian dog that would do a similar job.' He takes to cruising on the seafront, where he feels strangely liberated. 'If I didn't like the situation, I could walk away,' he recalls. 'And if I had to, I could run – depending on what I was wearing at the time.' An expedition to fetish-wear shop Expectations in London sees him return with the most provocative cruising outfit he can find: rubber Levi's shorts, rubber vest, black wrestling boots. 'And I remember wearing that along the seafront one night,' he tells me. 'I thought I was the best thing since sliced bread!'

By 1987, Terry is living in a tiny village in Lincolnshire called Eagle, helping renovate a house for a guy called Gareth, who is working abroad most of the time. Terry spends his evenings in the village pub, The Struggler, and joins their darts team. One night, a man who he's never seen before begins to ask questions. *Oh, you live in Gareth's house?* When Terry confirms he does, the man says, *Gareth's gay.* It receives a shrug. But the guy won't leave it. *That's really awful,* he says, starting to get angry. *It shouldn't be allowed, people like that.* Terry, with a sinking feeling, can see a fight brewing in this village pub. *I'm just here to have a drink,* he says, trying not to rise to the bait. By this time, the rest of the darts team have gathered round. Terry remembers what this means from school: he's about to get beaten up. Instead, the darts team turn on the aggressor. *You can leave,* they tell him, *he's our mate.* 'And they kicked the bloke out!' says Terry wonderingly. The landlord takes him aside and tells him, *You and your friends are welcome here anytime.* And so Terry makes sure he goes back the next night, a spring in his step.

Eventually, he becomes a nurse, a couple of long-term relationships taking him through the years, the most recent boyfriend becoming his husband. By 2019 they're living in the suburbs of Luton together, so that Terry can commute to his job at King's College Hospital in London and his husband can continue his delivery job in nearby Dunstable. Terry works in sexual health and transfers to the hospital in the town. It's taken some time for him to get to know the LGBTQ+ scene here, seemingly more based around hobbies and interests than pubs or clubbing. There's a gay outdoor club, and one for people into model trains. Some of the staff are involved with organising Luton Pride, and their clinic has a stall there. 'In the gay community in Luton we've got a very good reputation because we're such a mixed bag. We've got gays or straights or trans; we've also got a real cultural mix in our clinic.' Because of his job, he gets to meet a lot of young LGBTQ+ people in the town. Many are new to university, kids just coming out. His days are frequently spent helping young people whose drinks have been spiked in the town's bars. Like the theatre in Southsea, the clinic in Luton is allowing Terry to see behind the façade of the town. 'There's Greenhouse Sauna, and we run a clinic in the sauna. So we also meet people from all over, you get to talk to people who I suppose I would never do,' he says.

When he first arrives in Luton from London, he assumes the main issue for the clinic will be chemsex, as it had been in the city, but to his surprise no one initially seems to know what he's on about. 'I thought they were taking the mickey at first,' he says. 'I thought, *You know, tina, crystal meth.* No. *Cocaine?* No. But that's crept in over the last four years. Grindr's suddenly booming here. There's things I do see, a bit like the sordid underbelly, where people tell me how they've been blackmailed into having sex and things.' He gets speaking to one young lad who'd sent some pictures of himself to someone on Grindr but then starts to feel that something's not right. And his instincts are borne out, because the man takes those pictures and uses them to create a fake profile with which to blackmail him. *If you don't have sex with me I will keep the photos. I'll push this profile. If you have sex with me I'll take the pictures down.* So the young guy goes and has sex with this man because he's terrified of being outed. Terry is understandably angry when he hears this story. 'It's a whole new underbelly I didn't know of,' he says. 'I never heard about it before. It was quite shocking.'

It's 2023 when we speak, and his husband is undergoing treatment for cancer, but they're also doing up a house in Wales. It's near where the group Lesbians and Gays Support the Miners came to help in the mid-eighties. They attend a screening of

Pride in the local rugby club. 'At the end everyone clapped and cheered,' recalls Terry. Afterwards, they get chatting to their new neighbours, members of this former mining community. 'They were talking to us about how they remembered the people coming, and how much that meant to them. Because they wouldn't have survived.' Terry and his husband become well known in the area. 'We're known as the gays in the red house.' They're assured when they buy the place that they're not going to be the only gays in the village, but after all the different lives Terry has lived he's not really that bothered. Even so, it has exceeded all of his expectations. 'I've never felt quite so welcome,' he says. 'They're more about who you are rather than what you are.' It's a long way from the children's home.

Terry's husband dies in 2024. I hope they are looking out for Terry there, extending the feeling of belonging he's never felt in any of the other places he's lived. As he grieves for the beautiful man he's lost, I'm sure it's hard for him to see what a resilient survivor he has been, coping with all these different worlds and the secret sides of them he keeps having to decode. The future is something he will get round to facing when he's ready. For now, I hope the red house is proving to be the sanctuary he needs.

'There is a kind of freemasonry among homosexuals,' writes Bryan Magee in his influential and voyeuristic 1966 book *One in Twenty: A Study of Homosexuality in Men and Women*. 'A homosexual knows that wherever he goes – to a village, a farm, a coal mine, a factory, anywhere from an African township to the heart of the American Mid-West – there will be homosexuals there, and once he finds them he will be accepted as one of them.'[18] LGBTQ+ people are everywhere, it seems. He talks about how, for all the barriers, homosexuality allows people to break out of their allotted place in society, to mingle with queer folk of different classes and backgrounds against the 'poisonous' inhibitions of British class snobbery. All of which certainly paints a more exciting picture than the reality of, say, Luton, Woking or Penge in the mid-sixties might have presented your average LGBTQ+ person. The sixties are always painted as a decade of liberation and revolution, but that was often something experienced by small, privileged groups rather than accessible more widely.

But it is an era in which communications technology begins to play a role in liberation. From the mid-twentieth century, the telephone begins its creep into different corners of the suburban home. On tables in the hallway or hung on the wall, sitting beside the ashtrays and table lamps in the front room, or on bedside tables for an extended comfortable natter, shared party lines giving way to more privacy and intimacy. As families and friends move ever further apart to new towns and estates, it helps people maintain old feelings of community. But those private calls are not as secret as we might have hoped. At new telephone exchanges springing up in every district, operators are able to dip into the private calls being made and the conversations being had. 'Oh, we quite often hear them chatting on the line to one another,' one tells *Arena Three* in 1964.[19] 'Married women, y'know – husband gone off for the weekend up north or somewhere . . . So they probably get on the line to the old girl friend, y'know, and pass on the glad news the coast's clear.' A secret network of liaisons between married women, eavesdropped by the GPO. While few records remain of such conversations, just the outside acknowledgement of them is intriguing. More so than their male counterparts' calls, it would seem. 'The women are much more discreet than the male homos over the wire,' says the operator. Clearly, extensive sampling is taking place through the clicks and hum of the wires.

THE WOMAN WHO FELL TO PENGE

In the twilight, through the back bedroom window, Karen spies her again. The girl who lives in the house behind her family's home, illuminated by the light of her room, walking about in a nightie. She's a bit older than Karen, and it's not the first time she's seen her like this. She calls it 'Hitchcock spying', this obsession with the girl beyond the back garden whose room lights up with an amber glow in the blue dusk. 'Exciting moments before the curtains got drawn and the light was on at night,' she tells me. But not just the evenings. One dark Christmas Day, Karen is in her bedroom when her granddad comes in to see her. As they're talking about her latest art projects, the glue in the navy carpet, the gallery postcards on the walls, they both catch sight of something. It's the girl. This time she's naked. In the gloom of the winter's day she has put the light on, and Karen's granddad is speechless. 'It was just hilarious,' Karen recalls. Excruciatingly awkward. But at least it was something. 'When you grow up in the suburbs, you're constantly looking for something exciting to happen,' she says. 'Anything, even if it's someone having a bit of a row. It's the excitement of night falling.' Karen's room is big, and she has grown tall in it, ten inches more than her sister, who has the small box room next door. 'I felt like we were like plants,' she explains. 'It's scientifically proven, John. The size of a child's room will determine their height.' She pauses. 'It's *my* science.' Karen loves this room, the desk where she plays secretary, paints and draws, and sometimes intently examines the women's underwear section of her mother's Kay's catalogue. The room where she can discover herself.

In this small 1930s terrace in Penge, South London, all the furniture is brown, the curtains velvet, the wallpaper flocked. Karen has grown up looking like a boy, thanks to her mum roughly chopping her hair off. She has a difficult dad but a lovely mum, who works in the Irish sweet shop on the corner of her street, a place constantly at war with the Caribbean sweet shop at the other end. Alf Thwaite, one of the men who run the National Front, lives on their street and frequents her mum's sweet shop, and so Karen learns from an early age how good it feels to wind him up, taunting him by the pick 'n' mix. 'It's like being a tiny detective in suburbia when you're different, it's like birdwatching, isn't it?' she says. 'I was the alien that had landed. The woman who fell to Penge.'

She gets constant reminders of class snobbery that tell her neighbouring Beckenham is a cut above Penge. The constant judgement and the snide jokes. She grows up with 'an idea that I was less because of where I lived'. Perhaps it's that lack of excitement again, the constant search for novelty and meaning, that drives these restless class skirmishes. 'People will find anything to create hierarchy in suburbia.' But Karen remains proud of her maligned suburb, its council housing and diverse community. There's something about the way it has been marginalised and made into a joke that echoes with her experience of being a lesbian too. A parallel between her understanding of her sexuality and her pride in Penge. The two unexpectedly intertwined, in the way that so many of us find strange affinities with the place where we grow up that stay with us through our lives.

Aged nine, she meets Jenny, all blonde hair and quick tongue, and they spend their free time in Karen's big bedroom making up comedy sketches and shows, and later, acting out scenes from *Dallas*. Jenny is JR, Karen Sue Ellen. 'And we used to smooch.' One day they discover a porn mag, and she remembers 'looking at these women's bodies and parts and it changing the air between us'. She feels sensations as pleasurable as having an ice cream or being on the swings, but they feel different too, more intense. 'My eyes were opened around that time to an obsession, really, with a friend. And I think that was sexuality.' Jenny's family are working class made good, living in a private tower block nearby. 'I had this whole crush, not only on Jenny, but also the family,' she recalls. Jenny's mum is glamorous but complicated, suspicious of her daughter's relationship with Karen. And so suddenly Jenny is being whisked away every weekend on family day trips, and the intensity of their bond is broken. Eventually, Jenny grows up and marries a man. Karen now lives in that same block of flats, as if completing some kind of complicated chess move or audacious *Dallas*-style takeover.

There's seemingly no recognition of homosexuality in Karen's family at all, and so constructing an identity is tricky. She remembers seeing two girls in her comprehensive holding hands and joining in calling them 'lezzers'. 'I still regret that,' she says. 'To be gay at school was not a thing.' Years later, she discovers her English teacher was a lesbian. When she finishes school, Karen heads off to art college in Chislehurst, the bohemian soul of Bromley. There she meets local girl Jane, who remains a close friend today. 'She basically told me I was a lesbian,' says Karen. 'I didn't really believe her. But then she proved me right.' Much as Jane informs Karen of her sexuality, so too are Jane's parents the ones to inform their daughter she's a lesbian. 'I'd never heard anything like this. I thought this was incredible, that parents could be so accepting, and *know* it. It's like, *Well, how do they know these things?*' Karen finds Jane's confidence all a bit much and still feels deeply uncomfortable with her own sexuality, happier to express herself through art pieces where she re-enacts *The Sound of Music* by herself on a camcorder on some waste ground out the back of the art college. In an effort to prove she's right, Jane takes her to lesbian clubs in Brixton. 'It was exciting to go out and find this new world. But I was also really afraid of it. I had no idea what it meant. It felt very far removed from that just-kissing-a-girl-in-my-bedroom feeling.' At the same time, she finds she's drifting through her days as if stoned, with no understanding of why, until she's diagnosed with something called pink adrenaline, causing her to experience life as if out of body. 'But I was acting normally, trying to act like who I thought I was,' she says. 'That whole performance of self started then as well. I started to learn about performance as coming across as normal. And that I'd been doing that probably for a long time.' Performing normality is perhaps the ultimate goal of suburbia if you want to play by its rules. She's still living in her back room in Penge, where the relationship between her parents is becoming more strained, thanks in part to her dad's drinking. It all becomes a bit too much, and so when her course ends she applies to university far away in Cardiff. Here, she changes her name to Tom and completely reinvents herself, distanced from the complicated pressures of her past.

It's the early 1990s when Karen returns to Penge, degree finished and trying to find a way of making a living through art. She still hasn't come out to her parents. 'I had tried telling my mum that I was gay,' she says, 'but I didn't want to use the word "lesbian". And so we got into a misunderstanding.' Her mum keeps telling Karen how all the girls she'd been at school with are getting married and having children. 'It was all very heterosexual, very claustrophobic. And I just said to her at this point, *I don't like men, and I'm not going to have children.* And she looked at me and went, *Oh*, but I didn't say anything more. And I don't feel like she even knew what that meant, lesbian or gay or anything. I just said things I *didn't* like, but not what I *did* like. Which was a bit of a riddle for her. She didn't ask any more.'

In the city, the gay scene and the art scene are booming, and for a while Karen feels like she's on the edge of it all, working in banks and having a wild nightlife. She does occasional guest slots at Duckie, the queer performance club in Vauxhall, where she meets the hostess, Amy Lamé, who encourages her to enter something she has been organising: The World's First Lesbian Beauty Contest, to be held at the Café de Paris. Karen enters, and in a matter of weeks she ends up on the cover of the *Independent on Sunday* magazine with the other contestants. 'After that it was no longer a secret,' she says, with understatement. This is coming out in a big way. 'It was a massive thing. And Mum was really upset. Dad seemed to be okay with it. But then it didn't really even make things that much easier. Because I was still living at home.' However, her sister has moved next door, with a family of her own, and is much more sympathetic. Even though they never talk about it very much, just her knowing and being supportive means so much to Karen as she struggles next door.

Karen has kept on changing, and Penge has too. Changing, or perhaps just becoming more Karen and more Penge. These days she's a published writer and performance artist, and the streets of Penge feel more liberated too, thanks to the demise of Alf Thwaite and the rise of an unexpected street art scene. 'In the local park they have a Pride family picnic,' she tells me, 'which, let's just say it's not exactly the Gay Pride that I'm used to. But there's a lot of allies, clearly. There wasn't that many gay people there; it was a bouncy castle, children. Still, it's good to see.' Her mum still lives in the same house, these days just in one room because she has dementia, and Karen cares for her. She's also immersed herself in the suburb's artistic fray, through a comedy character, Barbara Brownskirt, known as 'Penge's poet laureate', an anoraked performance poet who leans into the quirkiness of the place. 'Penge definitely has tilted more towards the eccentric, if you ask me,' she says. 'It's just like where odd people feel free. And I don't even know how to explain that. Maybe it's because I feel that I'm free.' Barbara has become the bard of the 176 bus stop, just along from the Conservative Club. 'She is based on the invisible people and the people that don't get talked about,' Karen explains, 'the people who wear cagoules with their hoods up, who were often having a cheap cup of tea in the caff (or *not* so cheap cup of tea), the people that are not looked at, who go unseen. I think I'm still really drawn to writing in all sorts of ways about those people who don't really get a voice.' And Barbara allows Karen to bring together and celebrate the awkwardness, absurdity and joy of both suburb and sexuality. 'And it's almost like the arty little girl is acceptable now in this place,' she says. 'And so we've both come home to be whatever we are.'

The first issue of *Gay News* is published in 1972. It has grown out of the Gay Liberation Front, the radical young rival to the more respectable Campaign for Homosexual Equality. It's a confusing period, the early 1970s, where Victorian morality meets space-age ambition. Some of the content of that first issue is thoroughly distasteful now, not least an interview with Jimmy Savile. And while the focus of much gay life at the time is clearly in a few big cities and university towns, this first issue hints at a much wider audience for the publication, and for LGBTQ+ life generally. 'Things are a bit quiet in this "respectable" seaside town,' writes Brian Hart from Folkestone, 'and any leafleting, campaigning, etc. has to be done by myself at the moment.'[20] There is a sense of isolation away from the established gay communities, but of excitement and possibility too. No one knows what might happen off the back of publications like *Gay News*. Will everywhere be able to sustain an LGBTQ+ community of some sort? Or will it just hasten a gay flight to the cities, where there is a critical mass? Five years after the partial decriminalising of sex between two consenting men in private over the age of twenty-one, the yearning and hope are palpable.

Also in that first issue there is a list of Gay Liberation Front groups. Twenty-nine are listed, and most are in the places you'd expect – London, Manchester, Oxford and Brighton – but they have appeared in much less cosmopolitan places too. In Bedfordshire (in the towns of Bedford, Luton and Dunstable), Chelmsford and Southend in Essex, Cheltenham in Gloucestershire, and Reading in Berkshire. And – perhaps most speculative of all – a group in Higham Ferrers in Northamptonshire, a historic market town with a population of just eight thousand.

Back in Folkestone, Brian describes how during a screening of *Sunday Bloody Sunday* in the Odeon 'there were loud gasps when Murray Head went to bed with Peter Finch, about half a dozen people walked out!' For campaigners like Brian, pushing at the boundaries of what a place like Folkestone might offer, the mere presence of a film with gay characters going on general release and being screened in the local picture house adds to a feeling that the world is changing, even if it does bring out the performative and controlling aspects of heterosexual disgust.

THE NEW MALDEN ROBOT

Summer 1989, and Mark is working the phones at London Lesbian and Gay Switchboard in Housmans bookshop, King's Cross. The location is kept secret to avoid them being raided or firebombed. He has warned the teenage caller that the Switchboard's number will likely turn up on his parents' phone bill, but they keep talking. The teen is lonely and isolated and needs someone to talk to. 'We weren't trained as counsellors,' he tells me, 'we were really there to hand out information. And we had this 20-foot bookcase full of clippings and notes about everything we were likely to need. So we had the information at our fingertips, and everything else was just empathy.' Evenings are busiest, and all the lines are in use. Around him are the other volunteers, engaged on calls of their own. 'It was people who worked on oil rigs, it was lawyers, it was architects, it was all sorts of people who were confident in themselves and achievers,' he says, of the people staffing the phones. 'And they were just, like, dozens of role models. All ages, some unemployed, but all people who had found their feet and were confident that they knew enough to help others on the phones.' Mark's caller is from a suburb of Daventry in Northamptonshire. He glances up to the map of Britain above the phones, colourful pins marking out pubs, clubs, youth groups and more. He locates Northamptonshire, then Daventry. No pins. 'There were these huge swathes of the country that just had nothing,' he says. 'And that's even in suburbia. You're disconnected. But these are people who are geographically in dire straits.'

Mark feels a great empathy with the teenager. He's born in 1961 and grows up in New Malden, in the London Borough of Kingston, not far from Surbiton, in a mock-Georgian house on a small estate, 'everyone competing with cars and brands of lawn mowers but not actually getting into each other's lives. There was very little socialising. You'd be nodding and *hello* when you brought the milk in, but there wouldn't actually be people going around for coffee mornings and stuff.' As a kid he can play on the street, but by the time he's a teenager there's nothing to do. He realises he's gay fairly early on, but the boys' school he attends is full of that suburban staple, performative heterosexuality: 'Everyone else is doing their best not to be gay,' he says. Everything – earrings, white socks, hair products, personal grooming – is seen as a giveaway. 'We had our own word for it. *Mo*. And it took me a long while to work out what *mo* was, and it was part of *homo*. But it was used as a verb as well. Someone's *moing* someone else. There was *poof* and everything else, but *mo* was the main slang word you just didn't want to be.' Mark spends his school days desperately trying not to give himself away. Such is the fear of limp wrists that he adopts a stiff-armed stance and clenches his fists in his nervousness at being seen. Two years in a back brace only magnify that. He tries dating girls and finds a couple of like-minded lads to experiment with, although it all feels very limited and fearful. But he does find a crowd, a corner table of straight lads who enjoy drinking, moaning and talking about music. But mainly drinking. 'Not alcoholism. I wouldn't drink at home.' From the age of fourteen he's putting away four or five pints of beer a week. He manages ten pints at a school disco and is violently sick afterwards. It's not doing him much good.

What saves Mark is not escape, but escapism. If he can't physically flee the suburbs, he can ride above them with film and music. He powers his way through post-punk, new wave and ska, until a Saturday-night show on Capital Radio sparks a new obsession with acts like Donna Summer. 'Every time electronic sounds came on in film or in songs, my antennae went up,' he says. 'I was like, *What is this? I cannot imagine where this sound is coming from.*' Vangelis, Tomita, Gary Numan: the space-age soundtrack to New Malden's very own teenage robot. 'I like dancing, but I was petrified of dancing in public,' he says. 'In parties and when they finally did big discos at the youth club it would be more like the Darts and Showaddywaddy, that kind of "lads' dancing".' And there is nothing to appeal to Mark in the machismo of the day. 'It was acceptable to be a flabby super-hero and be a flabby action hero or being an ancient action hero like Charlton Heston.' Despite the disappointments, with four cinemas in Kingston to choose from, Mark is there for it all, be it horror, disaster movies, action films, car chases or rock operas. It's eye-opening being a young gay man in the audience. 'If a gay character turned up, someone in the audience would go, *Eeeurgh* – you'd hear a young male voice in the audience expressing physical repulsion, just to signify that they're very straight.' Even when he watches these films today, he can still hear a chorus of homophobia punctuating them. In *Freebie and the Bean*, where the villain turns out to be trans, 'as soon as the wig came off there would be an *Eeeugh!* I think *The Rocky Horror Picture Show*, *Phantom of the Paradise*, just anything with a gay character or someone, someone being explicitly sexual would get a comment.'

When he's sixteen he discovers *Gay News*, and through it a couple of venues: a pub that has a gay night in a back bar, a place he fails to find on a drunken first attempt; and a Sunday-afternoon meet-up in Wimbledon, which he's too scared to attend in case he's recognised by schoolmates or family friends out shopping.

Instead, pent-up Mark lives for the day he can escape to university and be himself. When he finally gets to the University of East Anglia at the start of the 1980s, he thinks, *At last, I can be more open.* But as soon as he arrives, he meets his neighbour in halls. The university have put him next door to someone from his school in Kingston, and immediately Mark knows he cannot come out, convinced news will travel back home. The robot is back. It takes him two years to join the Gay Soc, and a weekend trip to Sheffield with them for an NUS conference of gay groups is a turning point. 'When I got back from that trip, the guys on my corridor asked me where I'd been, and I just told them . . . and that was it. I just spent the next couple of months telling everyone!' When he tells his parents, they say they had already suspected because he has never brought a girl home, but they're still upset. He makes sure he's living in Norwich when he tells them, so he can retreat if it all goes wrong. It's the hardest thing he has ever had to do, he tells me.

After two years of refusing to join his university housemates on the dance floor, it becomes their mission to get him to dance. They make him practise at home, dress him up, dye his hair and take him out to a club. His friends have even placed bets on whether he will or won't start dancing. 'But I did!' he tells me. 'I did the robot and all sorts of other stuff. To the Human League! And *that* started me dancing. Again, like coming out, it was bloody late. Like, I was twenty, twenty-one. That broke the ice and I was ready for *the* gay club in Norfolk.' Pretty soon they can't get Mark off the dance floor. On a trip to Heaven he accidentally finds himself on a stage, and is still dancing up there long after his exhausted friends have given up.

In 1987 he gets a job in London and moves back in with his parents in the mock-Georgian house in New Malden. His dad is commuting to work at the National Coal Board offices in central

London ('I don't know what marvellous things they were doing with their memos and letters and stuff,' says Mark, remembering a day there with his dad, 'but it just didn't appeal whatsoever'). By contrast, Mark is commuting to London for a social life, for the clubs and bars. Somehow, his metamorphosis into out gay man bypasses New Malden entirely, where he has gone from closeted teen to adult whose life is elsewhere. His sexuality feels invisible here. 'Going back to live with your parents in your late twenties was a step backwards,' he explains. 'I said, *I'm not doing mealtimes, I'll do my laundry and do my own meals.* I just couldn't do the teenage regimen, family meals any more. And of course, it cramped your style, and late trains didn't even run back home.' Instead, he is on the night bus, followed by a mile walk at 4 a.m. Given that these club nights are mostly on weekdays, it makes for a tough working week. It was, he says, 'not a good way to live'. Soon he has left forever, off to a flatshare in Camden, a job in TV post-production and volunteering at Switchboard.

It's 1990, and Mark has met David, who will later become his husband. David's parents have headed off on a golfing holiday, and as Christmas draws near he has nowhere to go. And so to Mark's surprise his parents invite David to join them for Christmas dinner in New Malden. Crackers are pulled, bad jokes read, paper hats worn. 'He was delighted to join in with my comparatively stable and traditional family life,' says Mark, the steady suburban flow suddenly feeling like it has a place in his life after all. Soon, they're going on family holidays together. Thirty years later, and David is still here with Mark, and has helped take care of Mark's parents in their final years. The two sides of Mark's life finally meeting in New Malden, no longer having to keep it all in.

The drinkers have not seen anything like it. Through the etched glass door into the dark pub, ten of them spill in, men and women, each wearing a badge announcing the arrival of Harrow Gay Unity. All eyes stare as a bubble of cheery bonhomie floats them across sticky carpet towards the bar, through thick clouds of cigarette smoke. *Seems like a nice boy!* someone calls. There is muffled swearing and whispered incredulity, dirty chuckles. But mostly there is silence and watching from behind pint mugs and Woodbines. It might be 1972, but there are limits. The group face the landlord, orders are teased out, a round is in the offing. But the barman is stony-faced, feeling all eyes on him, knowing they're all waiting to see what he will do. *You'll have to go elsewhere*, he says. *This is a respectable pub.* Even the regulars baulk at this. They may be many things, but 'respectable' isn't the word any of them would use. But they know what he means. He means they're not like *them*. *Could you please leave*, he says. *Our money is as good as anyone else's*, says one of them, Janie. *This is my pub*, says the landlord. *And I want you out.* He comes around the bar and ushers them back towards the door, the pavement, the world beyond: Harrow, in all its buttoned-up splendour. *We are ready to make a public issue out of this*, says Alex. *You do that*, says the landlord. *We don't want your sort round here.* Janie is not budging from the bar. *But then that's the thing, isn't it?* she says. *We are from round here. And we'll be back.* And she leads them from the pub, to catcalls and jeers and a golf clap for the landlord, who shakes his head in wonder.

Once outside, they regroup and make a decision. Give up and go home? Admit defeat? Never. On to the next pub! The group was set up in 1971 in confrontational circumstances, after a spate of arrests and harassment of men in the local cottages. They may have become a little less political since then, but they still have a social purpose. They have set out to visit all the pubs in the local area, to test out what would happen if they announced themselves to the people of Harrow. In most, it results in strange conversations with the drinkers, sometimes a bit of aggro, often puerile and uncomprehending. 'There are fewer suitable places in the suburbs,' group leaders Alex and Janic write in *Gay News* in November 1972.[21] 'Some of the fear about police and public hostility disappeared, and a personal social network of friendship and support developed the beginnings of a real local alternative scene.' They have made friends with the local Women's Lib group and the Harrow Youth Movement, and take to advertising in the local library and newspaper. 'We want to get in touch with more of the gays outside the usual scene,' they write. 'There are the kids still living at home who need to get more acquainted with gayness, and come out more. Then at the other end, there are the older men who haunt the cottages. For them, at the moment, this is often the best way for them to see, or take part in, sex.' Out here in Harrow it's all just part of the flourishing queerness in suburbia, thanks to the Gay Liberation movement, which, while short-lived, ignites a new generation in the struggle for recognition and equality, and brings that struggle home.

ESCAPE FROM EDGWARE

It's not easy to clamber out of an upstairs bedroom window in platform boots. Trickier still to haul yourself down to the lid of the wheelie bin below, and then jump to the drive. But So is an expert at it now. Aged sixteen, they have been doing this for at least twelve months, sneaking off to gigs and clubs, their family quite unaware. Combat trousers, plaid shirt, band T-shirt; it's a Camden Market look, but from Topshop, Tammy Girl and C&A. There's an army surplus kit bag bought for a fiver, covered in hand-drawn band logos and slogans ('I'm probably going to die because of those permanent markers that you shake'). Then a walk to Edgware station, not far from Harrow, where those bold 1970s Gay Libbers had once pub-crawled, through the pebble-dashed suburbs of outer North London, at the very end of the Northern Line, clinging on to the city like a rope.

Our conversation makes Edgware sound like the setting for a zombie movie, a place to be negotiated with caution and guile, avoiding contact with others as much as possible, climbing through windows and lurking in deserted Underground stations. Because this is the end of the line, the Underground staff always leave the gates of the station open at night so the drunks and sleepers can stagger out, blinking, to the high street in their own time. On the way back from a night out, So watches all the revellers, shift workers and people with nowhere better to be disperse slowly from the Tube carriage. When finally alone, they reach up and, with a practised hand, free a large printed card from its frame on the carriage wall. 'It's so badass,' says So. 'I used to steal

Poems on the Underground.' This one is May Sarton's 'A Glass of Water' – a taste of sanity in a rough world. They're wearing an oversized man's coat, from a friend of the family who sells department store seconds. 'It was grey. It was awful. It was my favourite coat of all time.' It's also the perfect coat for the job, easily big enough to hide a stolen poem beneath. The next day, they retreat to their room with hammer and nails: Poems on the Underground are too heavy for Blu-Tack. Positioned above the bed over the ditzy rose wallpaper So begins hammering, hoping this isn't the time they're going to be electrocuted by hitting a wire. Sarton will join Christopher Marlowe, Sappho and Lorna Goodison as part of a stolen anthology, literally writ large. Although they soon realise the Tube is full of other bored readers of poetry and let the rest of the placards be.

Edgware lies out on the edge of the green belt, on the northern extreme of the city. To most Londoners it's as remote as a distant airport, the word merely a destination at the end of a train line, a place that's hard to picture. And to those huddled further into the suburbs, it seems like a hinterland of farmsteads and wilderness. 'People would joke about *Oh, did you tie your goat up on the way to school today?*' So recalls. 'I'm coming in on the Tube, and they're like, *No, but you live in a field.*' People tell them it's *leafy suburbia*, but Edgware is not like that either. 'There are definitely leafy suburbs, like Hampstead Garden Suburb,' says So. 'But a lot of suburbs are just wedged in between an A-road and a train line,' as is the case on the road where they live. 'It wasn't like there's kids playing in the street, because we lived on a rat run as well. If you played in the street, you'd be run over by someone trying to get on the A41.' It isn't sleepy, but also it doesn't feel like the metropolis. London is where they go to see their great-grandparents at Christmas, enjoy a school trip or visit a museum. Edgware is zone 6. It doesn't feel like it has anything

in common. So grows up in a conservative Orthodox neighbourhood, part of a wider and more varied Jewish community that
stretches from glamorous Golders Green all the way up to the
rather less fashionable borders of Barnet. 'In some ways, it was a
transplanted shtetl in a suburb,' says So. Their mum's family were
East Enders; their dad's rather more local and suburban. 'I was
aware that there was this other London and other Jewishness in
London that was more secular, was more worldly, frankly, more
fun. But we never got to go and see it.'

Recently, So encountered a wave of nostalgia from a strange
and unexpected source: the George Michael documentary on
Netflix. George Michael's dad's restaurant was in Edgware. 'We
weren't allowed to go there because it wasn't kosher,' they tell me.
At what they describe as 'exactly Wham! age' (forty-five), So still
finds it mind-blowing that two boys who'd gone to a local school
had experienced such phenomenal success. But it isn't just that
which So finds affecting, it's the detail of the locale. A rush of
seventies clothing and suburban furniture, things they haven't
thought about for years. So's mum still lives nearby, so they go to
visit with their partner, but even now So refuses to go through
Edgware, despite it having changed a lot. Culturally, at least.
Physically, it's still streets of sad-looking pebbledashed houses
stuck, bewildered, on the edge of fields.

So's parents are the first in the synagogue community to get a
divorce. 'My parents' marriage was deeply unhappy, and my dad
was very abusive.' He finally leaves when So is seventeen, and
they describe those few years as a war zone. In such a tight-knit
religious community, their mother finds little support, everyone
taking her husband's side. So finds suburbia gossipy, conservative and judgemental. It feels like an utterly binary existence:
kids at their school with shaved heads go on a protest against the
Poll Tax and get suspended for throwing things at the National

Front, but at home the Jewish community vote Conservative and keep their heads down. Any sign of difference has to be hidden, whether it is alcoholism or domestic violence. 'It was a *shonde* – a shame.'

Part of that feeling of exclusion grows from a realisation that So is queer. Their secondary school is known as the dyke factory. But signs of LGBTQ+ life are not just confined to school. A local woman has transitioned – 'or in the parlance of the eighties, had a sex change', recalls So – something everyone knew about because of Christine Jorgensen, a trans pioneer, who travelled from the US to Denmark in 1950 to undergo gender reassignment. So has this highly visible symbol of LGBTQ+ life in the neighbourhood, even though the community implicitly understands there are barriers to her life. 'She was probably going to live with her mum for the rest of her life, not participate fully in whatever having an adult Jewish life meant.' There was also the daughter of another neighbour, who leaves to live with another woman. 'And because she was from within the conservative community, her family sat shiva' – the seven-day mourning period observed by Jewish families – 'which means they acted as if she died. So they had a full week's mourning for her.' Not to mention So's uncle – 'the nice relative' – who they consider to be gay too. 'He never married, lived with his parents his whole life, he'd go on holiday with his closest male friends. He was very, very religious, but very closeted.' Glimpses of LGBTQ+ lives, but with no sense of a community.

So finds their own queerness reflected more in pop music. As a child they're obsessed with The Kinks' subversive single 'Lola'. One day, they're at a caravan park in the Home Counties with their father's parents, and it comes on the radio. So starts to sing along, and suddenly there is their grandmother, literally washing So's mouth out with soap and water. 'You think it's something that only happens in books,' says So, 'but no! Oh, and she said, *You're not allowed to sing songs like that.*' But this was very much a tale of two grannies. So's other grandmother lives in the East End and her best friend is a sex worker with a son and daughter who are both queer. They end up having a kid, the son becoming sperm donor for his sister's partner. As a small child, So listens to their grandma tell these incredible stories, and even though the details might not have meant much, the idea that there might be alternative ways of living seeps into their brain. Maybe you didn't need to get married? Maybe women could work? They could even be prime minister, though Margaret Thatcher wasn't proving to be much of an inspiration for So. 'It seemed like you had to wear very unattractive clothes and carry a handbag.'

So's saviour isn't a person, it's a place. The library. They'd moved up to the adult library aged nine. *I'm sorry, I've read all the books.* Once in there, a whole new world opens. Mainly thanks to a librarian who has faced out all the LGBTQ+ books, perhaps in protest at Section 28. So gives *Giovanni's Room* a go because they like the cover. Then Jane Rule's *Desert of the Heart*. By the time So is thirteen, they're encountering their first-ever non-binary character, in a graphic novel, a flawed depiction but still powerful. 'I sort of knew I was different. But the way that that was identified was that I was clever. Which was a very gender-weird, boundary-line thing to be. I was told lots of things like, *You're learning this so you can teach it to your sons.*'

So's family are sitting around the TV. A prestige new BBC drama: *Oranges Are Not the Only Fruit*. When it becomes obvious what it's about – a child in a strict religious family discovering her sexuality – So's dad switches it off. That doesn't stop So reading Jeanette Winterson's book, or indeed from falling in love with their best friend. Later, by mistake they get to see Derek Jarman's *Blue* on television with their mum, who has confused

Jarman with Dennis Potter. *This is someone very important who has died,* she tells So. *He's done this amazing, interesting TV thing. Watch it. Blue,* the film Jarman makes in the final months of his life, is one of the most moving and magical pieces of art to have emerged in the midst of the AIDS crisis. And while their parents are getting divorced, a new form of escape comes to Edgware: a Blockbuster video store. Soon So is a regular, fighting with them for not stocking LGBTQ+ titles like *Go Fish* and *Priest,* and enjoying all the queer film-making that has instead sneaked unnoticed into the World section.

All of these early-1990s events feel part of a wider culture that sweeps teenage So along. *Everyone's androgynous and bisexual,* people are saying. 'I knew I wasn't a girly girl, like all the girls who wore full face make-up and fancied Tom Cruise. But there was still enough of that gender and sexuality crossover think-ing that I can think, *Oh well, my gender positionality is different because of my sexuality. Like, I want to wear carpenter jeans and climb ladders, and that's sexuality.*' By the time they're eighteen, they're heading out from Edgware to dyke bars and queer indie clubs. Suburbia, by contrast, 'became this surveillant, creepy, dark space that I had to walk home through, very drunk, with my keys out through my fist, in my horror-Satan clothing that their neighbours commented on. It just became a non-place, and everything began at the Tube station.' Even George Michael has moved to Hampstead. 'I mean, who wouldn't?' Soon So will be off too, to Cambridge, escaping the place they associate with all the confusion, control and family disintegration, and the binar-ies of gender too. Those stolen Poems on the Underground, that heroic queer librarian, the forbidden films and songs will inspire their own writing. But I wouldn't put it past So to still exit the odd situation through the window, zombie apocalypse style, should the need arise.

While for many LGBTQ+ people So's desire to escape for the city will strike a chord, for some the urge to stay and defend the suburbs has been equally powerful. 'There are a great many homosexuals living in the provinces and the country, to whom the gay world, as expressed in London, is neither desirable nor understandable,' writes David Richardson from St Albans in a letter to *Gay News* in 1972.[22] A month after the first issue is published, and possibly to David's dismay, the capital hosts its inaugural Gay Pride march. It's a discreet affair, not least because it's held at night. It comes in a period of huge change for the LGBTQ+ people in Britain. The founding of the Gay Liberation Front for one, whose energy, radicalism and optimism are at odds with the more pragmatic line being walked by existing groups such as the Campaign for Homosexual Equality. For the women's movement in Britain, 1970 had been a pivotal year, from a pioneering conference in Oxford to a protest against the Miss World beauty contest at the Royal Albert Hall.

But progress is not assured. In 1977, *Gay News* is successfully sued for blasphemy by moralising campaigner Mary Whitehouse after it printed a poem about a gay centurion's love for Christ. Five years before that, Richardson, that reader from St Albans, has a suggestion for readers of the paper: 'I would like to see a series of organisations, without political message or dogma, existing in the provinces to bring together all homosexuals . . . so that in my town there would be no need for any man to remain alone and lonely.' And he goes further: 'I wish to ask all homosexuals in St Albans and surrounding areas, to write to me so that we can arrange to meet: all of us with each other . . . If we are to be civilised then we must care for each other: care, not because we are beautiful, witty, erudite, or anything exceptional; but because we are all homosexuals.' It feels a modest ask in an age of revolution, but every step, like on the moon just three years before, is a giant one.

BETWEEN THE WORLD
AND NEW ADDINGTON

Up on the windswept estate, where trees grow at acute angles to the hilltop, Kate is saying goodbye. Goodbye to her family, to New Addington, to England. It's 1977, and in two days she will be off on the first leg of her journey to Melbourne, to join her new girlfriend – if that's what she might become – for the adventure of a lifetime. Kate is twenty, and this is her trajectory, like a slingshot from the council suburb on the edge of the woods to as far away as she can get without climbing into orbit. But first she has something to do. To sit her parents down and tell them something. Something she has kept entirely separate from her life on the estate. It's the most nervous she has ever been with them. As she's speaking, her dad just keeps rolling a cigarette. It's a moment that seems to go on forever. But when they finally speak, they are fine. Better than fine. 'They both said that they loved me,' she says. 'That was it really, that they loved me, and they loved me as I am.'

Kate was born in 1956, the youngest of four siblings in a family who at that time were living in a halfway house. They had to share a kitchen and bathroom with three other families. Her sister was scared of another of the lodgers, a man who was often drunk and would follow her to the swing park. These were times of struggle for her family, with barely any money coming in and precious little in the way of security. But the post-war period was a boom time for council housing, alongside the blossoming of the welfare state and the NHS, and so the family found themselves caught in a safety net, pulled free of the halfway house and deposited on a sprawling council estate on the edge of Croydon. Kate's dad finds work as a labourer on the factory estate next door. Her mum stays home with four small children to look after, but as soon as she can she takes occasional evening work, cleaning factories or the local school. By the 1970s it's been a long time since her parents have ventured far from the estate, and so neither Australia nor lesbianism are guaranteed a welcome, but they greet the news with all the love and positivity she could have hoped for.

The three-bedroom brown-brick council house is a miraculous change after the uncertainty and jeopardy of the halfway house. There's a big bedroom for the boys, a smaller one for the girls, though for a long time Kate shares the bigger room with her brothers. A coal fire, a repurposed school desk as a dining table, a serving hatch for the endless cuppas. She recalls searching down the back of the sofa for enough money for school dinner, and playing on the street until dusk, when they can't see to carry on and are called in for tea. Their house backs onto the woods and fields around the estate. 'It was like living in the country, really,' she says. They'd explore the wrecked and rusting cars in the undergrowth, climb trees, have adventures. Her impulsive mum sometimes joins in the fun of a summer water fight, chasing them down the street with a bucket of water, wilder than the lot of them; her dad is more at home with Beethoven, *University Challenge* and *Play for Today*. Kate describes her mother as loving but not affectionate. Later, Kate will experiment, kissing her hello and goodbye, to see if that makes a difference. She shakes her head at the memory. Come Christmas, the hall would be stacked high with drink, like a bar, the presents all paid for with loans from the Provident. Two streets over and fifteen years later, much of what she describes is true for my family too. Life on this working-class council estate changed little from 1956 until the Right to Buy kicked in in the 1980s.

Kate thinks back to all of those street games with her brothers. She describes herself as a tomboy. There's a couple of photos of her as a small girl in a dress, and then something happens, she's not sure what. After that she's got up like her brothers, in shorts and trousers, free to play. The transformation occurs without her even really knowing how or why. She watches her dad play football with the boys, and joins in. 'I hung out a lot with the boys. It was great, and also weird, sometimes risky. Sometimes I fitted in, sometimes I didn't.'

But the safety of this suburban bubble is pierced one day, when Kate passes her eleven-plus. She goes off to grammar school – two long bus rides away in Selhurst – and begins to glimpse another world. Some of the teachers wear academic gowns that set the tone for the school, one where fawn woolly socks, a beret and a briefcase are part of the uniform. *What the fuck?* she thinks. The uniform is bought on the Provident, and it's only a matter of weeks before the fawn socks are around her ankles, the briefcase bashed up, and she's carrying her books around in plastic carrier bags. 'I started that thing of traversing two different worlds in a really big way,' she recalls. 'I left that security of just being me in this place that I'd always known.' Sometimes, she's so tired after such a long day of travelling between school and home, and of performing the different selves this requires, that she falls asleep and ends up shaken awake by the driver at the end of the route.

It's the early 1970s, a time of power cuts and strikes. Lurid emerging pop cultures and rising feminism create a heady atmosphere where the world seems to be exploding all around her. Yet nothing can prepare her for what comes next. In her third year at grammar school, there is a teacher who is popular and cool. What begins as a crush quickly turns into something else. Even now, Kate finds it hard to talk about. 'Some of that sits between abuse and this other thing, which is, *Was I in a relationship with that person?*' There's no one she can talk to about it, to ask for help, and so in the isolation of a sexuality that is invisible, and a massive imbalance in power, she finds herself adrift in something she cannot control. When Kate turns sixteen, it becomes a sexual relationship.

The whole experience forces Kate to come to terms with her sexuality, and at that point, with little lesbian visibility in the world around her, it's scary. 'Fortunately, towards the latter part of my schooling, a couple of my friends were lesbian as well,' says Kate. 'They were later in coming to terms with that for themselves. They knew this teacher, and I was able to share some of what had happened with them, but prior to that, I couldn't really share that with anybody.' For her family she's still going out with boys, as a cover story. Some evenings she walks out to a red telephone box on a small green and calls her teacher; it's a claustrophobic space in which much of her coming-of-age is enacted. No one walking by realises what a strange other life this schoolgirl is having as she stands in the booth jamming in two-pence pieces, or hoping someone has rigged it so she doesn't need the coins. 'That compartmentalising,' she says wonderingly, 'I don't know how we do that, but we've all probably done it at some point.'

At the start of the 1970s, when she is in her early teens, Kate sees Germaine Greer on TV, and it makes a lasting impression. The women's movement is heading overground. Gay liberation, too, is filtering through, even to New Addington (not that I noticed), but it's feminism that captures Kate's attention. On an exploratory trip into London, Kate, then seventeen, visits her first lesbian club night. *Oh my God, here I am*, she thinks, full of excitement. A large room, DJ in the corner spinning the hits of

1974, women dancing with women, a sense of freedom and elec-
tricity in the air. *It's fab*. Then a slow song, 'Candle in the Wind',
and Kate spies a woman she's taken with. And so Kate asks her to
dance. Because in 1974 that's what you did when the slow songs
started. And it feels really exciting. She might be a teenager, but
for *all* of the women here, regardless of age, something extraordinary is happening. Something new. It doesn't matter if you
are one of the new political feminists proclaiming your radicalism, or one of the much slighted 'bar dykes' – women who a few
years before knocked on the shuttered doors of secret clubs, like
Gateways in Chelsea, and spent the evening in fear of it being
raided. Here, in the music, the alcohol, the heady thrill of bodies
moving in rhythm, in the lights and the cigarette smoke, they
are all together. Maybe just for one night. The room feels electric
with a new spirit. *Fuck! We haven't been here before together*. 'It
just felt tingling,' Kate tells me.

Some of the women she meets are from a squat in Vauxhall.
They take Kate under their wing, this teenager just beginning to
explore her lesbian identity, London and life. One runs a club
night at the Festival Inn. 'It's quite a long journey out of New
Addington,' says Kate, 'where there was nobody like me that I
could see, into these other places where I had a different life.'
From the council estate to the squats and discos of the 1970s,
she'd traverse the gap between these disconnected worlds. It
makes her wonder 'what you do in yourself to be able to re-enter
while you're carrying this other life'. Something that thousands
are also dealing with, an age-old tension increased by the social
mobility of the times. And she is searching for an identity too. 'I
was a butch young thing, really,' she tells me, 'and trying to find
a language for how I felt that wasn't just *butch*. It's a bit like now
with gender non-binary. Young people who are going, *All I used
to have before was drag, that was all I had, but actually it's more than*

that. And all the language I had was butch and femme, but that didn't quite fit or wasn't enough for what my experience was.'

Her parents know she goes off to women's dances, but not really what that means. They hear instead about the endless bus journeys and train rides in the dark. *How was it?* her mum asks when she gets in. *Did you have a good night?* She responds with something positive but non-committal while making some cheese on toast, before settling down to watch *Match of the Day* with her folks. The same evening containing utterly different worlds.

'At that point there was the whole burn your bra thing,' she recalls, and so she disposes of hers. Off to an anti-National Front demo in an elephant-print top and a pair of flares, anti-fascist badge proudly displayed, her mum is worried. *Oh my God, you're not going out like that.* Kate is unbothered. *I'm off. This is it.* Her mum is filled with anxiety. *What if someone sees that badge?* While Kate is boldly exploring new worlds, her mum hardly ever leaves the estate. 'I can't imagine what it was like for her, me going up into London and entering into this life that she had no idea about,' she says. Although perhaps she has *some* idea. One day, the pair of them are watching a Dirk Bogarde film on the TV. In *Victim*, he plays a married lawyer being blackmailed for his secret gay relationship. Kate sides with his wife, played by Sylvia Syms. *He's being a shit!* says Kate. *What's going on here?* She's mystified by why her mum seems to be supporting him. It's only later she begins to think their disagreement might not have just been about film criticism.

It's through Kate's adventures in Vauxhall that she meets an Australian woman she fancies, and they begin to get involved. But before they can work out what's going on, the woman has to return to Melbourne. Kate's dad has been in the merchant navy and is full of stories about his travels around the globe, and so his intrepid daughter feels inspired to follow his lead – and escape the estate for the other side of the world. But before she goes, she needs to say something to her family, so it's now, at the age of twenty, that she decides to come out. She tells her sister and her husband first. *Yeah, we know*, they say. *We've guessed. We knew that all along.* On the one hand, Kate is delighted; this is as easy as it gets. On the other, she is left thinking, *Why didn't you say something to me?* Burdened with this huge secret all her life, a bit of help wouldn't have come amiss. Her parents react calmly and with love. Finally, she gathers the whole family together for a going-away dinner at her parents' house. *I have something to tell you*, she says. But before she can continue, her brother-in-law interrupts, saying, *Did you tell Darren* – a bloke who Kate once had a date with – *that you're gay?* Her brother butts in: *What? Did I hear that correctly?* So Kate takes the plunge and comes out. A few minutes later, and her brother is saying, *Wow, what a great family we are, no one's batting an eyelid.* Okay, so her sister-in-law has got upset and leaves the room, but here is Kate, unburdening herself so she's light enough to fly around the world. 'I didn't think I could have stayed in New Addington and lived as I lived at that point,' she says. 'I went and lived in Melbourne, and I had a very free life. I went to women's dances. I got involved with various people. I built a political life, got very involved in the women's movement, involved in gay liberation. I just couldn't have done that, I don't think, if I'd stayed in New Addington.'

In cosmopolitan, arty Melbourne in the late 1970s, Kate's life is transformed. She runs a small disco that she sets up with her partner. Later, in Sydney, she becomes a carpenter. And part of a community of women pushing the boundaries of what is possible. 'We all did that,' she says, 'we stepped into this thing. There was a risk, there was some danger, but there was a lot of excitement.' These are women firing off each other to create something new. 'I feel very lucky in terms of the times that I lived in, recognising that it could have been much harder for people before me and the scenes that they had to make. The level of courage that people had and needed to have. And you see that now, don't you, in young trans people finding a language for themselves and making a space for themselves. The courage it takes to do that is tremendous, really.'

She lives there for over three decades, but frequently visits Britain, and New Addington, where her parents continue to live in the same house. She recalls her dad bringing her and her partner cups of tea in bed in the morning, and feeling she could not have been luckier. She also becomes friends with a group of lesbians who live in London, and uses them as a quick getaway when being stuck in New Addington gets too much. The contrast between her life in Melbourne and the one she left behind on the estate is stark. Once, she was secretive and powerless; now she is defining who she is, and how she wants to live. As she walks along the wide, wind-blown streets of the housing estate, past the dump and over to the parade of shops, she's at a loss to even be able to describe how strange it is to be embedded in both of these worlds.

Kate loses her parents in the late 1990s, and after her mum dies, she returns to help clear the council house that was her family home, needing to vacate it within three weeks. A decade or so later, she returns to the UK full-time and drives around the old estate 'feeling the air, and the air felt like home'. She thinks she's returning to a culture that she belongs to, but it all feels slightly different – she's changed, and it's changed too. The old house is still there, but the garden has been dug up and paved over, and a massive SUV stands where once her mother had chased them with buckets of water. She sits there a while in the car, and then to her surprise an old next-door neighbour opens her front door. *Kate! Come on in! Look at you!* Suddenly,

she's inside, hearing all about this woman's dead husband, a gar-
rulous tumble of gossip about people she can barely remember
or has never met. Kate finds herself smiling at this woman's particular way of telling stories, the complete lack of interest in her
after all this time, despite the remarkable transformations that
have happened in her life. The years in Australia, her adventures
and experiences, her partner and work: nothing. But it takes
her right back. 'My mum could have been sitting there, and we
could all have been having a cup of coffee together.' No distance
at all, suddenly, between the poles of her existence, and the years
that have passed. The different worlds she has inhabited all there,
rising in the steam of the Nescafé and the breeze that rushes over
the rooftops and up into the chilly afternoon sky.

'I walked up the stairs to the flat and paused before knocking on the door. Should I feel so apprehensive, even nervous?' wrote journalist Antony Seib in the *Thame Gazette* in November 1973.[23] Seib is visiting a flat in Gayhurst Road, High Wycombe, to meet members of the Chilterns CHE group, not far from where Quentin Crisp once lived many decades before. 'The door opened, not on scenes of the wildest imagination, but on a welcoming convivial atmosphere.' The founders, George Broadhead and Roy Saich, move to Chesham in 1969, Roy working in insurance, George as a teacher. But without any networks already in place, the age-old question remains: how do you find other LGBTQ+ people in your area? Broadhead and Saich's solution was to contact people and organisations that may have encountered gay people through their work. And so they speak to GPs, churches, magistrates and social workers – groups who likely have identified them for all the wrong reasons – asking to hear from isolated gay patients, parishioners, defendants or vulnerable people. The call goes out across Aylesbury, Bletchley, Harrow, High Wycombe, Leighton Buzzard and Watford. As I read the article, I realise this includes the area I live in, where the new town of Milton Keynes was only just starting to be built. This would have been the group I'd have signed up to, if I wasn't three at the time. A curiosity to the local paper, sure, but bold enough to put themselves out there, to see if the people of Thame lived up to their name or not.

So successful is this strategy that by 1972 there are seventy members, meeting in The Beech Tree pub in Beaconsfield.

'Everyone I met that evening behaved perfectly normally,' writes the intrepid journalist. For which you can't help thinking the Chilterns CHE have let themselves down a bit.

VAPOUR TRAILS OVER CROYDON

In his box room Alan is concentrating, carefully gluing together a Messerschmitt 109. The Second World War might have ended some sixteen years before, but still kids grow up filled with stories of danger and derring-do. Later, when the model is dry, he flies it around the house, arm sweeping it in imaginary dogfights across the landing and down the stairs. Joined by his older brother with his Spitfire, he takes it out into the long back garden, 90 feet of uninterrupted airspace, where they prop them against a wall of garages at the very end. Back at the house, Alan's brother lifts the air rifle and fires. Together they destroy the models, rifle pellets pounding the rough concrete walls of the garages or disappearing into the foliage, only occasionally hitting their target. The brittle plastic shatters as the metal pierces it. Soon, the models are completely destroyed. The boys return to the house, filled with noisy tales of destruction and mayhem, chattering about how they would go to the woods at the edge of New Addington later, to explore and fight and climb and hide in their territory, being whatever they want to be. Disappearing.

Their mum is just back. She's a charwoman and has been out cleaning houses in Shirley, a suburb of Croydon as wealthy as New Addington is poor. On weekdays, a group of women can be seen leaving the estate on the 130 bus, and disembarking with their buckets and mops, crossing the road at the roundabout to clean the large middle-class homes with their arched porches and exaggerated pitched roofs. Alan's mum chars for three families. One passes on old copies of the *Beano* and *Commando* when their children have finished with them, and Alan and his brother eagerly devour them. Another has a grown-up daughter who buys and discards clothes with alarming speed. They're passed on to Alan's mum, who becomes the most fashionably dressed char-woman in New Addington, in the latest chain store designs of 1961. It's the same era and a few streets away from where Kate lived, before she flew away to Melbourne,* and the next street over from where I would later grow up. None of us ever had the faintest inkling the other existed. And, back before the internet, how could we? Would our lives have been different if we'd known there were fellow travellers round the corner? Very probably, yes. But that was the twentieth-century suburb for you: a place of endless mystery and suspicion. Back then, the estate is still new, and feels unfinished, not yet settled into the hilly landscape on the edge of Croydon, a loose doodle beneath the flight path of the jet fighters from nearby Biggin Hill airport. They whistle and roar over the houses with a promise of exhilaration and excitement, and Alan stares up at them, imagining himself a fighter pilot, escaping the mundane world of the ground into the clouds.

At school, one of the boys finds a discarded copy of *Parade*, a pin-up magazine in the days before it goes full pornographic, and the kids crowd round staring at the girls on display. When one day the boys share a magazine that has pictures of men with women, Alan suddenly realises his attention is drawn in a way it hadn't been before. He knows he feels different from the other boys at school, but he doesn't worry about it. He's calm, patient, keeps a low profile. It's all very well being different, but what sort of different is it, and what does it mean? There is no one Alan can talk to or ask. And so he becomes expert at pouncing on the slightest piece of information.

* See the chapter 'Between the World and New Addington'.

It's a blazing October day, and Alan is fifteen, entering his last year at school. He's not paying attention in class, his mind wandering as he glances across at a classmate, a handsome Anglo-Malaysian lad, a rarity among the white working-class kids of the estate. He's roused from his teenage reverie by one of the trigger words buzzing in his head. Another boy is asking the teacher, *What is a homosexual, sir?* 'Homosexual', a long, cumbersome and provocative word, especially among boys who usually only get as far as *homo*, or even more commonly, just *mo*. 'We used to talk about *those people*, you know?' says Alan. '*Are you one of those?* Not really knowing what *one of those* was . . . You didn't really know what they were on about, you know? Just men that did funny things to other men.' But here it is, the word 'homosexual', plain as day. Perhaps it's a genuine enquiry; more likely it's laid down as a challenge to the teacher, to disrupt with the trickiest subject of the day. The room holds its breath. And then the teacher answers, explaining with functional sincerity. The teenagers sit there, astonished and engrossed, unused to having their questions about more worldly matters answered when there are the rules of grammar or long division to grapple with. 'Now I definitely knew I was a homosexual by this point,' says Alan, 'and I must admit, I thought he was quite brave, actually.' Alan goes out of his way to play straight at school. He's seen what happens if they suspect you're *one of them*. Merciless and relentless bullying, name-calling and humiliation, that's what. Alan doesn't even know if the target is gay or not, and as far as the boys at school are concerned that doesn't seem to matter. Even if he isn't *one of them*, this boy acts as if he might be, on the edge of the group, nervous and sensitive. A boy destroyed.

Yet changes in the wider world are filtering through to Alan's too. He's fourteen when sexual acts between consenting men over the age of twenty-one are decriminalised in England. 'Homosexuality was in the news a lot,' says Alan. 'And I gradually realised that they were talking about me. And I always consider I was very lucky to be brought up as a teenager, fourteen, fifteen at that time, because I knew what was happening, and I knew what it was.' He watches a news programme, *Panorama*, a whole episode focused on homosexuality in Britain, interviewing gay men and women about their sexuality, how the law affected the way they could live their lives. 'I remember my dad saying, *If either of you turn out to be like these people, you'll be out*. It never happened. But I remember that. It gave me an inkling and I knew what it was.'

Perhaps it's this that fires Alan to say it out loud. He hasn't meant to, but loneliness has worked away at him for years. In 1968, at the age of fifteen, Alan tells his mum. Even today, in the world of *Heartstopper* and *Everybody's Talking About Jamie*, this is a remarkable move, but back then, three years before Britain's first Gay Pride march, it's an amazing thing for a fifteen-year-old boy to be doing. She's remarkably calm about it. *Don't tell your father. And don't tell your brother. It'll just be a secret between us two at the moment.* 'I just thought I had to tell someone,' says Alan. 'I think I didn't get on that well with my brother at that time. I think if I told him, he would have treated the whole thing as a joke, and maybe told friends of his who would have told the younger brothers in the school that way. And then obviously, there was loads of gay boys at that school, because I mean, it was a huge school.' Not that Alan knows any of them. On the one hand, telling his mum helps release some of the pressure, but it adds new ones too, for him to somehow follow through with it, to become an adult. 'If I could give myself advice now, if I could go back in time, I'd say, *Don't! Don't come out. Leave it for a bit longer.*'

There aren't many gay role models for Alan to cling to. He listens to Kenneth Williams and Hugh Paddick as Julian and

Sandy on *Round the Horne*, talking in Polari and unashamedly a couple, and sees Dick Emery on TV as Clarence, the outrageously dressed, flirtatious character in his comedy sketch show, greeting blokeish men in the street with a cheery *Hello, honky tonks!* and often heading off with them at the end of the skit. 'I love those characters,' says Alan. 'Because in their own way I suppose they were rebellious, weren't they? They didn't care . . . They just carried on as they wanted to.' His grandparents offer him a different reference point, in tales from the antique trade in the fifties and sixties. His mother's parents run a house clearance shop in South Croydon, and one of the dealers they know is a camp man called Bob. His life cannot have been easy, living as an openly gay man in suburban Croydon at a time when strict moral codes were reinforced by harsh laws and sentencing. When Alan's family visit his grandparents they tell hair-raising stories of Bob, this week arrested for picking up men in public toilets, the next assaulted by a violent homophobe. *He'd really been beaten up badly the other day*, they tell them. But despite the wider moral panic Bob remains a family friend, someone Alan never meets but hears countless tales of, a remarkable outlier.

Fourth of August 1969, a couple of weeks after the first moon landing, and sixteen-year-old Alan sits in Grants department store on an induction day. Grants is a venerable Victorian establishment, once a huge draw for French tourists who flew into glamorous Croydon Airport in the 1930s, but by the late sixties beginning to look out of place in the psychedelic world of modern retail. Alan is going to be working in the shop's travel bureau, booking holidays and arranging flights. On his first day, he sneaks out at lunchtime to get some cigarettes. As he steps out of the staff entrance, a man gropes him. It's a manager, much older than Alan. 'And two days later, on the Wednesday, he had sex with me,' says Alan. 'So I can tell you when I lost my virginity: it was the sixth of August 1969, between, say, 1.30 and 3.30 in the afternoon.' The manager takes the new boy back to a flat around the corner from the shop. 'I wouldn't say exactly he raped me, it was more consensual than that. But I didn't really know what I was consenting to, you know? But anyway, it was uncomfortable, but it wasn't unpleasant. And this became a regular Wednesday-afternoon thing for quite a few weeks.' Until one day he takes Alan back, and another man is waiting there for them, a stranger. 'And that sort of freaked me out. And I thought, *No, I couldn't cope with this.* So I wouldn't see him after that.' The gentle, softly spoken sixteen-year-old escapes an abusive situation.

The labyrinthine back rooms of Grants would introduce Alan to a number of other gay men too. A few months later he meets Harry, who is working as a courier for the travel bureau, accompanying groups of package holiday customers on their trips, still a novelty for many in the late 1960s. Harry, in his mid-twenties, feels impossibly sophisticated to Alan: he can speak multiple languages and is a member of the actors' union, Equity. Alan recalls how Harry took him under his wing. 'He showed me how to behave, and how to say no and not let people take advantage of you. And then of course we had sex, but it was in a very nice, friendly way. And fully consensual.' Harry always insists they use condoms, which is highly unusual at the time. Alan wonders if it's a kink, but Harry tells him, *You should use them too. Because the last thing you would want to do is to go to your doctor because you've got a case of the clap in your arse or in your throat. How are you going to explain that?*

As the 1970s begin, Alan is allowed to go on a cruise as part of his job, although because of his age he has to get his parents' written permission. Alan glows as he remembers it. 'It was great fun, being gay on a cruise . . . I could be completely who I wanted to be.' He's away from Croydon for ten days, and when he returns to work it all falls a little flat. Sophisticated Harry moves away to another store, then the Ideal Home Exhibition and on to a chorus line. But before he goes, he introduces Alan to a lad who'd become his first boyfriend: Jeffrey. At last, this is a lad the same age as Alan. Jeffrey also works at Grants and lives with his mum in a block of flats in central Croydon. She's a busy single mother, and while she's out the boys take the opportunity to hop into bed as often as they can. 'I don't think it was more than two lads just getting their legs over,' says Alan. 'No more than that. But I think given time it would have grown into a real relationship.' But all too soon Jeffrey is whisked off to the fleshpots of Basingstoke, when his mum gets a job there with the AA. They exchange letters and postcards. 'We said we'd keep in touch,' says Alan. 'But we never did, because we were just two young lads. Two children, really.'

The 1970s see Alan drifting from job to job, discreetly navigating the era of free love in the red-brick working-class estate on the edge of London. But times are changing. Gay pub and club nights start to crop up in Croydon. The Star holds a disco once a week, as does Dr Jim's, which is what Alan describes, with authentic period flavour, as *a discotheque*. 'It used to have a gay night on a Tuesday,' he recalls. I imagine Alan there, quiet, smiling, nodding along with the beat, mid-length hair bouncing for emphasis as he's dragged reluctantly to the dance floor. He describes Dr Jim's music policy as 'the disco sound', which he was never into. No, Alan's scene is jazz – Duke Ellington, Count Basie, Benny Goodman, the big bands. As nostalgic as his enduring fascination for the vintage aircraft of Biggin Hill.

Just as Alan found the beginnings of gay life through his work, so the job he gets in the late 1970s – working in reservations for Dan-Air – liberates him beyond his wildest imaginings. 'Being gay in an airline is absolutely no problem at all,' he says.

'It's just accepted, and you can be who you want to be. It's a fantastic environment. And I think Dan-Air was a particularly gay-friendly airline.' With the job comes cheap travel for employee and spouse, and Dan-Air is one of the first to accept homosexual couples as partners, decades before the law caught up. But that isn't the only perk of the job. 'Airlines were of course gigantic cruising grounds,' he says. In 1982 the office relocates from Croydon to the small town of Horley near Gatwick, and Alan finds himself trapped in a daily commuter hell of British Rail signal problems and breakdowns, stuck on slam-door trains with their smoking carriages and wooden floors. He looks to move closer, and is helped by having recently started dating Neil, an Irishman living in Crawley who works in the operations department of another airline. They rent a flat above a shop in Horley from a pilot, landlording being one of the many side hustles of pilots in those days, including, Alan recalls, florists and video rental shops. Neil works shifts, so they can sometimes go days without seeing each other.

We're used to historic stories of gay life in Brighton, London and Manchester, and numerous university centres, but this small Surrey town had one of the highest concentrations of LGBTQ+ residents in Britain, thanks to the airline industry. Alan and Neil socialise in the town's pubs, like The Three Bells. 'Completely gay,' says Alan, 'because it was an airline town. Everyone worked for the airport or worked for the airlines, knowing what a gay-friendly environment it was. There was never any problems about being gay, being with a boyfriend and that in Horley.' He's never had such a busy social life. 'Everyone mingled, straights and gays together. It was just a lovely loving environment. Very like going into a gay-friendly pub. Couples of mixed sexes, couples of women, couples of men.' The Horley of the 1980s is an unlikely haven of hidden queer suburbia. And with Brighton and London on the train line, there were plenty of escapes for them too. 'It was when I worked for the airline that I really started to live my life more or less openly as a gay man. Although, as I say, I never really went about publicising it, so people said, *What you doing here? This is a gay pub.* I said, *I know! I'm gay!*' Always drawn to travel and escape, Alan is delighted that a perk of the job is that he can take his parents away on holiday. Together with Neil, he takes them to Amsterdam, sometimes Jersey just for a day, and one time Venice too, his parents enjoying the decadent thrill of it, off with their son and his gay partner, trading in the council estate in Croydon for the Grand Canal.

In 2004, after twenty-two years together, Neil is diagnosed with lymphatic cancer. 'It was very quick,' says Alan. 'From diagnosis to him dying was only a matter of weeks. I think he was probably ill for some time. He always seemed to be getting colds and flu . . . It was a shock, you know? It took me a long time to get over it.' Circumstances around his death made it much worse. 'When Neil died, I had to get out of the flat, which was in his name,' says Alan. Neil's large Catholic family blames Alan for making Neil gay and can't bear it. 'As far as they were concerned, it was all my fault. I led their boy astray. So they were really fairly unpleasant.' After a hostile silence, Neil's sister rings Alan and tells him the date of the funeral. Alan goes along with some friends from Neil's airline. 'We had to sit at the back of the church, and I wasn't allowed to take part in any of the, you know . . .' Alan trails off. 'It was really, really sad.' AIDS took away many of their friends too. He recalls one week going to two funerals. All of that hope and liberation and love hollowed out through loss.

After that, Alan leaves Horley and heads back to New Addington to look after his dad, who's had a stroke, and later his mother when she gets ill too. 'So I've ended up back in the house I was born in,' he says. 'With about seventy years of clutter.'

He doesn't hide his sexuality, but isn't particularly open about it either. 'If people would say, *Are you gay?* I'd say, *Well, yeah. So what?* But I never volunteered it to anyone. I think the neighbours suspect.' When his mother dies, Alan realises he feels quite isolated out here, with no gay friends around. So in 2019 he looks online to see what there might be in the town, and finds out about our old friend, the Croydon Area Gay Society, still drifting on in a very different era from the one in which it was founded. 'I just wish that I'd found out about CAGS when I was a teenager,' says Alan. 'It would have made a big difference because it's recently had its fiftieth anniversary. It was certainly going when I was in my early twenties.' Of course, because Alan came out so young he even steals a march on the society, which began in 1971. He tells me about how much things have changed in his lifetime. 'I think one of the biggest examples of that is Croydon Pride,' he says. 'The fact that the police take part in it now. Whereas in the early days of the Pride marches, the police were there – they weren't keeping an eye on the people watching, they were keeping an eye on the people marching.' He feels how important this change is, how it sets a tone and helps people feel comfortable being out. 'It's lovely to walk around Wandle Park,' he says, thinking back on the marches he's been on. 'And, you know, just seeing couples. I remember seeing two elderly women sitting next to each other on a bench, just kissing.' Like Alan, pioneers, leading the way so that the rest of us can follow. But also, for much of their lives, invisible in the sprawl of the suburbs. Life for the generation before him must have been really tough, he thinks. Coming out when he did, just as the law was changing, meant he was entering a world his LGBTQ+ forebears dreamed of but couldn't really imagine. 'Especially not really knowing what it was like to be homosexual before. I was so lucky . . . I grew up at just the right time.'

It's 1974, and the august representatives of Tunbridge Wells Borough Council are meeting. Internationally renowned concert pianist Peter Katin is due to perform a recital at the Assembly Hall. A prestigious guest – how wonderful! Except this event is in support of the Campaign for Homosexual Equality, and there's been an objection to using a council venue for such a scandalous activity. The councillors hurriedly refuse permission. This is *Royal* Tunbridge Wells, after all. Yet rather than receiving thanks for defending the heterosexual honour of the town, the councillors find themselves ridiculed in the local press by a stream of letter writers. 'We do not want these persons mincing in our magnificent Assembly Hall and soiling the seat cushions with their effeminate clothing,' goes one. 'I am sure that all respectably minded gentlefolk of Tunbridge Wells will heave a sigh of relief as the Entertainments Committee ushers in a new era of clean, decent, heterosexual entertainment such as Bingo, Wrestling etc.'[24] The council hurriedly rescind their ban, but too late. They get their wish, and Katin never performs in Tunbridge Wells, Royal or not. But off the back of it the pianist receives other letters, darker threats than the council can muster, anonymous this time. *I wouldn't let a little boy in the same room as you, you are the kind of man who murders small kids. Why don't you die. Look out we will get you, a silent shot, we are waiting for you.*

Katin is one of post-war Britain's foremost concert pianists, known for his passionate performances of Rachmaninov at the Proms and his tours of the US and Europe. He lives in a large house in the suburbs of South Croydon with his wife, Eva, and their two sons. He's also bisexual, and has been a public supporter of homosexual law reform since giving a fundraising concert at Wigmore Hall in 1966. Katin's house is big enough to have a dedicated recital room, and when he joins the Croydon branch of the Campaign for Homosexual Equality in 1971 he gives the first of many concerts to his fellow members. Eva goes to the theatre that night, as she elects to each time he has one of his CHE evenings, leaving Peter to it. The kids stay behind, and so in the kitchen one of their sons is earnestly asking a couple of flight crew from Gatwick about the performance of the Boeing 707 while they're trying to get away to mingle with the adults. The evening is a huge success, a remarkable coup for a small local group to have pulled off out here in the stockbroker belt.

It's interesting that during the 1970s the codification of both suburbia and LGBTQ+ people – particularly gay men – reaches some sort of peak in British culture, not least through the hugely popular TV sitcoms of the day. Images of both are cemented that will prove stubbornly hard to shift. Suburbia is seen through the prism of snobbery in *The Good Life* or oppression in *The Fall and Rise of Reginald Perrin*. Gay visibility in the era mainly involved characters such as Melvin Hayes's make-up-wearing soldier Gloria in *It Ain't Half Hot Mum* or John Inman's turn as camp menswear assistant Mr Humphries in *Are You Being Served?*, which many of the people I spoke to for this book brought up as one of the only visible representations of gay life they saw in the media at the time. These were stereotypes from another era, filtered through the work of straight writers and directors, and sometimes performers. Affectionate or not, these became the LGBTQ+ signifiers of the day. But sometimes life does take a sitcom turn.

Following on from Katin's successful recital, his parties become a regular treat for the officer class of Croydon, usually at home but sometimes requiring an outside venue. 'At a Boxing Day Party in the mid 1970s Peter played the piano and flirted politely with all that caught his eye,' recalled Ray Harvey-Amer of the group some years later. 'He participated in all the party games, and as night merged into morning he was only tempted to leave when told that the taxi driver was like a dream unfulfilled.'[25] Croydon CHE is a respectable middle-class affair, all sherry and Chopin, but one evening Katin opens the invitation out more widely to the homosexuals of the town. I think of Alan and Kate, my fellow gay New Addington residents, who were both living in the borough at the time. Would they have been tempted to go along? I doubt it. It sounds extraordinarily intimidating. And what a sight Katin's house, recital room and guests must have seemed to people usually excluded from these kinds of events. 'It was like any other gay party of a rather less desirable kind, where people had screaming rows,' Katin recalls in an interview with Peter Scott-Presland, and the stage for class-based situation comedy is set. 'I said no, this is not why I organised this. I don't know where the silver's going to go. They really weren't very nice.'[26] And so disharmony rules around the grand piano as the different sorts of LGBTQ+ suburbs briefly collide, in class conflict over the sherry and canapés, to fuel gossip and grudges for years to come.

RUNNING AWAY TO SUBURBITON

Josep sits in his bedsit in Tolworth, exhausted after a long shift at the nursing home. He has grown up in a village outside Valencia in Spain, a place that considers itself rural, where everyone knows everyone else's business. But he longs to escape, to explore who he really is. And now, in 1999, recently graduated, here he is, in the suburbs of south-west London, within rumbling distance of the Kingston bypass. Homesickness drags at him, even as he makes new friends at the nursing home. But in these first few difficult months not everyone has been kind about his accent and hesitant spoken English. So it's good to have somewhere he can escape to. 'At the end of every month, I had a moment with myself, where I thought, *Okay, has this month been easier than the month before? Because if it's not been easier on the whole, I'm leaving.*' He turns on the small TV. 'And these boys are rimming each other,' he says. 'I'm like, *What the fuck? What paradise have I arrived in?*' Britain at large might not be ready for this now-famous scene from *Queer as Folk*, but this boy – who has never even seen a same-sex couple kissing either end on screen before – certainly is. Up until now, the weight of having started a new life in a new country has been holding Josep back day by day, making him wonder if he's doing the right thing. But suddenly he can see a chink of light too. 'Okay, so it was difficult,' he says. 'But at the same time, it was exciting.'

A few months later, and Josep has a new job as a nurse at Kingston Hospital. With a couple of Spanish friends, he finds a three-bedroom 1960s house in nearby Surbiton to rent. 'It was green and leafy, big maple trees, and by the river.' It's a place mythologised in British culture as the home of *The Good Life*, the archetypal sitcom of suburban snobbery. 'There was a South Asian older couple that we got on very well with because the wife was very nice to us. We didn't look after the garden, and we were the only house that didn't look after the garden. She was like, *Okay, I'm gonna come and do this with you.*' Now this is a reboot of *The Good Life* that I want to see. Soon it's just Josep and his friend Maria living there, renting the third room out temporarily to housemates when they need the cash. They have dreams of moving to somewhere bohemian in central London for a more exciting urban life, but the landlord doesn't put the rent up, and so a decade later he and Maria are still living there. 'The life that we had, we were not students, but we behaved like students,' he says. 'We're professionals, but we lived together, we travelled, we didn't look after the garden. Our values were very different from the others'.' Something chaotic at the heart of well-ordered Surrey. But something else strikes him about the set-up. Although his housemates are straight, they all seem to be living queer lives, 'because of the lives that we lived and the relationships that we had. My friend Maria, who is straight – ostensibly straight – we used to go out and do things, like, *Okay, let's see, who can snog more boys tonight*, you know? So that's a very common gay thing, right?' He smiles. 'We were definitely different from the common man plus woman plus child households in the street. We were the queer household.'

It takes a while for Josep to adapt to living on the edge of this huge city, and Surbiton comes into its own as a life-support system. 'At the beginning I was quite conservative,' he says. 'So it allowed me to explore things at my pace.' The first time he goes to Kingston's gay club is with straight work colleagues from the hospital. They take safety very seriously here: three bouncers on the door, encourage you to get a cab straight away as you leave, the suburbs not to be trusted with their precious LGBTQ+ cargo. His first time at G-A-Y at the Astoria in central London is a similar story of a straight friend dragging him along. 'She was like, *Okay, enough*,' he says. 'I was very shy.' While the sheer number of guys in the clubs in London is exciting, 'I felt a little safer in the one in Kingston,' says Josep. 'I still remember very well the guy at the cloakroom, he was a very femme boy and super nice, older than us, but super, super welcoming. And sometimes we went to bigger clubs and people will be catty.' He also feels less vulnerable in Surbiton. 'When I have encountered homophobia I was in town. It's always been in town that I've held hands with boys because of a sense of safety in numbers,' he recalls. 'But in Surbiton I felt safe.'

The protective streak, it turns out, works both ways. Josep becomes a fierce champion of Surbiton. 'Whenever anybody said, *Oh, that's not London*, I was like, *Yes, it is! It's still a zone!* But definitely it was very suburban.' His London friends mockingly call it Suburbiton. When guys hear where he lives, Josep is used to them saying, *The suburbs? That's not London*. 'There were quick judgements about where you live. Also at night, if you wanted to spend the night with someone, living in the suburbs made it tricky. Because you had to get a night bus that wasn't very reliable. And by the time you got there, you had snogged for so long that you were exhausted.' Poor lambs, imagine. He looks back now and thinks he was blissfully oblivious to how people perceived his life there. He recalls Jean Genet saying that you're gay because other people make you aware that you are. 'So when he says that you're called into the world as a queer man, it was a bit like that,' says Josep. 'I was called into the world as a dweller of the suburbs. And I was totally unaware that that's what I was.' Here he is, *openly* suburban, flaunting it.

The concept of queer space is more developed now, but even at the time Josep was a keen observer of the distinctions and territories around him. 'Queer was my room basically at the beginning, when I lived in Surbiton,' he says. 'And the river. The river, particularly at night if the weather was nice, was cruisy.' He quickly discovers that LGBTQ+ life in Surbiton is either very private and hidden, or very public. Unlike fellow Surbiton dweller Seena,* Josep throws himself into the hidden life of the suburb. 'I did a lot of cruising around Kingston, Richmond, Epsom, and you got all the guys that were married to women. Because you saw them in the market on the Saturday with the women, or in John Lewis choosing a sofa.' Younger guys Josep's age tended to be out and on hookup sites like Gaydar or Manhunt. 'And then there were semi-closeted guys that had boyfriends but they didn't have an open relationship. But they were cruising without the boyfriend knowing. So there was quite a bit of that. There was a couple where both of them I used to meet for cruising, but they used to say, *Oh, do not say anything to my boyfriend. He doesn't know I do this.* I'm like, *Okay, you need to have a conversation.*'

For somewhere so famously middle-class and proper, Josep finds traces of more transgressive, marginal ways of life. 'I always identified with the more seedy side of Surbiton rather than the clean, freshly painted side of things.' When he arrives there he discovers brothels, advertising themselves with red lights like it's the 1960s. His suburban adventuring is something that still fascinates him. The lover who works in a huge mock-Tudor nursing home. The middle-class flats and bachelor pads of men who were air crew or staff at hospitals or prisons. And students from the university too. Josep recalls one particularly memorable resident. 'Oh my God, the guy with the bleached arsehole,' he says.

* See the chapter 'Love and Hate in Surbiton'.

'Everybody knew he had a bleached arsehole: my boyfriend, his lovers, everybody. And he had a lovely, lovely place by the river. These were men with money and taste.'

For several years, he dates a guy from nearby Epsom. They regularly throw parties or have film viewings at his house or his boyfriend's flat. They're creating their own network of local queer friends, making a fraction of an otherwise fairly invisible community work and cohere. He studies philosophy as a mature student at Roehampton University and becomes a secondary-school teacher in Surbiton. 'I was the English as a Second Language guy,' he says. 'So I had my own students who came from Korea, Pakistan, Bangladesh, India, whatever. I loved it.' Connections to yet more diverse aspects of this stereotyped sprawl. He's there for a decade, before becoming a library assistant in New Malden, trying on as many of the hats as the suburbs have to offer. Eventually, he leaves south-west London for Edinburgh in 2014. 'I haven't been to Surbiton for a while,' he says, 'but over the time that I was there, it really didn't change. The same-sex hookups and lovers. Yes, there's been a proliferation of apps, if you want, but people are still cruising the same places.' Did it work for him, moving from a village in Spain to another country to start afresh? 'I think if you had asked me this question, like, ten years ago, I would have said I could have ventured out earlier and lived more of an urban life where I'm closer to things that matter to me, like galleries, bars, cafés, clubs, queer spaces, you know? But now I think it was good while it lasted.' Once he had felt an outsider here; now his observant eye has catalogued the hidden history of the place, a side of Surbiton most of us never see. The good life.

'Bucks Wants Lesbian' runs the front-page headline in *Gay News*. It's February 1975, and Veronica Pickles is that lesbian, convenor of the Milton Keynes branch of the Campaign for Homosexual Equality – a new group for a new town, both only just under way. The CHE runs a regular disco in The Cannon, a quaint pub in the old coaching town of Newport Pagnell. By August the group will receive a grant from the new town's development corporation and find a more permanent base – in the Bakehouse, a base for community organisations in the new town. And so in Milton Keynes the LGBTQ+ community is officially acknowledged and embraced right from the outset. It's one of the first places in the UK to be built on any scale that openly welcomes gay groups to its heart at its foundation. It feels as if here in this new suburbia both the utopian experiments of Edward Carpenter and the garden designs of Richard Sudell have reached an unexpected flowering. Maybe my own gaybourhood makes more sense now. We are living the Milton Keynes dream. In 1975, *World in Action*, ITV's weekly investigative series, ran a documentary following the work of the group and the challenges faced by its members.

But that's not what this *Gay News* story is about. It follows Veronica Pickles' interview for a job in the NHS as a health visitor. She's been upfront to the panel that she's lesbian and makes a point of mentioning her CHE work. 'The panel of interviewers showed an unbiased interest in the reasons for starting a gay group and its aims,' she tells *Gay News*.[27] In fact, they're so positive their main consideration is that, should her sexuality become common knowledge, they'll support her if she needs it. 'I am naturally proud and pleased with my achievements to date,' says Pickles, 'and hope that my success will be an encouragement to the thousands of gay women and men in the National Health and allied services to come out and fearlessly proclaim their right to be gay.'

But all is not as rosy as it looks. A couple of months after her interview, Buckinghamshire Health Authority withdraws its offer of a secondment to become a health visitor, because of her high-profile work with CHE. 'If they're saying,' says Pickles, 'if I qualify as a health visitor, in eighteen months' time, people are gonna start slamming the door in my face, I think they must be mad.' The offer of training is withdrawn in March. *World in Action* airs in June. 'There have been repercussions,' she tells the show. 'This is another point about homosexuals coming out. We have responsible jobs. We have an image to uphold, and we are criticized because of what we're doing.' The discrimination she encounters isn't coming from the public, she feels, but from her employers. Once her plight becomes public knowledge Pickles receives a huge amount of support, not just from the local LGBTQ+ community but also from the wider population in the new town. Her story is taken up by the local and national press, with rather less positivity. Yet it has recently been retold by Eden Storm and Judy Goss in their 2025 book *MK Q:mmunity Tales*, telling the story of the new city's LGBTQ+ history since 1967, from shared houses of gay Open University staff in the 1970s to protests against Section 28 outside the central library in 1988.

Some forty years after Pickles' ordeal, in 2020, many gay and lesbian people working in the NHS and social care report a significant level of discrimination from both patients and colleagues due to their sexuality. So those battles continue among new generations, in the footsteps of pioneers like Veronica Pickles.

THE OTHER LESBIAN
IN PRESTWOOD

The doctor has written the prescription, and Katie, then in her early twenties, is getting ready to leave the surgery, when he says, *Let's talk about contraception.* She shifts a little uncomfortably in her seat. He's always overly chatty, and here, back in the days when doctors had a bit more time to talk to their patients, he's just making sure this young woman is getting all the advice she needs. *What are you using?* She imagines he's thinking, *Well, you're not on the pill.* So Katie puts him straight. *No, no, I'm a lesbian.* This just sets him off in another direction. *Oh, that's really interesting,* he tells her, in his matter-of-fact tone. *Yeah, there is one other in the village.* 'And,' she tells me years later, laughing and still cringing, '*I know who that is!*' *I never meet lesbians,* he says as she gets up and backs towards the door, trying to make it clear the appointment is over. *You won't be wanting these condoms then!* he adds as she heads out. 'It was very uncomfortable for me,' she recalls. 'It's tricky finding people. Certainly in small villages. I needed to tap up the doctor, I think.'

Katie grows up in the 1980s in a dormer bungalow on a private road in Prestwood, a village near High Wycombe in Buckinghamshire, effectively a suburb of a suburb. It's not far from Milton Keynes, or where Quentin Crisp had once lived, observing his beloved Soho from the Home Counties. 'I fancied my teacher in middle school,' she tells me. 'I was probably about ten.' She doesn't have a word for it, but senses this is something she needs to keep secret. 'I was terrified that whenever a letter was sent home – and it would probably be telling them about a parents' evening or whatever – I'd always think it says in there, *Katie, there's something wrong with her, and she likes Mrs Horrigan.*' She describes her home life as 'pretty standard' – parents, sister, dog – but since her realisation she finds she's becoming more secretive around them. Perhaps her parents think it's just a part of growing up, which of course it is. Katie keeps a watchful eye out in case there are others like her at school or in the neighbourhood, but years pass and there's nothing. Apart from one boy at school who seems to her quite obviously gay, and who, in an unwelcome turn of events, relentlessly bullies her for years. Later, she discovers that her best friend from childhood, a girl who went off to grammar school, is gay too, but they never see each other after she goes away. 'But that would have been amazing,' she says. 'To know that she was gay as well, that would have just been fantastic. Because I would have known her just when I was about ten. I wonder what two ten-year-olds back in the nineties, what kind of conversation would you have had?' Instead, it's not until she's fifteen that she comes out to her friends, in the hope that one of them might say, *Yeah, me too.* 'And then we'd just dance off into the sunset and go to all these gay bars and stuff – but that didn't really happen until a little bit later.'

It's isolating, feeling like the lone lesbian in Prestwood, in the days before her GP has confirmed she's not the only one. 'That's the thing in a small town, you're not immersed in any of those cultures. You don't see those people around you.' Instead, Katie's in her bedroom listening to anthems of teenage angst, otherness and longing from bands like Radiohead and Bush. But when she goes to college, things start to change. For one, her best mate Aaron comes out. At last there's someone to explore the local scene with! 'You make the most of the places that you can find,' she says, 'those little pockets or little bits of community that you can connect with.' She's adopted the full Avril Lavigne skater look – baggy Dickies jeans, boxy tees, airline-style belt – clothes of rebellion that also hint at who she is, coded signals that only the most attuned will pick up on. 'It was a difficult balance, because you wanted people to recognise you as a lesbian. But you also wanted to hide in conservative Home Counties.' One day, in her family car, they pass a pub outside Wycombe that catches her eye. Decorated entirely with rainbow flags and called The Pride, it isn't hiding what it is, even though it is tucked away. ('Were we pushed out?' she wonders aloud as we talk. '*Maybe*, now I'm thinking about it.') Okay, so it's mainly full of gay men, with a handful of older lesbians, but it's still some sort of community, somewhere she and Aaron can go and feel at home. One time, there's a boy she recognises from school, the one who'd tormented her for all those years. She's feeling brave and tells him, *You weren't very nice at school. You're a bit of a bully.* She's expecting this to be one of those stories where he says, *I'm so sorry I did that, being gay myself. I should have known better.* Instead, it's a case of *I don't even remember who you are.* Infuriated, but unable to do anything about it, she heads off, thinking, *God, I hate you even more now.* Even safe spaces have their trip hazards.

One day, she and Aaron are leaving The Pride with some straight friends when they find a guy on the ground, glasses broken, queer-basher fleeing. 'We ran over – *Oh my God, what's happened?* – and we were helping this guy up and his glasses are all broken, and we're fishing around for them and making sure he's okay. And I remember my other friends, they didn't come over, my straight friends. They just carried on walking. They were quite frightened.' She wonders if she and Aaron ran to help because they are gay too and could empathise with him and his plight. Another time, in High Wycombe, a group of girls start mouthing off at Katie and her girlfriend. 'That was quite a horrible experience,' she recalls, 'them lashing out and kicking and just being skanks. Just horrible.' Again, it's her gay mates who come to their aid, along with a straight friend who has a lesbian sister. The others hold back. 'I think people just have a bit more empathy when they've been around gay people a bit more,' she says. Unless you count that boy from her school, obviously.

The Pride is great, but she spends more of her time in an alternative pub in High Wycombe with her mates, which is where she manages to find most of her girlfriends. 'That worked out pretty well!' she says. Better still are the pubs in Wycombe that start to hold LGBTQ+ nights on random evenings during the week. ('You're allowed to be in town at this point,' she observes dryly.) One day, when she's nineteen, she's at home pairing socks when her mum starts asking her about a new friend she seems to be seeing a lot of. *Yes, she's my girlfriend*, says Katie. Her mum does not take the news well. (A few weeks before, a conversation about Aaron is equally tricky. 'She accepted it,' she says, 'but I could see her heart breaking as soon as I told her that my friend Aaron was gay. Her face dropped because she thought me and him were together, and I think then she realised why we had a connection.') Luckily, at that moment Katie's girlfriend turns up. 'And I was just, *Yeah, bye*,' she recalls. 'We just got into her car and I was like, *Just drive anywhere. Let's just go somewhere. I've just come out, let's just go.*' And so they spend several hours driving round the Chilterns in a Mini Metro because there's nowhere else to go. 'Whenever I've had therapy, it's always come back to that. I've broken down. *And I'm gay! I'm coming out to my mum!* It always goes back to that. It's like a shame, or fear of my parents not being proud of me.' She thinks her mum's reaction was partly because she didn't know any LGBTQ+ people in real life, just characters on the telly. But in Prestwood they don't have a nice lesbian couple round the corner who her mum could get to know (or maybe they do, but it's complicated). Still, if Katie thinks she's at least managed to come out to her mum, she is in for a shock. Because every time she tries to introduce a girlfriend into the conversation, she gets what she calls 'a lot of *Oh, are we still talking about that thing?* And it felt like I had to come out over and over and over again.'

Salvation comes in the form of a lesbian bar in Reading. The Granby is run by a lesbian couple, and it's the first time Katie's been to an LGBTQ+ venue that didn't primarily aim itself at gay men. 'I was like, *I've landed! I've found them finally!*' She goes along first with someone she's met on Gaydar Girls. 'She quite liked me, but I wasn't that into her,' she recalls. 'But then we did end up going out, because it's a small pool of people, isn't it?' She remembers going back to The Granby with a girl she was on–off with. 'I remember that she seemed to be more into me than her new girlfriend, and I was enjoying that immensely.' Soon, she is venturing into lesbian bars in London too – all closed now, she reflects sadly – these LGBTQ+ spaces allowing her to move from being one of two women in a Home Counties village to being part of something wider, a community where she has friends and rivals and possibilities, without having to worry about constantly having to come out to her mum all over again.

If you think suburbia is an enclave of exclusive heterosexual privilege – and it is – could I also direct you to organised religion? For centuries, Christian churches have offered sanctuary for the persecuted and abused. But for LGBTQ+ people, that sanctuary has usually been conditional on renouncing identity and sexuality. But, as with suburbia, the Church also has a rich seam of queer history, participants who have lived within the confines of its rules or been brave enough to rise above them.

And so when in the modern confines of St Alban's Church in Crawley a heated exchange is taking place, it's no surprise it's not a theological issue. It's March 1975, and four officers from the Campaign for Homosexual Equality have been asked by the local vicar to speak about their work. As might have been expected, the crowd is not entirely supportive. The CHE officers find themselves heckled repeatedly by members of the audience. But the hecklers aren't the church's usual crowd. They're members of the National Front, who initially threatened to picket the event, and then when they realised there weren't enough of them for that, joined it instead. To bolster their thin ranks, they've drafted in the big guns – five local schoolboys recruited for the evening. But as they attempt to jeer and provoke the CHE officers, each put-down is elegantly extinguished with that most deadly of weapons: information. By the time Mr Clark, a local resident, stands up and addresses the church, the atmosphere is a little wild. *I'd be happy if the money for the local CHE branch was taken out of our rates*, he says.[28] The vicar adds, *If CHE could stamp out some of the prejudice and ignorance that has been evident at this meeting, I would support it wholeheartedly.* At the end of the evening the small band of NF members leave, having achieved little more than appearing as aliens in this sacred space. All these years later, in a time of rising tension and intolerance, trans and non-binary people would tell you that those words from the vicar still hold power. Prejudice and intolerance are all too easily weaponised against the powerless. And in suburbia it can be hard to feel the solidarity and support from neighbours and family.

ENTANGLED IN SNARESBROOK

Robin's mum watches from the bay window as her son climbs into her little mustard-yellow car, slams the tinny door shut and sets off. He's told her he's going to see some school friends in Romford, not far from their 1930s semi in Snaresbrook, East London. Instead, when he gets to the end of the road, Robin heads west. He's off to Earl's Court, 11 miles away, over the other side of the city entirely, to see Billy, a guy he's met through a classified ad in *Exchange and Mart*. They've spoken on the phone and Billy says he's going to show Robin the gay hotspots of West London. In 1975 Robin is seventeen, and desperate to see a bit of life. Billy, a gay youth group leader, takes Robin first to leather pub The Coleherne, and then to The Catacombs, a place as famous for its poppers-soaked atmosphere as for its pumping American disco sounds. 'It really opened my eyes,' Robin tells me. A night out with schoolmates in Romford can't compete. But when he gets back in the car, the gear lever comes off in his hand. Cursing his luck, and not sure what to do, he finds a phone box and calls his parents, and has to explain to them that he's broken his mum's car and somehow he's stuck not in Romford but Earl's Court. 'They asked what I was doing there. And of course my brother said, *Oh yes, Earl's Court, that's where all the prostitutes go. He's probably seeing a prostitute.*' He still sounds a little mortified by it now, almost fifty years later. He has to lie to his respectable Jewish family, but at that moment it seems preferable to the alternative.

Behind the pebbledash, they've done fashionable sixties modernisations to their thirties house: the handsome wooden panelled door making way for a frosted-glass version with ornate wrought-iron frame; original fireplaces swapped for marble-effect Formica and new electric heaters; windows replaced with draughty louvres that don't shut properly. Out the front there's the garden fence, replaced with a brick wall, the wooden gates with wrought iron, the once manicured lawn and flower beds with tarmac. And for his mother's car, beside the garage rises a wooden-framed carport with a corrugated plastic roof.

At the start of the 1970s, Robin is just becoming a teenager, and his parents are worried he seems quite solitary, so they send him to see a psychiatrist in Theydon Bois, Essex. 'My dad drove me there,' he says. 'I only went there two or three times, but then my parents heard that the psychiatrist was cheating on his wife with someone, so they stopped me going.'

By the time Robin is a teenager he knows he's gay, but it's not possible to come out quite yet. There are not many positive role models. 'For many years from the 1960s my mum used to go to a local hairdresser who was effeminate and who wore a bad toupee,' says Robin. 'Gay men were considered sad characters. I know she felt sorry for him.' He recalls going to the Golders Green Hippodrome to see Danny La Rue in pantomime, because his mum was a big fan. Robin fancies the son of one of his parents' friends, who is slightly camp, and his father says, *I hear that Paul might be a bit gay.* 'They were often warning me off people, in their minds for my own good,' he says. 'My parents used to be very suspicious and protective.' Instead, they're keen for him to make some Jewish friends, particularly girlfriends, and so he's taken along to specially organised dances in West End hotels and nightclubs. 'There was a time when I was going to these Jewish dances and also going to gay bars,' he recalls. And he's obliged to go on dates with some of these girls. Entangled with all of that, Robin goes to an evening class in car mechanics, where he meets a guy called Jon. 'He'd been going out with a girl but he had an earring,' he recalls. 'And my parents, they were shocked by his earring. They were convinced that he must be gay if he's got an earring.' Jon is very good-looking, and he and Robin begin to hang out together. And it's through Jon he's introduced to the nearest Gay Youth Group.

It's 1978, and Robin is climbing the stairs at the back of a shop on Holloway Road. He's heading to the Gay Youth Group, which was for anyone below the age of consent, then twenty-one. Robin is twenty. There's about fifteen of them up there, with the long hair, wide lapels and tight-fitting trousers of the day. There's a guy there he recognises, but isn't sure why. They get chatting and he realises Steve was in the year below him at school. In no time they become good friends, knowing all the strange history that comes with a place like Snaresbrook, where everything is interconnected, the streets like a vast spider's web, every movement causing vibrations that are felt somewhere, signals to be alert for. Robin remembers Tom Robinson visited the group not long after his song 'Glad to Be Gay' was released, and Matthew Bourne was a fellow member. 'I've never spoken to him since,' says Robin, 'but I've been to a few of his ballets.'

Robin doesn't have the opportunity to choose the right moment to tell his family, because one day soon after he turns twenty-one his mother receives an anonymous phone call outing him. He thinks it's someone he's spurned from the youth group. 'I got home from work and my mother confronted me,' he says. 'She was always volatile. She never hit me or anything like that, but she was always very verbal. Very, very loud. The guilt thing, the Jewish mother thing.' *Someone's phoned me up and said that you're homosexual. It must be a phase you're going through. You're making my life hell.* 'Trying to make me feel really, really small.' He later finds his family have been having discussions about his sexuality, and they have decided it's all because of his mother, 'because she was so forceful and so in your face all the time that it forced me down this path'. So much for agency. They make it clear it must remain secret from their friends and wider family. *You wouldn't tell your grandmother,* his mother says, *you wouldn't tell your auntie about it, would you?* He's under no illusions that there is a terrible stigma to being gay.

But by this time his life is much less bound up with his family's. They have moved from the suburban semi to a large flat overlooking a golf course in Woodford Green, a little further out, following one of his mother's whims. Robin decides to take a break with Steve, his pal from the youth group. 'We went on holiday to Sorrento together in 1979,' he recalls. 'But my mother didn't like this at all. She managed to find out Steve's address. And she used to have phone calls with Steve's mother about why we were gay – basically, what they could do to stop it.' And his family continue to persevere with the idea he might actually be straight. His brother pairs him off with one of his female friends, a larger-than-life American woman visiting from Los Angeles. So Robin takes her to a drag night at the Vauxhall Tavern. 'Initially, she was horrified,' he recalls. 'But she actually quite enjoyed it in the end. Although I remember her asking me which role I took in bed, the man's or the woman's.' His brother never tries that again.

Many years later, in 2005, Robin and his partner, Andy, buy a house in the grand suburb of Buckhurst Hill in north-east London. The school teacher who sells them the Victorian semi falls in love with them as soon as she meets them and dismisses all other offers. *Oh no, you need to buy it,* she says. They live there for several years after Robin takes early retirement, and move once his partner retires. 'I got bored with suburbia,' he says. He finds Buckhurst Hill 'fine, but very straight'. They meet up with a few other gay men locally at the Toby Carvery or Harvester. 'We used to refer to ourselves as "The Fine Diners",' he says.

But when Robin leaves the family home back in March 1980, he heads off to a small terraced house in decidedly urban Forest Gate. His neighbours Elsie and Bill have been there since 1936, and Elsie's sister turns up next door for a bath every Friday because there isn't an internal bathroom in her house. Robin suspects they guess he's gay, not just because of his fashionable clone look ('short hair, moustache, Levi 501s, check shirts and DMs') but more likely because of his constant stream of male visitors. He's at Heaven when it first opens, and frequents The Coleherne and The London Apprentice in Shoreditch. In Brompton's, he often sees (and is sometimes mistaken for) Freddie Mercury. In 1985, in the midst of all of this excitement, he wants to continue a family tradition of volunteering and starts work at a new charity: the Terrence Higgins Trust. The volunteers first meet at County Hall in the last days of the Greater London Council, and work together in one room in Holborn. 'At our first meeting we were told we'd either be a buddy to a PWA' – a person with AIDS – 'or we'd be on the telephones or help out with publicity,' he explains. 'But in the end, we just did everything because there weren't enough people to do individual roles.' *Robin's doing wonderful charity work*, his mother tells her friends, with lofty vagueness. 'I don't know if they thought I was at risk. Because I was,' says Robin. 'Many of the men I knew and others I'd had sex with in the 1980s and '90s died of AIDS. I somehow managed to dodge it, I've no idea how. And most of these were guys in their twenties and thirties.'

Initially, he helps to staff the helpline, but before long he's meeting with PWAs at their homes or in hospital to provide moral support. After the TV public information films are shown and leaflets about AIDS are distributed, Robin has a regular

Sunday telephone shift at the Broadcasting Support Services offices in Acton, answering calls from worried people round the country, mainly gay men. He's also providing voluntary support to sexual health workers in clinics, meeting up with their PWAs at Newham General Hospital and the Royal London in Whitechapel to provide friendship to those facing this disease on their own. 'It all happened at the same time, like a massive bubble had just suddenly burst. And there weren't enough people to deal with it all.' He continues until 1992, when he suddenly realises he can't do it any more. 'I had sick friends of mine who needed support,' he says, 'so I decided to do my best to support them.'

In 1986, through one of his volunteering roles in a local sexual health clinic, he meets Kenny, a young man who lives in Gants Hill, a 1930s suburb of Ilford. A couple of years younger than Robin, Kenny lives with his parents, who do not know he's gay. 'He became very ill quite quickly,' recalls Robin, 'which was common with many PWAs.' Initially, they meet up at the house in Gants Hill or talk on the phone, but soon he's visiting Kenny at the Royal London Hospital as his health worsens. 'He'd had a very close friendship with a childhood girl friend,' explains Robin. 'And even though she knew that he was gay, they decided towards the end of his life that they would get married.' Kenny's doing it to please his parents. The groom is too ill to travel, so the ceremony takes place in the hospital, Robin helping him dress because by now he's too weak to manage it himself. Kenny's parents make sure they're home at eleven o'clock every morning for their habitual cup of tea and a digestive. Despite how entangled these lives are, these feel like two discrete worlds, the elevenses in Gants Hill as two frightened people cling to a routine to try to help make things feel normal, and the frail young man in his hospital bed, kept to a quite different routine, of tablets and visiting times and doctors' rounds.

'The last day I visited him at the Royal London, not long after his wedding, was just hours before he died,' says Robin. 'I remember that he was almost delirious when I arrived.' His parents leave as soon as Robin turns up, saying, *He doesn't know we're here.* But although Kenny's in and out of consciousness, Robin knows his presence is felt. *Robin, why are you walking away from me?* says Kenny, but Robin hasn't moved. *Why are you walking away from me, Robin?* He becomes more restless, and so Robin helps him from bed to chair, from chair to bed, 'because he just wanted to move, and he wanted me to hold and hug him'. Eventually, Robin has to go home, but gets a call at 2 a.m. to say the young man has died. Driving away from the hospital that night, a voice sang on the radio, *I just died in your arms tonight.*

'There were so many friends that died,' Robin tells me, 'people in addition to those who I was trying to support through the various AIDS organisations. I remember so many of their names, but there are names I can't remember, and they're in my memory as shadows. And that hurts and saddens me. So many died as strangers to their families, and now I can't remember them.' But Robin was there when they needed him, devoting years of his life to looking after these men when so many did not or could not: their friends; their lovers; their families. Robin is part of a different sort of network from those suburban wires of Snaresbrook, one that vibrates still with half-glimpsed memories of arms holding, dressing, caressing.

I'm sitting in the Bishopsgate Institute, reading through their collection of newsletters from the Croydon Area Gay Society with alternating feelings of amusement, warmth, bafflement and alarm. The collection begins in the late 1970s and provides a rich monthly record of their activities up until the 1990s. One of the first I read recalls an evening in October 1979 when members are converging from every corner of the borough – Caterham! Shirley! Sanderstead! – on a venue in the centre of town. The society haven't always found it easy to fix on somewhere to meet. They were once barred from a pub in Addiscombe by the landlord, who hadn't realised his regular monthly booking was for an LGBTQ+ group. Well, not until the police had been called by a suspicious neighbour to spy on them through the windows as they planned theatre trips and dunked their Ginger Nuts. Apparently, unacceptable. Tonight, they're on their way to a talk in a community hall by Jane Newland, a producer for London Weekend Television who has been making a series intriguingly called *Gays*. Just as Ray Harvey-Amer, the chairman, is leaving home, his phone rings. It's Jane: overrunning hospital appointment, she can't make it after all. Disaster. They're expecting fifty or so people to turn out for this, and it's too late to cancel. He arrives breathless and heavy-hearted, and gathers a huddle of his fellow board members to break the bad news. They can't just magic up a suitable speaker at such short notice, so what *can* they do to fill the void? Then someone says, *What about coming-out stories? A group of us sharing our experiences?* There's some umming and ahhing and nervous laughter, but no one has a better idea, and so with members already taking their seats, seven unprepared volunteers shuffle their way to the front and get ready to share their tales.

Those hurried into participating don't have time to panic as they stare back at an audience of friends and strangers. Alan, one of the group, kicks off the evening. He shares the time he wrote to the *Croydon Advertiser* about the policing of cottaging in the town. The day after his letter's published, he arrives at work and, because of it, is immediately sacked. Next up there's Mike, whose family are supportive when he comes out, but who is still racked with anxiety. Because of that, he doesn't want his partner to do the same, or to come out at work. Then there's Ian, who tells his brother he's gay, only for him to gleefully inform all the kids on their estate of the fact, ensuring he's followed around by children calling him names in the street. There's Ray, who lacks confidence and is still in the closet to family and friends. His story of not coming out chimes with some in the audience, who have joined the group in secret. Andy has come out to his family but not at work, although he's considering testing the water. And finally there's Pete. He works for an airline where everyone knows he's gay. In contrast to many, his experience is exuberantly positive. Being out at work has made it easier to meet other gay people and help those who are having trouble accepting their sexuality. Each man who speaks has had a different experience, and in that room, as the stories land with each of the CAGS members, the resonance is profound. Here are people facing a reckoning with their own coming out, men either coping with the fallout or thriving in the disparate scattering of suburbia.

THE MIDDLE SPACE OF PINHOE

Lou and Sarah are sharing a quick kiss on a train on a bleak and dreary May Day. They're on a trip to see the Wallace Monument in Stirling. 'Sarah is from Edinburgh,' says Lou, 'so I guess her idea of romance was a nice factual trip to learn about how English people killed the Scottish monarchy.' As they kiss, they become aware that a boisterous group next to them have gone quiet. Twelve women, recovering from a hen party the previous night in Edinburgh, are openly gawking. There's whispering, and Lou and Sarah hear the word *lesbians* spoken with distaste. *That's disgusting*, says one. *I don't want to see that.* Phones are out, the ostentatious click of camera shutter noises advertising what is going on, the intimidating urging of others to join in. Then the tapping of keyboard sounds. Somewhere on Facebook, a post goes up: *Oh . . . boke 2 girls givin tonsil tennis wi each other.* Sarah gets up, Lou follows. They're going to look for a guard, for a safe space. *I hope you're proud of yourself*, says Lou to the women as they leave. Once they're out of the carriage the spell is broken, and after holding it together Sarah begins to have a panic attack. This is not the battle they had set out to commemorate. Later, they see the women depart at Alloa, a small station dwarfed by an enormous Asda. Houses straggle beside the line as they pull away, new homes on old industrial land, making the centre feel like the edge. As the train begins to move, the group are as boisterous on the platform as Lou and Sarah are subdued in their carriage.

Almost twenty years before, in the late 1990s, Lou is gazing out of a bedroom window. It's a rather plain 1920s semi on a small side street in Pinhoe, on the outskirts of Exeter. The bedroom is at the front of the house, and from their vantage point Lou is trying to make sense of the world. Once, Pinhoe had been a village, but now it was being overtaken by the city's galloping sprawl. From up here they can see through the endless housing estates right into the city, and also out to the fields of the West Country, tamed and timid, and beyond to the wilds of Dartmoor and the Exe Valley. They can hear the hum of the motorway in the background, the sound of birds and lawnmowers. A teenager at the edge of the city, at the edge of the century, looking both ways. The room had once been a shrine to Winnie the Pooh. Now it's a hippie cave clouded in incense, soundtracked by Jamiroquai. Looking out and looking in, Lou is confused. But no one seems able to help. At school, in the shadow of Section 28, there can be no advice. More than that, Lou's confusion is compounded by more everyday assumptions. Why should they have to wear dresses, for example? Why were they put with the girls to play netball? And why couldn't they play football? 'I don't think at that point in my life I was really able to separate my confusion about being dyslexic and having ADHD, and being a queer child as well,' says Lou. 'The muddle and the mixture between all of those things, of being trans and non-binary, ADHD, dyslexic, those are diagnoses that are now split into a constellation of understanding in adulthood.' Increasingly, Lou's love of sport becomes a solitary activity, barred from the team games they so love, and going on solo runs while bunking off the group ones in cross-country. 'I remember being absolutely devastated when I hit puberty and had my first period, and was just like, *This is horrendous. This is life-ending, I will never be able to climb a tree ever in my life ever again.* And I don't think that anyone really around me understood that grief.'

No matter what Lou does to try to fit in, they're branded a rebel. This, it seems, is where not conforming to your gender gets you.

The short hair, the trousers and shirts, the Doc Martens boots. So maybe the best thing is to pretend all of these signs are pointing at something else: music, perhaps, or fashion. Something that could create a distraction and conveniently explain it all away, while covering for the awkwardness of the truth. Tomboy is the name for the disguise, which Lou later supposes is a synonym for non-binary. 'When you are different, you have to lean into that,' says Lou. 'You have to become weirder and weirder so that you can hide the original weirdness. So that's what I did. I had crazy, brightly coloured hair. I wore a tape measure around my neck. Different bits of cutlery as badges. I looked completely bizarre as a way of hiding in plain sight. Hoping that no one would see the original instigation of that uncomfortableness and that difference.' One day, Lou is pulled into the headmaster's office for having dyed hair. *You cannot keep doing this*, he told them. *Next time you come in, you know, we're going to wash your hair in the toilet.* Lou is shocked by the aggression. 'I just remember feeling like, *Oh my God, I'm the worst person in the world. This is terrible. What am I going to do?* But also, *There's no going back from this. How else am I going to hide? This guy has literally taken my disguise.*'

The rules around what makes for appropriate behaviour or feelings aren't obvious at first. In the playground at primary school the kids are playing 'sex change', taking roles and then swapping them midway to be a different person for the rest of the game. Lou suspects it was made up just for them. *This is a fun game*, a friend tells Lou, *because it's not really you, you know. Like, you're not really a girl.* Lou recalls feeling, *Oh, that's nice to be seen. That's really nice.* But despite this sophisticated understanding among people of Lou's own age, the adults around them conspire to completely misunderstand them instead.

It's Christmas, and Lou is in the Jubilee Hall, where the amateur dramatics society's panto is being rehearsed. A play where women dress as men, and men as women, in extravagant, joyous drag. It has attracted all the outcasts from the surrounding streets, eagerly making the costumes and the music, putting together the lighting and the script. For a short time the hall is liberated from its sensible schedule of events – the scout groups, guides and jumble sales. Now something decidedly less sober is happening. Something quaintly queer. Not that anyone will identify it as such. An atmosphere of don't ask, don't tell pervades the space. And although Lou knows queer is a thing, they also know that it's not okay to identify that in others, to call people out. The seen has to remain unobserved. Yet it is here among the misfits and secrets that Lou feels safe and encouraged. At last there are people Lou can identify with. Even in this quiet corner of suburban Exeter, an alternative spirit exists. And it reaches them from back in time, showing all of them there is a history to their identities. It connects all of them back to the queer roots of commedia, folk art and music hall, where this is a space to be different, to cross-dress and tease the audience with things they'd never normally say out loud.

Then there's the family wedding, where the theme for the reception is medieval. Because why not? In a costume shop run by one of the outsiders from the panto, they each find the perfect outfit. Lou's sister wants to be a princess; Lou stumbles across the garb of a court jester. 'This is like absolute premium non-binary,' says Lou. 'It came with a wand with bells on it. I mean, it was fantastic. I took it to the front and was like, *Mum, this is what I'm gonna wear.* And she was like, *Oh really? It's a nice family occasion, do you not want to wear something nice?* I said, *This is nice! I get to wear tights that are different colours on different sides – it's great!'* Playing the fool, but not.

Some years later, Lou is locked in a bare room with a rat. They have been in here for almost twenty-four hours. All there has been to do is think and eat chips and feed them to the rat. If Lou needs to urinate, they have to do it in a cup and throw it out the window. Lou is not a political prisoner, but a fine art student at Goldsmiths College in London. Grimy, urban New Cross in the early 2000s, with the South Circular road roaring through, is a long way from a sleepy side street on the edge of Exeter, and Lou has come here to try out new ways of being themselves. Every day it's possible to try out being a new sort of person, and unlike at home, no one ever remarks on it. At Goldsmiths it's not just expected, it's demanded of you. For Lou, the anonymity of the city is thrilling. And the artworks they push themselves to produce are part of that, a way of testing the limits of possibility, to find out who they are without the sensation of being constantly observed. Although observed they are. Which is a curious freedom of visual art. 'You spend so long creating a kind of constructed identity to keep yourself safe,' says Lou. 'I remember doing all sorts of really weird artworks to try and push myself to be like, *There's the edge of the way out.*' Perhaps feeding chips to a rat is one way out? It's worth a go. One stop on a long journey.

It's August 2016, a year after the train incident, and Lou and Sarah are back in Alloa. But this time they're not alone. Instead, they have – accidentally, it seems – organised the first Alloa Pride march. It's just going to be a quick pint in town with some friends, but then the local queer youth group gets involved. Then come people from the big Prides in Edinburgh and Glasgow. Before they know it, a full-scale celebration is in progress. After the hen party disembarked from the train that May Day, Lou and Sarah couldn't stop thinking about those women. 'We were like, *This is horrendous that there are people who are stuck in Alloa, mostly probably kids, mostly people like us who have grown up with no representation, no awareness of queer identity. And these people are probably mothers and they're probably working in schools and they're probably actually influential people in children's lives.'* They reported the incident to the police and ended up winning a court case against the main perpetrator. And now, two hundred people are marching through the streets of Alloa, dressed up, a field of rainbows, shouting, *We're here. We're queer. We're not going shopping.* 'Which I didn't realise was an actual chant from Pride of yesteryear,' says Lou. 'I just thought it was a really strange thing about shopping.'

By the evening, they have retired to a local pub, and the celebrations continue. Lou thinks about the ride they have been on, from Exeter to New Cross, from confusion to self-expression. The events of Alloa show it's still not always easy being queer away from a big city. Yet curiously, suburbia still exerts a pull. Lou calls it 'a new-found love affair'. 'The middle space of suburbia feels like the middle space of gender, in a sense,' Lou says. 'There's a contested ownership to it all. There's this idea of people who've been there before and doing it the right way, and new people doing it the wrong way. And those battles happen in both spaces, and people feel their identity split in two directions.' Here in Alloa, turning an unpleasant memory into a positive, beautiful experience, pulling hundreds of people into the huddle, all of those feelings seem to have come together. 'You asked me about one of my proudest moments of suburban queer identity,' says Lou, 'and it's not in my own place, but that, a hundred per cent.' The revellers on the streets of a small town, full of joy, being seen.

As the 1970s draw to a close, a small group of gay men and women are standing in the Whitgift Centre in Croydon handing out flyers, and are finding it an unexpected thrill ride. Any passing shopper who takes a flyer and doesn't immediately bin it will spot a list of forthcoming events for a festival called Stonewall 1979. It's been ten years since the not-yet-famous-in-Croydon riot in Christopher Street, New York, and this festival has been dreamed up to mark that moment. Who could have imagined the ripples of that night reaching all the way here, to the people standing outside Dorothy Perkins on a Saturday afternoon with their badges and photostats, and the many they hand them to? This is the Croydon Area Gay Society again, as recorded in their newsletters. They've been busy, putting up posters around the borough, promoting events in the *Croydon Advertiser* and standing here for a third day in a row, meeting shoppers face to face and telling them about their events programme of discos, raffles and coffee evenings. I'd have been eight at the time, and the thought that such a public acknowledgement of LGBTQ+ culture was going on then in such a familiar and unlikely place blows my mind.

I'm reminded of this because in late 2023 a film is released that echoes my experience of that place, and it's not celebrating Stonewall '79. Instead, there are the shadows of so many of my gay generation's preoccupations: the AIDS crisis; the plea for acceptance from our parents and peers; those struggles with depression and loneliness. Andrew Haigh's *All of Us Strangers* has been largely shot in the director's hometown of Croydon, where the ghosts of protagonist Adam's long-dead parents allow him to have the adult conversations he was never able to have at the time. Haigh even filmed some of it in the house he grew up in, a defeated-looking 1930s semi in the stockbroker suburb of Sanderstead. A key scene in the film sees Adam, the central character, return to his favourite childhood spot, a café in the Whitgift Centre, near where those flyers were being handed out many decades before.

I worked for some years in a bookshop in the Whitgift Centre. Now a Waterstones, back in the 1970s and '80s it was called Websters, and each year they would have a window celebrating what was then Gay Pride Week. While many high-street shops shied away from carrying any LGBTQ+ themed books and magazines, Websters had no such qualms. In fact, here, a few doors along from a vast Woolworths, you could see books published by the new Gay Men's Press and lesbian literature from feminist publishers the Women's Press and Virago, alongside LGBTQ+ magazines and Pride badges all displayed in the window. Before the nineties concept of the 'pink pound', gay shoppers were used to not being catered for at all, or finding these sorts of publications carried as some sort of guilty secret, hidden away on a single shelf, away from the inquisitive glances of families. It's the only shop to stock *Gay News* in the town centre, and this flourishing of LGBTQ+ counter-culture proudly displayed in the window in the mainstream heart of suburbia must cause a flutter in the hearts of the LGBTQ+ shoppers passing by.

'Yes, we were ridiculed by some,' wrote one of the Stonewall '79 volunteers of their experience handing out flyers and advice. 'Yes, others responded angrily, but others (rather more than this optimist anticipated) stopped to give encouragement, support and thanks, and others sought advice. On the day of the carnival' – Croydon's annual family-friendly festivity of floats and funfairs – 'two total strangers who said they weren't gay stopped for half an hour to hand out leaflets!'[29] Here, in the heart of the suburbs, something that all of us strangers could benefit from.

CROYDON IN STAGES

The temp bustles in late. David, newly qualified as a solicitor in the mid-1970s, watches her settle herself. It's not a surprise she's late: she's been commuting every day to London's legal heartland in Holborn from the Isle of Wight, a journey involving a ferry, a long train journey from the coast and a Tube ride. David is upright, a little shy and self-contained. Mary is anything but, loud, chaotic and gregarious. But they both share a passion for the theatrical: in David's case, liberal doses of amateur dramatics; in Mary's, it's in the realm of spiritualism. She's supposed to be helping David with his casework, but instead is captivating the office with demonstrations of fortune-telling. David is initially standoffish about this, as it means she doesn't get any of the typing done, but soon he's as drawn in as everyone else, and Mary is examining his tea leaves and reading his tarot. She tells David he's the most self-content person in the firm. 'Not self-satisfied,' he tells me, 'but self-content. And I've always thought, *Actually, I think she was on to something there.* She also said I was going to fall in love three times. And one of the people was going to come back into my life at a later stage. That has intrigued me because I've tried to work out who the three people are that I'm supposed to have fallen in love with. Because I think there were more than three.' When I interview David in his house in South Croydon, he's an extremely dapper seventy-five-year-old. Surrounded by fashionable mid-mod furniture from the first time around, he's still wondering who it is that's supposed to be coming back into his life. 'It'd better happen soon,' he says, 'otherwise I shouldn't be here to experience it.'

David has lived most of his life in the suburbs of South Croydon. He's an only child, growing up in the middle of Davidson Road, an enormously long street of terraced interwar houses half a mile from the nearest bus stop. 'My mother hated the house,' he recalls. 'In fact, she used to see it occasionally when she went up and down on the train, and said, *I'd hate to live in one of those*. And ended up in one of those.' At grammar school in the 1960s there is a lad he fancies from afar, Michael, who is as good at PT as David is hopeless. Unexpectedly, they find themselves paired off for wrestling practice. 'He was more physical than I would have expected him to be. Innocent that I was, I never clicked, I never thought I could be in with a chance here. It was only several years later that someone happened to say, *Oh, by the way, of course, you know Michael was gay?* Gosh, missed out there, didn't I?' As it is, David sails through puberty unconcerned. He knows he's gay, and decides that there is no point falling in love, because in the hostile world around him, where it's illegal, he's going to be unable to act on it. Instead, he watches his contemporaries fall to pieces as they face the teenage trials of heterosexual love for the first time and keeps his own feelings firmly under lock and key.

By the late 1960s, David is at university in Hull. Roy Jenkins has just partially decriminalised gay sex for men over the age of twenty-one, and the Stonewall riots have taken place in the US, sparking the formation of the Gay Liberation Front in the UK. None of this filters through to David. He doesn't even look to see if there's a Gay Soc, let alone join it. 'No, I think I just decided that it wasn't acceptable, society didn't like it. I wanted to be liked.' And a sure way not to be, he felt, was to reveal his sexuality. But he's aware of the bind that puts him in. 'I gave up religion when I went to university, so I should have taken up homosexuality at the same time, shouldn't I?' At the start of the seventies, when the course is over, he moves back in with his parents. A job in central London means he joins the ranks of the kipper-tied commuters at East Croydon, but even the cover of anonymity the city affords can't bring David to act on his sexuality. 'I want to fit in, and I don't want to stand out and I don't want to be pointed out and looked at – *Oh, it's him* – I think that's why there has been that reserve in not actually taking the plunge until very late. That's certainly my excuse for not being brave.'

David's big escape isn't from the suburbs, but into the realm of amateur dramatics. In the mid-1970s his hobby takes him to Polesden Lacey, a large Edwardian house in the Surrey country-side near Dorking. There, in the open-air theatre, he plays a Roman soldier in *Androcles and the Lion*. In the story, Androcles removes a thorn from the paw of a wounded lion, and is later shown mercy by the same creature when forced into combat with it in a gladiatorial arena. Instead of fighting, man and beast end up dancing, to the delight of the crowd. One of the other actors is kindly helping young David apply the body paint for the per-formances. 'He did a very nice job of it,' he recalls. A week later, the cast reunites for a picnic to celebrate their performance. The actor spends a lot of time with David, and when they're alone makes a pass. David is shocked and affronted, not by the man himself, but by the insinuation that he's gay. And unlike the lion in the play, David savages his would-be rescuer. 'I was so horri-fied that somebody had seen through to the real me. What had I done? What sign had I given that I was gay? And so there was a complete rebuff. I mean, there really was a *complete* rebuff. And I got in my father's car and I drove home. I just drove away.'

Soon, his local theatre group are appearing at the Warehouse Theatre in Croydon, a small arts space beside the railway station. David is involved in a production of that most acid of suburban texts, *Abigail's Party*, and his antennae suggest one member of the cast he's attracted to might be gay. And so when he's directing the next play, Peter Shaffer's *Equus*, he casts the young man as the troubled central character. He puts in a remarkable performance. 'When that production finished, there was nothing to follow,' says David. 'There was no reason why we should be meeting. And I think at that point I realised I actually was in love.' He plucks up the courage to ask, *Would you like to go out to the theatre with me?* Soon, they're on what David describes as 'my first what I would call a date'. Afterwards, he invites himself back to the younger actor's place for coffee. He's worked out a very careful speech declaring his love. 'This was all moving very quickly, thinking about it. I mean, if I was doing it now, I think we'd go to the theatre several times before I got round to actually saying, *Can I come back to your place for coffee?* and then broaching the question.' All the while, hanging over him is the ghost of the lion from Polesden Lacey. 'So I do the big speech,' says David. *I mean, I'm sure you're not, but if you are, I really fancy you. But you know, if you're not, then that's fine. And can we still be friends?* 'He was very good about it,' says David. 'Because he was straight.' They have an amicable chat about future theatre visits, David having already prepared himself for this disappointment. 'And I think at that stage, I thought that everything was going to be okay.' He pauses. 'Except, of course, it wasn't. It absolutely wasn't.'

Instead, the normally contained and level-headed David finds himself overwhelmed by emotion. 'I went home and cried my eyes out. Went into work the next day, I cried my eyes out.' He can't bring himself to explain why – that he's gay, that he's fallen in love, that he's been rejected. Instead, all he can say is, *It's okay. I'm perfectly okay. Don't worry. I may burst into tears, but don't worry.* This goes on for a couple of days, until finally David decides to phone his friend Eileen, and at last comes out. She's very calm about it and assures him she's not going to reject him.

Perhaps now things will get better, he thinks. But they do not. And so he tells someone at work, and then someone else, and suddenly David has lost track of who knows and who doesn't, and takes the plunge and comes out to everyone there. *They're solicitors, they have seen it all*, he thinks. Though perhaps not a shy and self-contained colleague sobbing his way through the day with a broken heart.

By this time, David is forty. His father has died, and he decides not to come out to his mother, fearing she'll worry too much. David still finds the act of coming out painfully embarrassing. So long has he spent keeping it secret from everyone that it's hard to know who to trust. But then exasperation and impatience take over from caution and hesitation. 'I think, in fact, I did get to the point of *Oh, for goodness' sake, come out*,' he says. 'The period in which I grew up, that really does have an effect on you. I think that you don't want to be rejected or to be disliked, or people to think that you're disgusting. Whereas now, young people I'm sure will go, *But that's really weird. It's really strange that you should have that fear.* But to an extent, I still think that there is that.'

In his lunch break, David takes a ten-minute walk to a newsagent's in Holborn. There, on the top shelf, he finds a copy of *Gay Times*. As he leaves the shop, he folds it over so that no one can see he's carrying a magazine with the word 'gay' on the cover. Once he gets it home, he scours the contact ads, looking for men in the London area because he doesn't have a car. He tries meeting guys in bars and pubs, but despite all of his theatrical nous David realises he's fundamentally quite shy and doesn't have the confidence to chat someone up. 'Which may be where Croydon was, I suppose, more helpful,' he says. 'In that there was a society here in the suburbs. And it was going to be very social. And you got to know people very quickly. And therefore, it was much easier to go to parties without feeling the odd one out or somewhat isolated, which is what I felt when I was in the pubs and clubs in London.' Because one of the things he finds in *Gay Times* is the number of Switchboard, and from there he discovers the existence of the Croydon Area Gay Society. He goes along to his first meeting. I ask David if joining CAGS had been a liberation. 'Not really, no,' he says. 'It sort of ought to be, but no.' The social side is slightly lost on him. 'I don't think that I wanted to have a society that I could feel comfortable in,' he says. 'I think probably coming out so late I didn't really feel that I wanted that because I was quite happy with my heterosexual friends.' Instead, David joins because he wants to find a partner.

CAGS means parties. Mostly, they're jolly middle-class affairs round someone's house. A few drinks, a few nibbles. A couple of times they do fancy dress. But instead of finding a partner there, David is almost immediately drafted onto the organising committee, just as he has been in the local conservation group, and now his solid solicitor's brain can be channelled away from romantic pursuits and instead engaged in the mechanics of events, fundraising and, of course, newsletters. He hosts some parties himself in his modern South Croydon townhouse, no longer fussed if his neighbours know whether he's gay or not. In fact, he finds himself coming out in the most unlikely of situations. He's made redundant and for a while helps deliver Meals on Wheels. 'I was the assistant and there was the driver,' he explains. 'The driver was an ex-police inspector. And therefore I suspect probably actually arrested people like me, in the bad old days. There was a frisson, I think, the first time I told him that he was actually driving with a homosexual by the side of him.'

Pretty soon David becomes the chair of CAGS, which is a mixed blessing, as he finds he's not terribly interested in pursuing what he refers to as 'a gay agenda'. 'I'm quite good at keeping it all going,' he explains. 'But what I want is to actually integrate. I don't want to stand out. I don't want us to be any different from anyone else from the heterosexual world.' For David, these days gay people have got what they wanted – to be treated as equals in society – and so he now questions the existence of CAGS itself. 'In a sense, I don't really want to have a gay society at all,' he tells me. 'Some people find having that group of friends with the same outlook on life really useful to have. And that's why I want the society to continue for as long as it's needed: so that those people have that community. Because they like that community and they want it.' But for him the spark has gone, and it's a duty rather than a passion. 'My Conservation Area advisory panel that I belong to, I love those people in a sense much more – and they're all heterosexual – than I do the gay society.' I can't help thinking that ending up as the representative of Croydon's oldest LGBTQ+ organisation has created a new kind of closet for David, one where he is always publicly out in a way he doesn't really covet, the ambivalent poster boy for a gay life he's never quite embraced. But then for someone so experienced in amateur dramatics, taking on this role is perhaps a challenge he could not pass up, a chance to play a character while living another very different life inside.

Jackie Kay is having waltzing lessons. Aged sixteen, in 1977 she's preparing for a school Christmas dance. She's having to practise with two other girls, and has been given the role of the boy. The music is lumpy, the whole experience sexless, awkward and slightly absurd. But later that day, with her jazz- and blues-loving friend Gillian, she finds music she *can* move to. Gillian blows perfect smoke rings and is good at kissing. The kisses aren't just illuminating the moment, they suggest a life ahead with connections that Kay has not been able to imagine in the low-rise grey sprawl of Bishopbriggs in Glasgow. 'I thought I was the only black lesbian in the world,' she writes. And just as first love down the ages has cast its magic on each generation, Kay must surely be able to feel the presence of a wider world, to see far beyond the next sloping rooftop and the grey clouds above. In her memoir *Red Dust Road*,[30] Kay tells moving tales of how as a child she's given up by her Nigerian father and Scottish mother, and of her search later in life to find them. Adopted by progressive white parents in the creeping drift of suburban Glasgow, she faces racism and searches for an identity.

The progressive drift of the 1970s makes way for a more gendered and politicised climate, even in suburbia. Especially there. Even something as innocuous as home decoration falls under its spell. After a decade of louche experimentalism, 1980s suburban homes are suddenly dominated by hyper-feminine blousy florals and blokey wipe-clean black melamine, creating the sort of heteronormative retreat the mock-Tudor house had embraced fifty years before. There is flight from suburbia too, all of that yearning for escape being channelled into a new excitement at moving into the centre of the city rather than living on the outskirts. Many of those pioneers colonising squats or warehouse flats are young LGBTQ+ people fleeing life on the fringes for something more urban and anonymous, away from all that black ash and Laura Ashley.

Not that Jackie Kay's adoptive parents are anything like that, embracing progressive politics and a revolutionary spirit rather than chintz and bone china. Still, she soon becomes one of those young people who move into a squat in the city. But before then, she has her suburban school to negotiate. 'When she was teased as *a lezzie* in art class,' writes Lisa Allardice in the *Guardian*, when interviewing Kay, 'the teacher responded by asking her: *Well, are you, Jacqueline? Are you a lez-bee-ann?* She trills now, giving it the full Miss Brodie.'[31] In her words are glimpses of the strange reality of being a lesbian teenager out in the far scattering of the city, the rapid code-switching in a place where some gender roles are thrown at her by school and tradition, while others she chooses to explore more willingly. As the eighties dawn, there she goes, part of a generation pursuing city life in all of its chaotic richness and variety.

TODAY TORQUAY,
TOMORROW THE WORLD

Torquay in the late 1980s, and the cul-de-sac is very white. The people, the culture, even the houses. Not much has changed here since these semis were built in the 1930s. And so when Huseyin's family move in it's a bit of a moment, heralding the start of a slow shift, for them and for the street. 'I always felt like I'm in a place that's too small,' he tells me, 'there's not enough variety around here, because everyone looks the same. And speaks the same.' His dad, a Turkish Cypriot, moves to the UK in the mid-1970s and initially becomes part of a Turkish-speaking community in London. Then, moving on to Maidenhead there were still some echoes of that urban diversity. But Torquay? Not so much. 'We *were* them,' recalls Huseyin. 'There were half a dozen more, kebab shop owners, that kind of thing.' In Maidenhead there were Black and brown friends, 'neighbours from one country, neighbours from another. To me, it seemed a bit less interesting around here.' The move has been made on the flimsiest of pretexts. A Turkish friend of his dad's has set up home on the Devon coast, and when Huseyin's family go to visit they fall in love with the place. Before Huseyin knows what's happening, they have found a house down there on the English Riviera, his parents, a sister and a cat, in a place he describes as one big suburb. 'There was a certain isolation,' says Huseyin. 'In Torquay and suburbia I think we were a bit exotic.' He can recall there being one Indian kid at his school, and a Turkish boy – and that's no coincidence at all: that's the son of his dad's friend. As a seaside suburb, it's quite different from the drab semis of Southbourne or the Victorian grit of Southsea. Their house is at the top of the town, overlooking the bay. From their garden it's framed like a rather camp theatrical set, the palms and gleaming white houses and hotels putting on a show for the tourists, pretending to be looking out onto the Med.

Both his parents work for the NHS. Years later, after Huseyin has lived all round the world, he comes back to Torquay, and for a while joins them in the NHS, working in the local vaccine centre during the Covid pandemic. 'I saw almost everyone who lived in Torquay at least three times,' he recalls. It's a view of the town he never got as a teenager in the 1990s. 'I certainly wouldn't have noticed that there's lots of retired queer couples around. There's a big lesbian community as well,' he says, 'which was really fab to see.' Back when he was growing up, he didn't feel there was much LGBTQ+ life in the town at all. He has crushes on other boys and some of the *Gladiators* on TV, but everything remains hypothetical. 'All the boys at school were, *I love Jet the Gladiator. She's amazing. Don't you love Jet the Gladiator?* It was that thing where you just have to go, *Yeah* . . . Meanwhile, I like the guy with big muscles! *Okay. Anyone else?*' More obviously gay personalities on TV would be greeted in strange archaic code that would have felt more at home in the music hall era. 'My nan would say, *Oh, he's a nice boy.* And I wouldn't really understand what that meant.'

Going to school in the time of Section 28, there's very little information about sexuality around, and he finds it a pretty homophobic environment. But it's not without its heroes. 'One kid came out at school, came out as bisexual, and he was the talk of the school for two years,' recalls Huseyin admiringly. 'Realising people could just say that, without still realising it myself.' One day, they're doing a school project about Notting

Hill Carnival, and three festival veterans come to talk to them about it. 'One of them very clearly a gay man,' says Huseyin. 'No hiding it, an artist, fully out there. And one of the kids in my class had let out a slur.' At which the artist takes control, telling the class why we don't say those sorts of things or behave in that way. How we should be celebrating difference and not trying to crush it. The message sticks with Huseyin, a symbol of a different sort of life elsewhere.

His family's encounter with LGBTQ+ culture is suitably glitzy for such a theatrical town: a drag show in a short-lived bar, The Blue Angel, in the late 1990s. 'It was very much like we were watching it on the telly or something,' he recalls, 'all quite pleasant, little cabaret tables and sitting far away from the stage. Like it's a piece of art.' And not something that is speaking to Huseyin so directly, in all its subversive mischief, social commentary with sequins. Not the raucous club nights he will become more familiar with either. His parents have a ball, but they don't know their son is gay, so the whole thing feels very safe and distant. While the town's low-key LGBTQ+ life might not be setting Huseyin's heart on fire, there are other distractions. In the summer the town throngs with French, German and Italian students, all learning English at the many language schools. Young Huseyin is good at languages too, and this feels like a way out. He heads off to university in Bath – 'a pretty queer town' – where he starts to explore his sexuality. His language course launches him on a seemingly non-stop tour of different countries over two decades: France, Germany, Finland, China, the Netherlands and currently Malta. Quite the jet-propelled escape from suburban Torquay. 'I just got the hell out as soon as I can,' he says. Even when he visits now, he describes it as 'old me when I'm here, and it's new me when I'm away', his life as an out gay man happening in other places far from the cosy semis and arcades. In Amsterdam he gets into photography, using old camera lenses from the Soviet Union that he picks up in Sunday markets in Eastern Europe, and joins Dance With Pride, a Black queer collective, a group running counter to the country's current political culture. 'Unfortunately, there is a group of white supremacists, DJs, club owners,' he says. 'Not many, but there are some. And there are a lot of right-wing or very racist people.' Very much not the chilled vibe the country likes to project. 'For a place that says it's quite open,' he says, 'don't have a Turkish name.'

In his twenties, his dad's side of the family in Cyprus expect Huseyin to find a girlfriend and settle down. 'There would always be that question of *Who are you dating?* Then it was, after twenty-five to thirty-five, *When are you getting married?* And then, after about thirty-five, I just said, *I'm happy being single, thank you very much.*' During the Covid pandemic, when Huseyin moves back to stay with his parents in Torquay, he experiences suburbia-on-sea as an adult. Having spent so long away, he finds it a bit of an eye-opener. For one, he gets a job working for the charity Movember, which is based in London, but because of the circumstances he mainly works remotely. After being away from Britain for so long, he finds a generational shift has happened too. 'There's lots of under-twenty-five-year-olds there,' he explains. 'The concept of someone having a different sexuality is so normal to them. It's weird. For the first time I wasn't different . . . It's almost disappointing.' It's while he's working for them, visiting the office in London once a week, mired in Covid boredom, that a thought strikes him. 'I was on Instagram and I was saying, *There must be gay Cypriots. There must be.*' If there's 10,000 Cypriots living in London, there's got to be a hundred gay ones among their number. And his hunch is proved right. He finds a group, a start-up called Queer Cypriots. They meet at a bar, The Yard, in Soho, and their next get-together will be on a night when he's in the London office. So he goes along. 'Everything suddenly made sense,' he says excitedly. 'All of a sudden, I didn't have to explain any part of myself.' Not just the cultural references, the extended families and the food, but also a shared relationship with sexuality. 'They'd say, *Are you out to your parents?* And I would go, *Errr* . . . And they'd say, *Oh, I know* . . .' The peers he never realised he'd missed, living so far from them all these years.

While he's in Torquay, his niece tells him she wants to go see a drag show. Echoes of his family's experience in the 1990s come back to him, but this time it's all very different. 'We came out to each other,' he says. 'And it was brilliant, a lot of drinks . . .' It helps break the negative feelings he's been building up about the town, doing something he enjoys in a place where he'd never thought that was possible. Since Brexit he's found the town quite tough, a lot more racist sentiment being expressed. Outside a pub, an old man tells him, *If you were any darker, I'd think you'd come over on a boat.* 'At which point I thought, *I'm gonna go job hunting, find another place to live.*' Yet one thing does reconnect him to the town: a sense of awe, staring out to sea and wondering what is out there. And so once more Huseyin is off on new adventures, far from the whitewashed semis and cream teas. 'The world is huge,' he says. 'I want to see everything.'

It's a Saturday night in 1980 at the Star Gaze disco in West Croydon, where it's pumping out 'Xanadu' and 'Upside Down', and they're knocking back Babycham and Skol. The pub, The Star, opened back in 1973 and has been running South London's first gay disco in its back bar for four years. Janet is there with her partner, Jenny, and the three oldest of her six kids. 'In my view,' she writes in a letter to the local gay society newsletter, 'our relationship proves that two women can successfully bring up a family in a loving and caring atmosphere.'[32] The kids have taken to Jenny and the couple's gay friends in a way that might seem fairly standard now, but back in 1980 in the leafy streets of Croydon this is a pretty unusual situation, although by no means unique.

There are echoes of their relationship in a book of the time. In 1983, the Gay Men's Press issues a translation of Dutch children's book *Jenny Lives with Eric and Martin* by Susanne Bösche. It tells the story of five-year-old Jenny being brought up in a same-sex household, a fairly gentle tale of birthdays and going to the laundrette, given an edge by an encounter with a homophobic woman, which the adults have to try to explain to young Jenny. Three years later, in a moment of confected outrage, tabloid newspapers and Tory education secretary Kenneth Baker contrive to have the book withdrawn from the school library service run by the Inner London Education Authority. By 1988, Section 28 of the Local Government Act has been drawn up, forbidding schools from 'promoting' homosexuality, and *Jenny Lives with Eric and Martin* is cited as one of the main reasons for that. But all of that moralising huffing and puffing cannot change the fact that some kids are being brought up by same-sex couples, and that this is not a new phenomenon.

Certainly, back in 1980, Janet and Jenny's kids seem to be flourishing amid the cultural limitations of the day. 'The younger three (all girls) don't as yet fully understand,' writes Janet, 'but paintings and things they make at school always have *to Mummy and Jenny* written on them.' Theirs might have seemed an unconventional household at the time, but it worked.

CASUAL VIOLENCE
IN ADDLESTONE

Early morning on a school day in 1978, and David is on his paper round. He's on foot, pushing *Daily Mails* and *Daily Expresses* through the letterboxes of sleek sixties terraces and stodgy thirties semis with their black-painted beams. This is Addlestone, a commuter town in Surrey, and David is bored. But he's also lost in teenage daydreams. He's always dreaming about something: artists, musicians, escape. On that morning, he's thinking of something else. 'I knew that I was starting to have feelings for boys,' he says. 'No one in particular, really, I didn't have a crush on any boys at school, but I knew that I didn't particularly fancy girls.' That morning, there is a sense of acknowledgement. 'On this paper round, I remember one day saying to myself, *Well, that means you're gay then.* And once I'd said that, I couldn't really go back from that. I was fine with it. I was like, *Okay, well, that's it. I'm gay. I'll get on with it.* I didn't really have a lot of angst about it. I was quite comfortable with my sexuality.' For David, it's as simple as that.

Addlestone seems sleepy and innocuous, but for the children of the 1970s something unpleasant lurks on the fringes of the green belt. One day, David is hanging around down by the river with other kids from the estate when a man approaches them and says, *You lot, why don't you go off up the canal? There's something you need to see. And I'll look after your bikes with this one of your friends,* he says, pointing to a girl they're with. *She can stay with your bikes.* The kids agree, and run off along the towpath.

'We came back twenty minutes later,' recalls David, 'and she ran up to me and she said, *Oh God, that guy's really weird. He's been taking photos of me in the tree.*' The man is never caught, the episode instead submerged like a pebble in dark water, joining countless others. David sees flashers in the quiet crescents and cul-de-sacs. The place is full of hidden dangers.

At home in his room he's staring out of his window, day-dreaming again. Beyond the back garden are the grounds of a radar company, with a tennis court for the staff. 'I had this big, big crush on this guy that used it. A man, he must have been thirty or something. And I used to stare out my bedroom win-dow and watch him play tennis. I would be drawing, writing poems and yearning for escape. And I was a big reader and was always looking for more, I knew there was more. I was fascin-ated by people's lives, people that had done interesting things and arty people, and I would always be reading about them and wanting that life for myself in some way.' And that life is not in Addlestone, he decides.

He's not alone in wanting to rebel against the conformity of the town. 'The local punks would hang out at my house,' says David. 'There was one punk boy and one punk girl.' David's house is always the one where his friends gather. 'Cos my mum was pretty easy-going. And she liked them. She was quite up for all of that. I wasn't trashing the place and neither were they.' When they had PE on a Wednesday they'd hang out at David's instead of doing a cross-country run, before heading back to school. They'd lounge around in the living room, and if his older brother was about or his mum came home from work, they'd disappear to David's bedroom. 'I was obsessed with David Bowie, I really loved him,' he recalls. 'My dad, I remem-ber him looking at the cover of, I think I bought *Aladdin Sane*, and he went, *Oh, look at him. He's a degenerate.* And I thought,

Yeah, brilliant. I made the right choice.' He sees Boy George before he's famous, part of a similarly dressed group in the audience of a music show on TV, and even at that point thinks, *I want to hang out. I just want to be their friends.* Many years later, working on pop magazines like *Smash Hits* and *Number One*, he gets his chance.

But the dark side of Addlestone keeps resurfacing. Coming back from a friend's house late one night, David, then aged sixteen, is stopped by a couple of coppers in a panda car, who emerge as he walks by. It's quite a different experience from Daniel's brush with the law in Dudley.* *We need to search you,* one of them tells him. Being the good boy he is, David panics, wondering what he has done, what he might have got himself mixed up in. Before he quite knows what is happening, they have him spreadeagled over the bonnet of the police car. The frisking seems to focus on David's groin and legs. *My friend needs to do it as well,* says the constable, *because I don't think he thinks I've done it properly.* And so once more David endures being groped by a policeman. 'It was only afterwards I thought, *What the fuck was that?*' he tells me. 'And that was where we lived. There was shit like that going down. It's shocking, really.'

When he's sixteen his parents split up, and he ends up staying in the same house in Addlestone with his dad. A rebellious streak emerges. He cuts up the carpet in his bedroom and paints the floorboards white. Okay, he can't move the wardrobe, so he just cuts round it with a Stanley knife. How did his dad react? 'He went up the wall.' But he'd made it his, this room overlooking the radar company's tennis courts, as family life around him disintegrated. 'It'd be me and my friends in there smoking fags out the window and stuff like that. Smoking joints.' And as the

---

* See the chapter 'Neighbourhood Watch in Pensnett'.

1970s become the 1980s, he tentatively begins to come out to his friends, helped by his cousin Anthony, who'd already done so when he was fifteen. 'I remember telling this friend of mine, a girl, I said, *So did you know I was gay?* or something. She said, *Yeah, I am as well.* Another friend of ours, a guy, he was gay. It's not surprising the people I gravitated towards were of my type.' But not all of them accept things as easily as David did on that paper round. 'A friend of mine, he was quite conflicted about his sexuality. He was quite – what's the word? – straight-acting, or whatever. You wouldn't have guessed he was gay. And he had a job with BT digging roads, stuff like that. And he ended up cottaging quite a lot, and keeping it quite furtive and secretive. And ended up with a drink problem, so his was quite a sad experience.'

At this point David dyes his hair blond, stealing eyeshadow from Woolworths and buying green foundation from Boots for that desired New Romantic pallor. 'I used to get beaten up,' he tells me. 'I used to get punched in the street. So maybe I was more outrageous than I think I was.' One day, crossing the railway bridge at Addlestone station, a man walking in the other direction suddenly strikes him in the face. 'Didn't even say anything, not even an altercation, it was just *bang!* And that happened again, somewhere else, near the library. Walking home one night, I just got beaten up. But all of that didn't grind me down. It just made me realise even more that I've got to get out of this place.' It was the era of the casual, that subculture of watered-down mod styling mixed with laddish football tribalism. 'The town was full of them,' says David. 'It was us against them. The weird kids against the boys.'

In contrast to shy David, his cousin Anthony is more out-going, and before his sixteenth birthday has already hunted out the nearest local gay group he can find, in Wimbledon, and he and David start attending monthly discos on that popular gay-friendly night, Tuesday. 'It was very cloney,' David says. ''Tache, checked shirt. But I was just like, *Oh my God, this is amazing*, you know? And feeling real stirrings of, like, *Oh, I fancy pretty much everyone here*.' But while he might desire them, David isn't able to start a conversation with anyone, even while Anthony is off dancing and being chatted up. 'I hated the music,' he recalls. 'Hi-NRG.' The Smiths are on repeat in his bedroom. These days he regrets having gone to the club so young, losing his virginity at sixteen. 'I wasn't ready for it, really.' The whole experience would be topped off by that most teenage of suburban experiences: 'My dad used to drive to Weybridge station to give me a lift back,' he recalls. 'God knows what he was thinking.' By the time he's seventeen, David is heading up to the London clubs: Heaven, of course, but others too, long since closed. Spats on Oxford Street, and another called Stallions, which had fish tanks on the walls. While all of this excitement is going on, he comes out to his brother, who responds with an uninterested *Yeah, whatever*. The only people he doesn't come out to are his parents. 'They must have assumed it,' he says.

David finds it stifling with his dad, and jumps at the first opportunity to move away. 'I went to art school, and definitely wanted to get a place in London, and that's what I did. I got out like that. I knew I had to, I couldn't have stayed living there. I just couldn't. It was never an option.' He heads off to the London College of Printing, and ends up sharing a house in Streatham in South London, which he finds by ringing up Gay Switchboard. It's as far removed from his life in Addlestone as he could have hoped for. 'It was like the gay *Young Ones*,' he says. 'It was mad. It was four or five of us in this real dump in Streatham. And everyone was very, very different. There was a guy on the top floor who used to blast out hi-NRG; he worked at a bank. There was a school friend who ended up becoming an alcoholic, he lived with us. There was another rent boy. There was this big Black dancer guy who was outrageous and used to make us do aerobics in the living room. There was this quiet one that never said boo to a goose. So there's a real mix of people, but they were good fun, you know? And it was like, *Oh my God, I'm in London. I can go out and I can do things and I can find things*, and it was just like breathing oxygen at last. It was wonderful.'

David has never returned to suburbia. But he acknowledges the propulsion it gave him through the years, this desire to escape and find a life somewhere more urban and colourful. 'It's always been a place of fascination in a horror way, to me,' he says, thinking back to those dark shadows of abuse and violence on those butter-wouldn't-melt streets. 'And suburban towns and whatever, they're nice to see pictures of, but it fills me with horror. I'd rather be stuck on a hillside in Scotland. I would never want to live there again. Because it's just so boring.' Which, given everything that happened to him there, is a bit of a surprise.

'Old Bill is a-trolling!' The Croydon Area Gay Society newsletter in May 1980 is not just there for the drinks and nibbles; they're looking out for their members too. 'Reports are reaching us that the more "notorious" public lavatories in the borough are under police surveillance. One group member was stopped and questioned by two plain clothes police officers after using the convenience at Thornton Heath Clock Tower at about 11pm.'[33] And then it turns the tables with quite a flourish, giving detailed descriptions of the two policemen. 'Both were described as *quite dishy,*' it adds, quite aware of the honey trap being set. The report is witty and knowing, sure, but on the next page a comprehensive list of your rights if arrested is reproduced. This subversive article does not need to highlight the anger that lies behind it.

It's a bit of a shock to realise that it's only in 1980 that a bill decriminalising sex between consenting men over the age of twenty-one is passed in Scotland, and not till two years after that in Northern Ireland. It comes at the start of a decade where what will follow is a moral backlash against the LGBTQ+ community, compounded by the AIDS crisis and codified in Section 28. The first British Social Attitudes survey in 1983 showed that half of the public thought that sex between people of the same gender was 'always wrong', with only 17 per cent saying that it was not wrong at all. Then there were the 53 per cent of people who thought it was unacceptable for a homosexual person to be a teacher or hold any other prominent position in public life. When the AIDS crisis is at its height in the late 1980s, the number of people who completely disapprove of homosexuality reaches over two-thirds of the population. While there is greater visibility for queer people in mainstream culture and society, the tone of that coverage is often confrontational and humiliating, with tabloid newspapers greeting the new gay icons of the day – from Boy George to The Communards – with leering contempt and hysteria. It will take decades for the damage this 1980s culture war does to the LGBTQ+ community to disperse. It will fire up a whole new generation of out and proud queers, which I'm quite sure was the opposite of the effect the politicians and editors of the day had intended, and all the more wondrous for it.

GAYDAR GIRLS IN
MILTON KEYNES

The school leavers' ball is in full swing. They've been dancing to 'Common People', 'Country House', 'Lovefool' and, like her friends, Beccy is absolutely hammered. She's made it through all these years in Aylesbury, and now here she stands, on the brink of a new life, the world beyond the newbuilds and Friars Square shopping centre, away from her family and the expectations of everyone around her. In the haze of the evening, she spots her favourite teacher. Before she knows what she's doing she's coming out to him, and he seems delighted. So much so he calls a guy over and introduces her to his boyfriend. Beccy is overwhelmed – this is the coming-out story she's dreamed of, not just acceptance but the immediate opening of doors by other LGBTQ+ people. And the next day, as she surfaces with her monster hangover, realising she still has school to struggle in for again, she wonders if it was actually a dream after all. It's only later, when she catches the eye of that teacher in the corridor, that it all comes back to her, with the kind of turbocharged mortification only a teenager can feel. 'I could see he was trying to speak to me, and he said, *Oh, you're so brave for what you did*,' she tells me. 'And I was like, *Oh, thank you, sir, thank you*, like Kevin and Perry,' she says, doing a spot-on impersonation of Kathy Burke as the embarrassed adolescent. 'That was it really, it just wasn't spoken about.'

It's a subject she's hedged around for years. Her mum is a big soap fan, and one day Beccy sees in the paper that *Brookside* is about to feature a lesbian storyline, Anna Friel, as Beth Jordache, soon to be famous for having the first pre-watershed lesbian kiss on British TV. 'I was like, *Oh, Mum, let's watch* Brookside!' she laughs. She wants cool hair, but all the hairdressers in Aylesbury appear baffled; it seems impossible to get them to do anything that isn't the same as everyone else's. Her mum is desperate for her to keep her long hair, and so it's not until she leaves for the University of Leicester that she breaks free, with spiky hair and a nose piercing. Slowly, her identity is becoming more obvious.

When she does finally come out to her mum and her stepdad, it doesn't go quite as well as she'd hoped. She's nineteen, with a girlfriend visiting from university. 'It wasn't good,' she recalls. 'My mum took a week off work. She was just distraught. I'm pretty sure she said, *At least if you were into drugs there would be something we could do about it.* I say this now and people are like, *Oh my God*, but because of the shame that you have, you think, *Oh well, yeah*, you know?' Her stepdad compounds this. *You always wanted to be different*, he says, because this is, of course, the easiest sort of different. Beccy swiftly heads back to university and her girlfriend, just accepting that because of who she is, this is what happens. Eventually, they get to know her girlfriend and begin to calm down and accept Beccy's sexuality. 'But they stopped me from telling other members of my family,' she recalls, 'because my mum said, *I'll just go mad if anyone says anything bad about you.* But of course then you internalise that shame, don't you?'

When she finishes her course, she ends up back in Aylesbury for a while, county town of Buckinghamshire, a place of municipal estates and newbuild sprawl. She experiences both sides, moving when she's ten from a two-up two-down in mid-century Bedgrove to an eighties house near Stoke Mandeville Stadium when her mum remarries. These are spick and span closes of small faux-Victorian houses, with well-mown gardens and garages painted snowy white. 'It just felt like a bit of a judgy place,' she recalls, 'quite conservative in every sense of the word.' She remembers their neighbours disowning their son because he was gay. One evening, she heads out with some old school friends for a drink. *I'm glad you got over that dyke phase*, one of them tells her. 'I was just so shocked,' she says. 'But again, rather than being *How dare you* or whatever, I just sat there and ate my dinner and never spoke to them again.' Decades later, she takes a course on mental health first aid for her job, and has to give a presentation on anxiety in the LGBTQ+ community. 'I just put up a few phrases that people had said to me over the years,' she tells me, 'and everyone was horrified. And I'd realised from that reaction – they were apologising, *I'm so sorry you went through that*, these people from all over the place – and it was *then* I realised it was wrong. That was the first moment, which sounds crazy now, but I just think that shame, it seeps deep inside of you, this feeling that you're defective and that you should hide. It does take a long while.'

There is a gay pub in Aylesbury when she's a teenager, but she doesn't venture into it for some years. The first time she steps inside, she feels extremely nervous. *This is the place where evil happens*, she thinks, although once inside this just turns out to be Steps and a regular karaoke night. 'In queer spaces obviously the only thing you've got in common is you're queer,' she says. 'Everything else is probably totally different. Your age, your upbringing, your likes, your dislikes, your taste.' But she finds common ground, dressing in her Etnies trainers and baggy trousers and listening to Europop. 'It's all part of what makes you feel like you belong,' she says. She leaves Aylesbury for nearby Milton Keynes, which has taken its responsibility to its LGBTQ+ residents seriously from the off. For one, there's Pink

Punters, a massive multi-floor bar and club based in a sprawling mock-Tudor inn and prefab in Bletchley, just down the road from where Alan Turing helped break the Enigma codes. But this is a changed world from those wartime secrets and the persecution that saw Turing chemically castrated for being gay. For twenty-five years, the Pink Punters' rainbow double-decker bus has been a conspicuous symbol of the new city, picking up clubbers from around the many estates to bring them to the famous nightspot for karaoke, cocktails and non-stop pop. And in that time, Beccy has seen its customers change. 'Think of Pink Punters now, there's lots of people there who you won't be able to identify as queer or not,' she says, 'which is great in a way, because if you want to be really butch or really femme or anywhere on that scale, you can be that.' In the meantime, she makes the effort to be out at work, dropping in references to a girlfriend in watercooler chats with new staff, and on one occasion having her boss come out to her in turn. ('She said, *I had all the jobs. I was in the military, I was a plumber.*') It's important for her to be a positive example of an out lesbian.

In 2010, Beccy is on Gaydar Girls and spots a profile that looks interesting. They get chatting, and it turns out they both live in Buckinghamshire – the other woman, Katie, we met earlier when her GP told her she wasn't the only lesbian in her village of Prestwood.* They chat for a few weeks before deciding to meet up in, seemingly, the least queer space they can find, The Moon Under Water in Milton Keynes. All these years later, I'm interviewing the pair of them together. How did that first date go? I ask. 'We both had our awkward moments,' recalls Beccy. Katie mistakes Beccy's North Bucks twang for Brummie, and Beccy tries to say something clever about photography, knowing

* See the chapter 'The Other Lesbian in Prestwood'.

it's Katie's job, but it falls embarrassingly flat. 'I think we definitely had that attraction,' says Beccy. 'It was easy to talk to you,' says Katie. They recall what a palaver it was to arrange dates via Gaydar Girls, and about how cautious they both were. 'So we took things really quite slowly,' says Beccy, which was much to Katie's friend Aaron's outrage. *What, so you've not kissed her yet?* he asks impatiently after Becky and Katie have been dating for a few weeks. 'He was like, *You can't leave until you've kissed her,*' recalls Katie. 'And I remember his words in my head as I was saying goodbye to you and thinking, *I just can't do it!*' They marvel at the premise of 2024 lesbian dating show *I Kissed a Girl*, where getting off with each other is the first thing the women do. 'We were like, *Oh my God, there's no way I could have done that!*' says Beccy. 'I'd probably start walking peculiarly,' says Katie. '*Am I walking normally?*' 'Hitting yourself in the face randomly or something . . .' adds Beccy.

After a couple of Covid-based false starts, Beccy and Katie are married in 2022 in a wedding venue in the improbably named village of Newton Blossomville. When they first meet, gay marriage isn't legal, and civil partnerships have only been around since 2004. Initially, Katie isn't sold on the idea. *Why would anyone get married?* she remembers telling Beccy. 'I'd always felt awkward about things like that. We'd have to kiss in front of people, we would have to be very visible, we would be in white dresses. On a stage, almost. I don't enjoy things like that. So that's probably what I was thinking. Oh God, people talking about you in a speech and having to give a speech yourself, like, eurgh . . .' She suggests instead that it would make much more sense spending twenty grand going travelling. 'And much to Beccy's horror, I realised as I'd said that that this was not how you were feeling.' Beccy, it's safe to say, is more of a romantic. 'My mum and stepdad really were devoted to each other,' she says. 'I was really lucky, my grandparents were together as well. So I think I had some good relationship examples in some ways, close ones where I thought, *Oh, that's really nice being married.* So I liked the idea of it.' By this time, their families have both come round to the idea too, after a rocky start. 'It seemed like everybody was like, *Oh, thank God, we can all get together,'* says Katie. '*And it's not a funeral.'*

Planning it is an eye-opener for the couple. They go along to a wedding fair to get ideas. Do they want a magician, perhaps, or to release doves? Beccy gets chatting to a photographer. *So what are you wearing?* he asks. *Will you be wearing a suit?* 'And then he suddenly thought, *Oh shit, I said that out loud,'* recalls Beccy. 'Because it wasn't a relevant question.' They're fascinated by how gendered it all is, a bride and groom still standard on the invites and cakes, along with the bridal suites ('Not inclusive if you're two men getting married,' says Katie). None of it is awful; it's just a reminder that years after equal marriage, not all of the wedding sector has quite caught up, or perhaps wants to. The day itself is a huge success, partly because the freedom of a lesbian wedding means they can make it up. And so they both walk down the aisle. 'We've known each other's families for a long time,' says Beccy, 'so we get on well. Obviously our coming-out stories were not great. But a lot of time has passed since then. So it was just a really great celebration.' Even the photographer accidentally referring to them as the bride and groom doesn't cast a shadow.

For a while they live in Newport Pagnell, an old satellite town of Milton Keynes, where the neighbours are noisy young lads with poor taste in music and a dog that barks all night. Eventually, they make Katie feel a bit uncomfortable, and so she and Beccy move a little further out to Cranfield, a large and eccentric village with a business school and an airfield. 'We go to the football club down the road and other pubs, and it's pretty obvious people know we're a couple,' says Beccy. 'But I've never felt uncomfortable anywhere. I wonder what that would have been like twenty years ago? Maybe that wouldn't have been the same.' Now they're in a detached house, which means they can watch Stacey Solomon's house-cleaning show *Sort Your Life Out* and end up hoovering madly at 11 p.m., telling themselves, *I am not a hoarder!*

When I speak to them, they've just watched Eurovision with Beccy's cousin Gareth and his husband, Stevie. It was meant to be a bigger gathering, but they left it a bit too late. 'Last year's party was good,' says Katie. 'We decorated it all. We had all of the bunting crossing over, and banners and balloons, and I bought us sequinned dungarees and sequinned bomber jackets. There was a lot of sequins going on. A lot of commentary on all the acts.' The year before was slightly more improvised on the costume front. 'You didn't have an outfit, did you?' recalls Katie. 'Mum had a bag from Iceland, so I just cut the bottom out and you wore it like a T-shirt.' While their parents might not have had any LGBTQ+ neighbours or role models in years gone by, now Beccy and Katie are performing that role for the residents of Cranfield, and also for their nieces and nephews. 'They've grown up knowing that some people are gay,' says Beccy. 'They probably don't even realise that we would ever have got any stick for being gay,' says Katie, but Beccy is less sure. 'I think kids are still bullied for being gay, but still they've grown up with us leading ordinary lives. I think that is it, isn't it? We've got jobs, we go to the shops, we have the same worries as other people.' She thinks for a moment about the fact that Katie's old stomping ground of High Wycombe now has a Pride march, while her hometown does not. 'I wonder what it's like in Aylesbury now?' she says. And it hangs there, like one of the great imponderables of our time.

When the call comes in November 1982, Maidstone's gay community are ready for action. And that action is a jumble sale and raffle, raising £7. This will be enough to place three classified adverts in the local press for their new volunteer initiative: Medway and Maidstone Gay Switchboard. They have estimated some 20,000 LGBTQ+ folk live in North Kent, many living closeted lives in isolation, or in need of practical advice or mental health support. The Switchboard, set up that summer, is getting seven or eight calls a night. To help promote it, one of the operators appears on Radio Medway's breakfast show, and they also approach *Chatham News*, a local paper, to place a small ad for the service. They've honed the wording and got it down to 133 characters to meet their tiny budget: *Homosexual women and men – for information and advice phone Gay Switchboard. Medway 826925 every Thursday and Friday, 7.30–9.30pm only.*

Mike Souter, ad manager for the paper, swiftly returns their cheque. 'Unfortunately, it is not the policy of our company to accept advertisements of this nature,' he writes.[34] 'We are not totally surprised by the response of the paper,' a Switchboard spokesperson tells Kent Gay Action's newsletter, 'as it is not noted for taking a liberal line on any issue.' Their hopes had been raised, they said, because the paper had run a news story about the Switchboard some months earlier. It's clear now that this was not intended to have been positive. And so, infuriating the paper even more, that winter the director of social services

steps in with a grant of £50 to cover phone rental and advertising – should the Switchboard be able to find somewhere to
spend it.

THE HOUNDS OF YARM

It's mid-morning when Benjamin lets himself into someone else's house. An executive estate overlooking a triangle of tightly mown lawn, the bulky newbuilds have yet to settle into this character-less landscape. As he pushes open the door, two big dogs race up to him, but he's not alarmed. He's used to letting himself into houses all over the area, and much further afield too. He's not a cat burglar, he's a dog walker, and as such holds a privileged position in British life, being able to see inside countless homes, to glimpse different lives, and to come and go as he pleases. 'I've got a bunch of keys in my van for half of Yorkshire,' he tells me. 'We'll get people ringing us, going, *Are you still in the area? Because my wife locked herself out.* We often get that. You're like, *Okay, I'll go and let your wife in.*' He and his partner both left stressful jobs and now run a series of franchises from their new home, on the fringes of Yarm in North Yorkshire. His husband quit his job as a paramedic in 2006 after he was stabbed, and almost a decade later Benjamin eagerly leaves his, working with prisoners, to join him. Now it's the third-largest dog-walking business in Europe, he proudly informs me. 'It's weird because all the interesting jobs I've had in the past, this job is the one that people talk to me most about,' he says. 'And I'm like, *I just walk dogs. There's nothing special about it at all.* But people are like, *Oh my God. That's, like, my dream job!*' He wonders sometimes if he's not using the skills he's built up over a varied decades-long career, but then the reality hits him. 'I work for myself. I don't have to deal with people, which is the best part of it. I work with dogs. They don't answer back. They require the bare minimum. And they give the most love. So yeah, actually, if I think about it, it is actually a brilliant position to be in, a brilliant job to do.'

Perhaps it's Benjamin's access to the secrets of the estate, with its dense clusters of eighties houses and upmarket cul-de-sacs, big cars, low hedges and competitive planting, that makes it feel a little like a Middlesbrough spin on *Midsomer Murders*. 'We love it,' says Benjamin. Their neighbours are relaxed and accepting, and they've fitted right in, dog-walking an incredible fast track into the heart of the community here. 'We're very lucky. And, you know, we appreciate that every day. Because it's not always been like that. Our previous place was just awful.' They'd bought a cheap house in an ex-mining-community hamlet in County Durham. 'And we paid the price for that, ultimately, because I was reminded of those very old-fashioned backwater views that hadn't moved on.' After a lifetime of trying to be accepted and relaxed in his own skin, this was not what Benjamin or his husband needed. 'So we cut our losses: we sold up, moved.' Trying on another suburb for size.

But then Benjamin remembers feeling the same in the place where he grew up, a council house in a suburbanised village in the Midlands. 'It was a very alien place,' he says. Alveley's ordered streets of 1970s houses with neat grass and tall hedges are not a welcoming place for a boy who's made to feel different very early on. 'I would have loved the opportunity to have an urban childhood,' he tells me. 'I think I would have had more of a support network.' Instead, here he's severely bullied by the other children. 'I was quite effeminate,' he recalls. 'The boys really, really mocked me heavily, and just did all this limp-wristed stuff. *Oh, look at the way he laughs, look at the way he walks, look at the way he holds this or holds that. He's just like a girl.* I got that a lot,' he says. 'And it used to really, really hurt.'

These days, Benjamin is a bodybuilder, a mountain of a man, which he thinks happened as a reaction against all that went on when he was a child. The transformation has been profound, and when he attends a school reunion it appears he's not the only one who has changed. 'People were coming up to me, and they were like, *If I was ever a dick to you at school, man, I am so, so sorry,*' he recalls. 'And I was like, *I don't remember you being a dick to me. And trust me, I remember who was a dick to me, and if they were here tonight, I'd have hold of them up against the wall.*' But none of those people are there. Instead, there are more welcome surprises. One of the sporty guys who'd not been particularly pleasant to Benjamin when he was a boy is suddenly transfixed by his hard-earned physique, much to his amusement. 'He got drunk and got very, very touchy-feely, let me tell you!' he says, laughing at the turnaround.

When his parents divorce, he goes with his mum to Fenham, a sprawling estate of municipal red-brick houses in Newcastle, plain, sensible and cosier than frosty Alveley, and he remains in the area for years, gradually shedding the layers of damage all the bullying has done to him. He thinks back to his time at Kidderminster College, the teacher who, when he pours his heart out about being bullied, tells him, *My advice to you is get a girlfriend.* ('But that's Section 28,' he shrugs. 'She'd probably never met a gay person in her life before.') At nineteen, he comes out to his mum, who for a long time goes into complete denial about it, which is painful all round. 'When she did accept it, and when she was good, she was brilliant,' says Benjamin. 'And we cried a lot. And she hugged me. And she told me she loved me so much.' The transformation now feels complete, from bullied gay kid on the edge of things to a big man at the centre of a community. 'I don't have to live this lie any more,' he says. 'I can be myself. And that was just a breath of fresh air and incredibly empowering. I loved living that life. And that's what I wanted to be, and I wanted it for so long.' And that feeling, he says, has never gone away. Now, with his dog walker's keys and his access to the secret life of Yarm, he no longer feels like an outsider. Instead, he's experiencing the curious inner lives of these cul-de-sacs and closes, its most trusted resident, running with the dogs in suburbia.

The arrival of the Gay Men's Press and other LGBTQ-focused publishers in the late 1970s had a revolutionary effect on the cultural life of isolated people like me. Their books could be bought via mail order or picked up in larger towns and cities, or in specialist bookshops such as Gay's The Word in London. But it was not always straightforward, with many local bookshops treating anything LGBTQ+-related as porn, hiding it away on top shelves and making it as inaccessible as possible, if available at all. For some people with disabilities, access to these publications is even less straightforward. Large-print and Braille editions of LGBTQ+ titles are either frighteningly expensive or vanishingly rare, and in the eighties only the big publishers are producing audio books, on cassette, mainly for sale to public libraries.

And so in 1983 the Gay Men's Disabled Group decides to do something about it. It begins when a member records their collection of short stories onto three C120 cassettes for other members to buy or borrow. Another starts a gay men's tape library out of his home in Luton. It seems fitting that this, like so many LGBTQ+ enterprises, grows out of a suburban home, where boredom and isolation have created the motivation to do something positive. It's a bootleg affair. 'If you have a good reading voice and access to a tape-recorder, please drop us a line,' goes the newsletter. Budding audio book readers are invited to record their favourite gay stories for this under-the-counter Luton library. 'We also need to get the cassettes copied, so if any member has a two-deck cassette recorder for copying cassette tapes reel-to-reel, please do write in.'[35] It's a high-tech combination of disability activism, LGBTQ+ solidarity and Dolby Noise Reduction – a new way of escaping the suburbs.

AN ACCIDENT IN BILTON

A dark country lane outside Hull, and Peter is on his new moped. It's 1983, and he's sixteen, and it feels like freedom. He worked out some time ago that he's gay, and is fine with that, though he's yet to tell anyone. There's no rush. He has a great group of friends and regularly stars in skits in school assembly, playing Captain Kirk one week, and a magician the next. Life is good. He is flying. Ahead, he sees a car coming towards him. Without warning it cuts a corner, swerving onto the wrong side of the road. Before Peter can do anything, the car is upon him. They collide head-on. There he is, flying over the bonnet, onto the tarmac. When he makes it to hospital, they confirm he's broken both of his legs and one arm in several places. 'But the life-changing injury,' he tells me, 'was the nerves in your back going into your spine – and that network of nerves is called the brachial plexus – and they were literally ripped out by the impact of the car. So my arm is completely paralysed, and has been since the age of sixteen.' Brachial plexus injuries commonly affect two groups of people: motorcyclists and newborn babies. 'The act of actually being born can tear the nerves in the babies,' Peter explains. 'A lot of people have some recovery if the nerves are severed partway along, but mine were just ripped out at the base. So it was never going to recover for me.' He remains in hospital for three months, longer than a school summer holiday, and a lifetime to a sixteen-year-old. When he leaves, the terrible migraines begin, the vomiting, leaving him bedridden for days at a time. Meanwhile, the sexuality that he has just begun to get a handle on now seems like a relic from another time, before the accident.

Peter grows up in Bilton, outside Hull, a suburban-styled village with a large 1950s red-brick housing estate tacked on, all dormer bungalows and neat terraces of municipal houses. Across the ceiling of his bedroom a bold trail of black footprints march, painted in a creative moment, while cardboard birds of prey dangle on threads, joining the dance on the ceiling. In the mornings, ice forms on the inside of the windows, sticking the net curtains to the thin glass. His mother is the heart of the family, but when his parents split up he and his brother remain with their dad, a lorry driver who is away long hours. And so Peter and his brother learn to fend for themselves.

While home life is hard, Peter loves school; he hangs out with the cool kids and gets to act and be creative. But as he grows, he becomes more cautious about what people will see if he continues performing, so he gives it up and retreats into himself. 'I think there's a difference between knowing you're not straight but accepting that you're gay,' he says. 'I had no inclination to date girls, but no one ever, ever, *ever* suspected that I might be gay. I think they thought I was picky.' He's into sport and, as he gets older, having beers with his mates down the pub. But there are reminders all around that this might not be the best environment to come out in. 'We had a neighbour who was a detective. And they used to talk about going on "poof patrol". And this was going around the toilets, I think, and just finding people who are cottaging or whatever and arresting them. And I just found this absolutely horrific. But I couldn't say anything, obviously.' It's a parallel education, as is his dad's *Daily Mirror* with its routinely homophobic headlines. The agony aunt column occasionally offers glimpses of other gay lives, but even that's not the help it might be. 'There was a letter from someone who was my age feeling the same things that I felt. *Am I gay? I'm worried I might be.* And the agony aunt's reply was, *Well, a lot of people at your age can experience same-sex attraction, but it sometimes just passes as a phase.* And I clung on to that for a long time. And I think that was really dangerous to put that out there because I think that's probably a very small number of cases, actually.'

After the accident, Peter has to retake the final year of secondary school, 'which was the worst year of my life', he says. 'Because all my friends had gone.' In hospital he has had a lot of time to think about his sexuality, and of how the accident has interrupted his coming to terms with it. 'My whole life consists of pre-accident and post-accident. And I think the two things are very intertwined.' One summer during his A-levels, he goes on a lads' holiday to Salou in Spain. Peter isn't out pulling, but then neither are his mates. Instead, they're getting blind drunk. 'Drinking was the thing,' he says. 'Bacardi was cheap. And we were just getting on it the whole time. Thoroughly shameful. So even the girls were a bit of a side issue . . . I don't think any of them had sex. I think they just snogged girls.' He pauses. 'I don't even think they got that far.' Peter hangs back. He's gone from being the popular performer at school to finding meeting new people a challenge, and spends social situations trying to mask his disability as best he can or reluctantly coming out as disabled. 'I think as a result of that, I came across as quite a closed person. My vibes weren't *Come and talk to me.* They were *Don't come and talk to me.* Whether it'd be men or women.' Despite all the beers and laughs, he feels slightly on the edge of the group. 'But if I'm honest, I've always felt slightly excluded from most things. I've always felt a bit different, like I don't quite fit in. And that's not a big source of anxiety for me or anything.'

He ends up at Leicester Polytechnic, still feeling low, migraines in full effect. At the end of his first year he decides he needs to do something radical, to break this spiral he's in. 'Two of my friends were doing a round-the-world trip,' he recalls. 'And they said, *Well, if you're gonna give up your degree, you're welcome to come with us.* And I said, *Great.*' What he doesn't tell them is he has a slightly different plan. Their trip will take them through India and Thailand, before heading to Australia and continuing from there. But Peter just wants to get to Sydney and stay there. 'I never told them this,' he says. An Alan Whicker documentary about gay lib from 1973 has stayed with him all these years. In it, Whicker calls Sydney the gay capital of the southern hemisphere. 'My intention there was to come out. And I don't mean, like, have rampant sex or anything. It wasn't about that, it was just telling the people I was around that I was gay and see how it felt. I was on the other side of the world; there could be no repercussions of this to my other life back home. I made really good friends and it really worked.' He shares a house with a young Australian woman and meets her gay friends. They take him to extraordinary events, Mardi Gras and big dance parties. At last, here he feels euphoric and free.

He stays as long as he can, which makes returning home a bit of a shock. After being out and happy in Sydney, returning to live with his mum in a village a few miles from Bilton makes him feel quite the opposite. He needs to come out to his parents before he can tell any of his friends, because he knows that here in the suburbs of Hull gossip will quickly spread beyond his control. 'I told my mum, and she was very, very upset – accepting but totally bewildered.' The first thing she says is, *Who knows?* 'I don't think she was ashamed,' says Peter. 'She's very hyper-protective of me. And I think it was more about she doesn't want me to experience any hatred or abuse, or any negative behaviour.' When he tells his dad, he accepts it but doesn't talk about it. 'Very working class. My dad just found everything awkward to talk about, he just couldn't.' Peter tells one of his best mates, who says, *You're probably gonna have to move away. You're not gonna have any life around here*, 'which wasn't particularly supportive', he says. But the next one he tells is super cool about it and, flooded with relief, he asks her to tell everyone else. He's through with being in the closet, but the process of coming out is exhausting. 'And it felt comfortable, because I'd already worn that coat, if you like, in Sydney, had already felt what it was like.' His mum's immediate fearful reaction is replaced by incredulity. 'She was astonished that all of my old school friends reacted positively. She really couldn't believe it.'

Many people with disabilities relate a common experience of others assuming they can't do things, rather than the opposite. In some ways, suburbia can have a similarly limiting effect, presenting illusory boundaries rather than a sense of possibility or potential. Peter's experience of being disabled in the gay world has also been pretty negative. 'I've had a lot of rejection and stuff, even on online dating,' he says. 'Even if you mentioned it in the chat before you meet, people just cut you dead . . . I've had a couple of people say, *You should have told me this at the start. I'm not interested.* So it's pretty brutal.'

These days, Peter lives back in Sydney with his Colombian husband, Nando. His mum is eighty-five now and loves Peter's husband, as do his old school friends, who hang out with them down the pub when they come to visit. His mum lives near where he grew up, and so all the old haunts are still there, ready to ambush him every time he returns. 'I get a physical feeling when I go there. It's so boring and clinical, and there's nothing there.' But he recognises that this is only half of the story. 'When you've still got strong friendships from that period that are tied to the environment, it can't all be bad . . . I would never want that not to have happened. It was a very safe place to grow up and it was a very fun place to grow up. I had a lucky childhood, in some ways, sexuality aside. So it'll always be with me, perhaps a little bit grudgingly, in that I never want to live in a place like that again.' It's the limits of the place that have stayed with him, those boundaries thrown up by his accident and the sexuality he felt he couldn't share. Now he's flown beyond those barriers. Out in his new life the sun shines, and quietly, so does he.

A midwinter's day in mock-suburbia. The lawns straggly and unmown, street trees bare, privet slabs of vinyl green defending the margins. Decorations sparkle from the windows of drab brown-brick and half-timbered houses. This is 1986 in the village of Himley in Staffordshire, on a street of stodgy mid-century houses that sell the fantasy of cottage living. Despite the developer's optimism, you couldn't call it proper suburbia. Just as mock-Tudor isn't Tudor, this is mock-suburbia. In a village of fewer than a thousand people, these semis sprout from the tips of tendrils that creep from Birmingham through Dudley and beyond.

Into this scene of shy domesticity walks a group of youths. They could have been carollers going from door to door, and true, they're spreading a message of goodwill and love through the neighbourhood. Boisterous, nervy, full of passion, they have been distributing leaflets, pushing them through letterboxes, handing them to the few people they encounter. And now here they stand, a joyous, noisy overspill on a grassy strip of land before one of these semis. The house is the very picture of respectability, and on the grass before it stand members of the Lesbian and Gay Youth Movement. Neighbours, peeking from their windows, aren't sure how these youths have got here or where they have come from. But the obvious thing is, they aren't from Himley and so they aren't welcome.

The house belongs to a local politician, Bill Brownhill, Tory leader of South Staffordshire council. In the run-up to Christmas 1986, the health committee at the council has been shown a film made by the government. The 'Don't Die of Ignorance' HIV and AIDS awareness campaign has been spearheaded by the health minister, Norman Fowler. The ad is helmed by Nicolas Roeg, who'd directed David Bowie in *The Man Who Fell to Earth*, and is voiced by John Hurt, who a decade before played Quentin Crisp in *The Naked Civil Servant*. 'There is now a danger that has become a threat to us all,' is Hurt's sonorous opening line, accompanying images of exploding, chiselling rock. 'It is a deadly disease and there is no known cure. The virus can be passed by sexual intercourse with an infected person. Anyone can get it – man or woman. So far it's been confined to small groups – but it's spreading.' At this point a freshly carved tombstone rises, with the letters 'AIDS' etched at the top. It falls. 'So protect yourself. And read this leaflet when it arrives.' An 'AIDS: Don't Die of Ignorance' leaflet is thrown onto the grave. 'If you ignore AIDS, it could be the death of you. So don't die of ignorance.' A bunch of lilies is thrown on the grave, and a tiny caption reads, 'Issued by the health department of the United Kingdom.'

The video, and the accompanying leaflet, has a great effect across Britain, a shiver of fear bringing sex and the shadow of death together in a macabre dance. And in Staffordshire, councillor Bill Brownhill's response is raw and shocking. 'I should shoot them all,' he tells the chamber. 'These bunch of queers that legalise filth in homosexuality have a lot to answer for and I hope they are proud of what they have done. It is disgusting and diabolical. As a cure I would put 90 per cent of queers in the ruddy gas chambers. Are we going to let these queers trade their filth up and down the country?' His opposite number in the Labour Party, Jack Greenaway, rises to respond. But if anyone is waiting for Brownhill's vicious comments to be contradicted, they're disappointed. 'Every one of us here will agree with what has been said,' Greenaway declares. Their pronouncements make the national news the next day. 'Gas gays says Tory,' bellows the massive front-page headline in the *Sun*, a jowly Brownhill peering out from behind huge resin-framed specs. A subhead, short and blunt, declares, 'Answer to AIDS'.

And so the small protest is in full swing. A handful of young people from the Lesbian and Gay Youth Movement are standing on the grass outside Brownhill's semi-detached, chanting the slogans of the day. *Two, four, six, eight! How do you know your kids are straight? We're here, we're queer, get used to it.* They're making themselves visible, and they're making the injustice of his words visible too. Some are still teenagers, and their protest is brave, swift and heartfelt. Brownhill would have all of these protestors shot, he says, would see them in gas chambers. *Gas chambers.* In a country still puffed up by long-stale *We won the war* jingoism, the bleak irony of this appears to have missed the councillor and his supporters.

Soon, the chants are joined by something altogether more strident: the sound of sirens. One of Brownhill's neighbours has called the police. Vans screech to a halt and coppers jump out, boots on the muddy verge, ready for action. These are the days of riot shields and strike-breaking, of fifth columnists and mob-handed policing, Orgreave and Greenham Common. They're here to defend Himley from outsiders – *the queers* – and to protect Brownhill and all he stands for. The coppers make a grab for one of the protestors, and suddenly the rest are sitting on the cold ground, linking arms. *We shall not be moved.* A classic tactic learned from the lessons of generations of protestors, a human chain making themselves harder to shift. But the police know this game too and are having none of it. They grab the young people and start dragging them from the ground, pulling them up as if weeding the garden. Despite their stubbornness, determination and fear, one by one the members of the Lesbian and Gay Youth Movement are roughly lifted, still noisily protesting, handcuffed and bundled with much difficulty into the back of the Black Marias. One for the pub later, lads. One for the ages.

For the protestors, this, the shortest day of 1986, would end up casting a long shadow. They're taken to the station in Wombourne, each aware of the dangers and the more vocal of the group reminding the others of their rights. When the charge sheets are filled out, four of their number refuse to cooperate, defiantly giving false names and addresses, making themselves indigestible, blocking the system. Regardless, all twelve are charged with using abusive and threatening behaviour, while one makes a counter-complaint of assault against the arresting officers. In turn, they're charged with assaulting two of the officers, the oldest trick in the book. Twelve members of the Lesbian and Gay Youth Movement are kept there, the officers enjoying the novelty of their capture while they work out what to do with them. They let the machinery of their workplace – the anxiety, the powerlessness, the boredom – grind away on the group. Eventually, the young protestors are told that as the police cannot confirm all their identities, the whole lot will be remanded in custody for seven days. It's 21 December, and so they will be spending Christmas behind bars. They're split up: the four under twenty-ones sent to a borstal in Redditch; three shipped a couple of hundred miles to a remand centre in Surrey; the remainder locked up in an imposing Victorian prison in Birmingham. A week of fear, lost liberty, humiliation and lonely contemplation. Bill Brownhill enjoys his roast turkey.

Between Christmas and New Year, the twelve appear for a bail hearing at Selsdon Magistrates Court in the village of Wombourne. Eleven police officers guard the doors of the court, and a riot van is parked round the corner. Members of the Lesbian and Gay Youth Movement are brought up in groups of three and made to stand throughout the proceedings. It's theatre, much as the entire response has been. Finally, they're released, with a court date set for two months away. But by now they know something isn't right. The maximum they should have received for their protest – handing out some leaflets, chanting some slogans, sitting down in Councillor Brownhill's garden – was a small fine.

The Wombourne 12, as they're now being called, find their cause championed in the local gay press – particularly *In the Pink*, a new free lesbian and gay newspaper for the West Midlands. On their trial date, 23 February 1987, three hundred supporters turn up outside Selsdon Magistrates Court to protest. There are more leaflets: *Take on the queer-bashers! Lesbian and gay defence starts here!* Two marchers hold a banner that reads, *Wombourne 12 – Police 0. Fight Back!* The sleepy Staffordshire village has never seen anything like it. 'Are we going to let these queers trade their filth up and down the country?' Brownhill had thundered. And yet, here they are, his worst nightmare, and the answer appears to be a definitive *Yes*. One of the protestors that day, a Wolverhampton youth who had only recently come out, told me what a unifying, motivating force the case was for many young Midlands LGBTQ+ people. Brownhill's words, and the police response, inspire a new generation, but not in the way the councillor might have hoped. The Wombourne 12 are released without charge. Four of the activists sue for malicious prosecution and win £30,000 in damages from Staffordshire police. The other eight do not come forward for reparations, perhaps too traumatised by their experience or just keen to put it behind them and get on with their lives. And Bill Brownhill? He goes on to represent Himley for another eighteen years, after which he's named an honorary alderman, with a room in the local council chambers named after him. But where is the plaque for the Wombourne 12?

THE BASINGSTOKE SCREAM

The railway line snakes across Basingstoke, taking trains into London or on to the coast. Along the path beside the line walks Mat, a teenage goth in the mid-eighties, bored and yearning and making a statement wherever he goes. As he wanders down it, he spots some fresh graffiti beside one of the town's many round-abouts. Someone has drawn a pink triangle and scrawled 'Gay Rights' next to it. 'It was the most exciting thing I'd ever seen,' Mat tells me. 'Because I didn't know anybody that would have done it, and it wasn't my friendship group. I went, *Gosh, there are actually people in this town that feel the same way that I do*. And that was quite powerful, to suddenly go, *Oh, right. Okay, I'm not on my own*.' He has known he's gay for a few years, but now for the first time in the Hampshire suburbs he doesn't feel quite so alone.

Mat is born at the beginning of the 1970s, when most of Basingstoke is pretty young too. His parents move out there for work, his dad an electrician from Hull, his mum a teacher from the West Country. Basingstoke may have Roman origins, but it's predominantly a London overspill town that expanded in the sixties, a landscape of complicated modernist suburbs with a brutalist concrete core. Initially, he lives with his parents in a bungalow. 'Everybody I've spoken to that grew up in suburbia, I think we all had the same experience of just crushing boredom, especially in the eighties. No internet, three TV channels.' Not that he's home much at first to appreciate it, as he's sent away to boarding school until he's thirteen. He realises he's gay when he's twelve, and when he moves to a state school a year later he has what he calls 'quite a bad depressive episode, because I suddenly went, *Okay, so I'm gay. I'm definitely gay, I understand that. And I'm hated by all these people. I don't know how to process that.* And so I came out to my sister. I think I was fifteen. And then I came out to everybody else when I was sixteen.' This is November 1988, and he tells all of his friends in a single weekend. Rather than a quiet coming out, he explodes from the closet. 'I felt like I was in a glass closet anyway, because it wasn't a mad surprise to anybody.' Although he's very nervous of telling his best friend from school. And so one of his mates does it for him while he disappears off for a smoke. 'He was like, *Yeah, no, it's fine.* And then, maybe three years later, he said to me, *Oh, by the way, I'm gay as well.*' He tells his parents three days later. He has fallen for a local guy and wants to call him, but chickens out. Instead, he uses that nervous energy to speak to his mother. 'I said to my mum, *Can we have a chat about my sexuality?* And she said, *Am I going to need my cigarettes for this?* I was like, *Yeah, I think you probably do.* And so I told her, and her immediate response was, *I don't think you are, I think you're just around a bunch of people that make you think you are,* because she'd had a relationship with a woman when she was at college.' He explains that it has been going on rather longer than that.

By the time he starts A-level college, he has had enough of conforming. *I'm not wearing the uniform any more,* he decides. 'I bleached my hair and started wearing black nail polish, which didn't go down very well at church, because at that point I was a C. of E. churchgoer. Yeah, they're not very forward-thinking about boys with nail polish.' He paints his small bedroom black, the furniture gloss purple. On a small black-and-white TV with the volume turned right down, he watches Channel 4 arts shows and their pink-triangle queer programming, praying his parents don't burst in and catch him. They split up when he's seventeen.

Soon afterwards, his mother comes out. Another family member has done the same. 'We're kind of thinking it's karma,' he says, 'because my dad was so vile when I came out, he didn't speak to me for six months.' Mat, his mum and his sister move into a council house in the town, and so to feel at home he immediately paints his new bedroom black, this time with the furniture red instead of purple. There are records and books everywhere.

By this time he has discovered the Basingstoke Area Gay Society, or BAGS, who meet every Wednesday. 'They were those weird gay men that are not massively fond of women,' he explains. 'I took a lesbian friend of mine, and they were like, *Oh!* Which obviously sat quite badly with me.' Instead, he finds more soulmates and support among his growing circle of goth friends. There he is, in black eyeliner and white foundation, 'and that's just not what the gay community in Basingstoke is about', he says. 'There was a mismatch in terms of knowing what was going on for me and what was going on for them. And I went along to this group, and then everybody was talking about what sandwiches they'd had that day. I was like, *Oh God, is this what gay societies are like?* Just the most terrible, boring suburban conversation. I was just going, *Nobody's heard of any bands I like, nobody's heard of any films I like, what the hell am I gonna do?*' The most bohemian thing is when a guy in a nearby village holds an annual gay hog roast at his bungalow. In one of the local shops Mat bumps into someone he's met at BAGS, who is working as a plumber on the retirement bungalows along the edge of his estate. According to the plumber, all the old people have clocked Mat and are saying, *That boy's definitely gay. And I think his mum might be too.* 'Not obnoxious,' says Mat, 'just commenting.'

Then there's one of the sociology teachers at college, who asks if Mat would talk to his class about his sexuality. 'I was like, *Yeah, that's fine. I'm not averse to doing that.'* And so he finds himself in front of classes of sixteen- and seventeen-year-olds, talking about being gay and facing penetrating questions like, *How can you fancy men when women are really pretty?* 'Someone said, *What would you do if I called you a bender? And I was like, It's true. I am a bender. It's not my favourite word, but it's up to you. But then that means I can call you a wanker, because that's probably true as well, isn't it? We don't get anywhere by calling each other names.'* The shadow of Section 28 hangs over all of this. 'I did have to be quite careful,' he recalls. 'A couple of times I'd said, *Don't knock it till you try it.* And then one of the teachers had to go, *We can't promote . . .* And I was like, *I'm not part of your faculty. I can more or less say what I want.'*

He spends a lot of evenings at gigs or alternative discos, locally at the Caribbean Club near the hospital ('It was a surprisingly big alternative scene in Basingstoke,' he says), the Greyhound in Slough, or clubs in Reading and London. 'I spent so much time in Brixton Academy, choking on people's hair spray,' he recalls. He loves being a goth. 'I liked the attention. To be honest, it's quite good to shock people, especially when you're a teenager. It's the best thing on earth where you can come out of the bathroom and have both your parents go, *Jesus Christ!* You've done it properly then, you've really made it.' If being a goth at home is a challenge, being a goth on the streets and plazas of Basingstoke is a provocation too far for some. 'If we went anywhere in town, we had to go in a group,' he recalls, 'because I got assaulted three or four times.' One night, he's on his way back through town after being at a local goth-friendly pub, and a guy grabs him as he passes one of the other bars. *Are you a woman or a man?* he demands. 'And I went, *Whatever, dude.* And he went, *Cos you're the biggest fucking cunt I've ever seen.'* Suddenly, they're throwing punches and traffic cones, the lot. 'I learned to fight rather than run away,' he says. 'I was like, *I'm not running from this. If you attack me, yeah, maybe you might give me a belting. But you're not getting away with that without some sort of injury.*'

Mat is seventeen when he meets his first long-term boyfriend at a meeting of BAGS. He lives in Alton, a nearby market town, and they end up living together there for a while. 'He was very much on the alt side as well,' says Mat. 'He wasn't goth, but he was into indie bands like The Wedding Present, understood the culture I was from.' Outside one of the pubs in Basingstoke they're both on the kerb, drunk, Mat's boyfriend sat on his lap. 'The landlady came out and said, *What you doing? You queer or something?* We just went, *Yeah!* And she went, *Oh, er, oh, ah, er . . . !* And I was like, *That's your fault really, isn't it?*' He describes Alton as 'very like the village in *Hot Fuzz*. It's very buttoned down. Nobody says anything.'

Since then, he's lived in various suburban locales: Camberley in Surrey ('I found that the most dispiriting, because there is no direct train to London from Camberley,' he says. 'And that really lets you know you're in the suburbs . . . You've just been in this really vibrant environment, and you come out the station and it's just you and the kebab van'); Farnborough in Hampshire; and now Three Bridges in West Sussex. He and his partner weighed up whether or not to get a flat in Camden or a house with a garden in Three Bridges, and gardening and cats won. 'It's not suburban in a way where you feel suffocated,' he says. 'There's stuff going on. I walk down the street and people go, *I like your hair*, or *I like what you're wearing*, or whatever it is. It's a really different vibe.' A few months before we speak, this new accepting suburban spell is broken. 'Someone shouted the word *queer* out of a van as it dopplered past,' he says, 'and I was like, *How retro!* I've not been shouted at in the street for about twenty years. Amazing!' He grins. 'Still got it.'

The bedrock of suburban gay societies is the coffee evening. Apparently, they are held at members' homes because new recruits might find that less stressful than a pub or community hall, though anyone with a passing knowledge of suburban etiquette will know this is likely to be absolutely terrifying for newcomers, and it makes for a highly charged atmosphere. Not least for the host. 'I remember I attended a coffee evening and found that the host had plenty of coffee and biscuits but only two pints of milk,' writes Eddie James, the chairman of the Guildford Area Gay Society. 'He had never hosted a coffee evening before and had not sought anyone's advice. He was horrified when told how many might turn up.' In the event, there were twenty-six packed into his house. 'Luckily for him, the local shop stayed open late so we were able to buy extra milk.'[36] The newsletter follows that with a piece about a serial killer targeting gay men, which adds perspective.

By the 1990s, membership of these groups is dropping off, as LGBTQ+ bars and clubs begin to draw younger people away from the suburbs and into the towns. And so instead they start to become vehicles for nostalgia. 'John's evening started slowly amid his fascinating collection of novelty lighting effects and executive relaxers,' writes one member, Bernard, of a meeting a few months later. Guests are asked to bring along a song that means something to them, and for some it transports them back decades. One plays a romantic film theme, 'The Dream of Olwen', which brings Bernard 'memories of a large Polyphone 78 of the same piece being played on a walnut-veneered Ekco radiogram'.[37] Another brings Tom Robinson's 'Glad to Be Gay', recorded seventeen years earlier, and this group of older men talk about how a recent law change still criminalises young gay men under the age of eighteen, the inequalities living on in supposedly more enlightened times. There are also copies of old newsletters to hand, and they begin reading out to each other lists of social events from the late 1970s. 'It demonstrated how active the society was then,' writes Bernard. 'Long forgotten names prompted memories of past members . . .' Perhaps there is a longing for those more chaotic days of long hair and protests, or a sense of relief that things are settling down for this group of middle-aged men, once out fighting for their rights and pushing to explore how gay Guildford might actually be, and now nipping to the corner shop for a top-up of semi-skimmed and some Gypsy Creams.

A SUPERHERO FOR CHELMSFORD

The Essex Pride march heads down Viaduct Road, past a row of shops and former industrial units built into the Victorian arches beneath raised train tracks. They pass the indie record shop, the men's spa, the tattoo parlour, all of which display welcoming rainbow flags and messages of support. This is the bohemian fringe of Chelmsford, a hipster neighbourhood grown up in old industrial sites just beyond a strip of takeaways and dry cleaners. Halfway down, the marchers pass Dark Side Comics, where the greatest welcome of all awaits. The proprietor, Bucky, stands at the door, grinning and waving at the passing marchers. Around the doorway are clustered younger faces too, teenagers from the town too nervous to join the parade, or just curious to see it go by. 'I orchestrated it with Pride so that we would be the road to Pride,' Bucky tells me, 'to give people a route to walk down. I wanted them to be safe, and that they weren't going to get shouted at for carrying rainbow flags and stuff.' Bucky calls the teenagers 'my kids. I ended up having this community of fifteen and younger that congregated there,' they recall. 'A lot of them, their parents would not let them go to Pride.' Instead, Bucky suggests their parents drop them off at the shop so they can join in the festivities without their parents knowing and be there later when their parents drop by to pick them up. Two trans women come by to change into the clothes they want to wear, because they aren't out at home. And for younger queer kids, the shop is a staging post, somewhere they can hang out and watch it all go by without having to throw themselves into it. What had started as a small indie comics shop rapidly becomes so much more to the young queer community of Chelmsford. 'It was amazing,' says Bucky. And they know how needed this place is.

Bucky grows up in Great Baddow, once a village and now part of the wider Essex sprawl. 'It was lots of old people that say, *Hello*,' they recall. 'You see the same people in the village shop every day.' But youthful Bucky never really feels like they fit in. Perhaps it's the enormous backpack in the shape of Jar Jar Binks's head and the spider hairgrips that mark them out as different at primary school ('a strange little creature,' says Bucky, 'I think I've always been'), or the colourful hair, piercings and tattoos they acquire when they become a teenager. 'I had bright pink hair that was big,' Bucky tells me. 'I used to backcomb it like my dad did in the seventies.' Bucky's dad, who'd been a punk in Harlow, used to get all sorts of hassle for sticking out, and the secret was not to care. 'I'd go into town every Saturday and I would get spat at,' Bucky recalls, 'and you say it to people now and they're like, *What, for having pink hair?* I'm like, *Yeah!* Literally every weekend someone would try and start a fight or throw things at you.' Bucky would pass by oblivious. 'We would go out into town and people would be like, *Everybody's staring at you.* I genuinely wouldn't have noticed.' At home, Bucky is a keen comics geek when being one is not considered cool. 'I would hide my comics under my bed if anyone came to the house,' they recall. 'Like fifteen-year-old boys would be hiding porn, I was hiding comics.' Top of the list were those mutant outsiders the X-Men, 'which I feel like is every queer kid's experience'.

Growing up with parents who have been punks is a huge bonus, 'parents that were like, *Do whatever you want. It doesn't fucking matter what anybody thinks, dress how you want, do what you want, we'll help you dye your hair.*' Back in the day, Bucky's dad wore a lot of make-up and dresses, and ended up in fights because of it. 'It turns out a man wearing a dress walking through Harlow is not the best idea.' Bucky also has a gay uncle on their dad's side, but doesn't see much of him because he lives in Brighton. They don't have a particularly gendered upbringing, and when puberty hits it's a bit of a shock. *Oh, hang on. I don't have this neutral body any more. I don't identify with what it's turning into.* 'People would literally say out loud, *Oh, is that a boy or a girl?*' says Bucky. 'I'm like, *Actually, that's the question. Because I'm not either of those.*' But growing up in the 1990s there's very little information about being non-binary out there. An internet search when Bucky is in their mid-twenties changes everything. 'I read the term "non-binary" and read what it was. It was like, *Oh my God, oh my God! I've just read this sentence and it's just explained my whole life!*' It's like a new beginning. 'I wish I'd had the vocabulary and information to explain that a lot earlier. But it just wasn't there.'

Being bisexual feels more straightforward, in part heralded by a youthful obsession with Lola Bunny in *Space Jam*. Everyone at secondary school seems focused on having boyfriends and girl-friends, while Bucky is happy just to go home and disappear into comics. Going to college in Southend, with its cohort of arty, alternative and queer students, changes all of that. 'I was like, *EVERYONE'S attractive,*' says Bucky, slightly astonished. 'There's been attractive people *this whole time.*' Not that they can do much about it, what with being extremely shy, but it's good to know that they're out there. Meanwhile, they finally find a group of local friends too, alternative kids from all the other schools nearby, who start to hang out together in the park. There's just four of them to begin with. Pretty soon, the group has grown beyond all expectation, just as later Bucky's shop will too. 'I've got a brilliant Polaroid of thirty to fifty kids all sitting together.' On a sunny weekend the park would be full of what they call 'these absolute weirdos. You'd have a group of goth kids, then a group of more emo kids, and then the little skateboard kids, but because they were all weird in their own spaces, they would all come together.' Fearless – well, some of the time. 'In the summer mostly, otherwise we would get wet.'

Bucky is twenty-three when they open Dark Side Comics. 'I was just like, *I want to open a sho*p,' they say, '*I want to make it somewhere cool that people can come and feel comfortable, sell some comics*, that's all my expectations.' But from that starting point, something much bigger begins to flower. 'The community that grew around it, it was just the most loving, welcoming, diverse, amazing community of people from all different backgrounds, all different ages. So many young queer people, older queer people as well. But so many youngsters coming up.' People who no longer want to hide their X-Men comics under the bed, but could be out and proud about them, who want to find a friendly shopkeeper to geek out with about Captain America for hours, their enthusiasm running so bright Bucky could run the lights off them. 'But even with those intentions it became something so much bigger than I had ever anticipated it being.'

After six happy years the shop closes, but many of the customers are still in touch today. 'I get messages from those kids, and they've finished uni and they're going off to do jobs. They're all out and proud and being gay all over the place.' Bucky has even become friends with some of their parents, the connections and community living on beyond the railway arches. The kids had wandered into the shop often feeling isolated and lonely, but through the community there left with a whole group of new friends. 'I would have loved that as a kid,' says Bucky. And for them, it wasn't just the shop but the shopkeeper that made the difference. Many had not met a non-binary person who was successful and happy in their life. 'A lot of them said to me, *You made me feel that I would be okay.'* When Bucky was growing up, there wasn't a generation above them that they could look at and go, *Oh, there's the non-binary people, I get it.* But now they have accidentally become that person to a new generation of kids in Chelmsford.

'I got top surgery a few years ago,' they tell me, 'and I was like, *You can all see the gory pictures,* because I think education is important.' But getting people to understand the journey is not always straightforward. Which is why the most unlikely connections can sometimes be the most rewarding. When one of their aunts gets a boob job, she tells Bucky, *You've just had the opposite of me. When I had my boob job I suddenly felt, Oh my God, this is what I've always wanted to look like.* Bucky is delighted, this is exactly how they felt too, and how wonderful to encounter such empathy. These days, Bucky is asked to talk about their experience in local schools. 'I went to a secondary school that, to me, is quite progressive, they're quite on top of it, they do really well. Their teachers will have pronoun badges and all this sort of thing. Even then, there was a girl there who was maybe year nine, she was like, *I think I might like girls and boys, but I'm not sure, is that okay?* That was it. That was the question. I was like, *Of course that's okay. You can like girls this week or boys next week, it doesn't matter. You're figuring it out.'*

'I'd always said, if my dad was born now, I'm pretty sure he'd be non-binary,' says Bucky. 'I think at this point, he's leaned so much into the masculine.' One day they're having a conversation about what he would do if he woke up and he was a woman. 'He was like, *But everyone's wished they could be the opposite gender, haven't they?* And I'm like, *No, Dad! No, not everybody has.* It was like, *I don't think I'll unpack that.* I was like, *Okay.'* Even a fearless superhero like Bucky has their limits.

At last, Edith gets through to the Samaritans. After thirty years of marriage to Norman in the respectable suburbs of Coventry, she has fallen in love with a woman. A woman who Norman has met, taken a dislike to and scared away; a woman who has since moved on from Edith and found a new partner. Edith has overheard her sisters saying lesbians are disgusting and should be shot. And so now here she is, pouring her heart out to a stranger on the phone, unable to keep it all in any more. As she's speaking, the woman on the other end begins to laugh. *What do you do when you're with your husband?* asks the Samaritan. *Do you lie back and think of England?* Shocked, Edith puts the phone down. 'I was so lonely. People just don't realise. I couldn't ever tell anyone,' she explains to Jane Traies for her remarkable book of lesbian life stories, *Now You See Me*.[38] Many years later, after Norman's death and at the age of eighty-five, Edith comes out to her children and grandchildren, the weight of the secret she has carried all of these years finally beginning to lift.

IT'S DIFFERENT IN GATESHEAD

It's never easy knowing when to tell people. Mark's sister is doing Christmas dinner; it's just easier now their parents are divorced. Like many an eighteen-year-old on Christmas Day, Mark has a hangover, but knows he needs to make the effort as his dad is here. 'And I was sitting talking to me dad,' Mark tells me, 'and I looked down and realised I'd left all me nails on. And he was staring at them.' At this point, his dad is the only member of his family he's not out to. The previous night, Mark had staggered into Newcastle in full drag. 'It was a struggle to find a size-11 pair of high heels,' he recalls. 'I just about managed to get over the complexities of tights and things like that.' Mark is a big guy, and the only dress he found that fitted was from his mum's wedding from her second marriage. There were big dangly Pat Butcher earrings. A punk friend – the magic punk friend becoming an unexpected saviour to many a suburban queer in these tales – came over to help him and his mates with their make-up and hair. 'It was an experience,' he says. But now here he is, halfway through roast turkey, and his dad is staring at his chipped and painted nails. So he plunges in and tells him, *Dad, I'm gay.* 'He went, *Oh, I always knew,*' says Mark. 'When you turned eighteen in the North East, there was a massive working men's club scene up here. So part of your rite of passage was your dad would buy you your working men's club membership card, and you would go for your first pint. He did that with my older brother, who joined the army. I've got a younger brother who's nearly two years younger than me, and he did that with him.

And he never did that with me.' Not, he adds, because he was ashamed, but just because he always knew Mark was different.

When he tells his mum she seems disappointed, but he's not sure if that's because he's gay or just because she's worried about him in the mid-1980s with the AIDS crisis and homophobia to deal with. His sister has been told by fellow hairdressers that Mark has been seen in Rockshots, Newcastle's gay club, and so she asks him about it. *Well, that's fine*, she says, when he comes out. *I'm here to support you*. Up until this point he's dogmatically convinced himself that it's just a phase, and that it will be over by the time he's eighteen. But when he passes that milestone and he's still very much gay, he finally begins to accept it, and so that year, 1986, becomes a significant moment in his life. He even travels down to London to attend his first Pride. 'I remember being on the Tube with all of these gay people and thinking *Wow, for the first time, I'm in a majority rather than a minority*, and feeling part of something.' It's quite a moment for a boy who's still living in the Victorian suburbs of Gateshead. He's also lucky to go out and about with a friend from school who's gay too. All these years later they're still best mates, hanging out together.

A year later, and he's living down the road with a guy who identifies as straight, but who goes out with Mark for some time. One day, builders working on the flats see them through the window asleep in bed together. 'And they stopped working on the flats,' he recalls. 'So that had an effect.' And when he moves to another flat nearby, one morning he finds homophobic graffiti sprayed on his front door and 'RIP' on his car. 'So that was difficult,' he says, with some understatement. 'It's a different time, and the North East was a different place,' he says. 'I'm not making excuses for it, not in the slightest. But this is a suburb, this was an industrial area. And people just didn't talk about those kinds of things.' But they did, it seems, spray-paint them.

For a long time Mark lives in Edinburgh, but now he's back in the suburbs of Gateshead again, this time living with his partner. He's also the primary carer for his mum, who has Alzheimer's, and when we speak is looking after his sister too, who is suffering from long Covid. 'I think it's responsibility that keeps us here,' he says, a familiar story to carers everywhere. He has dreams of retiring to Greece to open a taverna. 'I think I'm too old now to live in a city,' he says. 'I think I've suburbanised myself.' Yet he still feels uncomfortable holding hands with his partner out and about, especially due to the right-wing cultural climate, the casual hate that increasingly greets trans and non-binary people reminding him of the prejudice he faced as a young gay man. He does notice younger queer couples on the bus holding hands though, which makes him happy. It reminds him of how, in his clubbing days, he would only be able to be himself for a couple of hours, until it was 'back to the suburbs and hiding everything again'. These days, what he yearns for is a safe space to go out to where he can just relax with his partner and his friends, a coffee shop or quiet pub rather than a banging club night. 'I think as an older gay person, you start going back onto the fringes again,' he says. 'I think it's come round that I'm no longer in that community. I'm lucky that I've got a partner and I'm lucky that I've got a friend and we can be a little community.' Mark drifting back to the edges, and hoping for a better world there.

Rochford in Essex reminds me so much of New Addington. Maybe it's the curving streets of brown-brick post-war munici-pal houses set behind low hedges and lumpy verges. It's largely unremarkable, save for its fame as the founding place of the Peculiar People, a Christian offshoot of Wesleyanism that rejected frivolity, medicine and war. These days, its reputation for peculiarity rests on a different source, after being labelled in the press as *the straightest place in Britain*. The 2021 census for the first time included questions on sexual orientation and gender identity, and the data yielded this particular nugget, where only 1.6 per cent of the town's population identified as lesbian, gay or bisexual (against a national average of nearly 4 per cent), along with a trans and non-binary population in the area numbering 145. One in twenty Rochfordians didn't answer those questions on the census, more than double the national average. Perhaps its conservative ageing population was the reason for a lack of diversity? Maybe its proximity to the coastal towns of Essex, or the capital, had drawn gay residents away? Or perhaps people there just didn't feel able to respond honestly to that part of the census? In reply, Chris Taylor, a Rochford resident, set up a local LGBTQ+ Facebook group, which now has 173 members. It soon begins to receive trolling and hate, the old control mechanisms of suburbia taken online, the poison pens of invisible neighbours. 'I know there are going to be people out there against it,' he tells the *Guardian*. 'But they can't dictate to us that we can't be who we want to be in our community.'[39]

In contrast to Rochford, Britain's smallest Pride event has recently been held in the Warwickshire town of Rugby; more specifically in Batt Close, where forty neighbours organised their own celebrations for LGBTQ+ people and their allies, marching 80 metres past the newly built semis. Sponsored body-waxing raised £100 for the Terrence Higgins Trust, while home-made costumes and decorations, and high-heels races up and down the close, helped promote it as a safe space for all (apart from those who find it hard to run in heels). Taylor Wimpey, developer of the estate, produced their own expression of pride on their website. 'It is hoped that the residents at Batt Close will continue to host Pride events for years to come,' they wrote, beside features promoting their new house types, called things like The Gosford and The Plumdale.

Much of the cultural snobbery about suburbia has hinged on the idea that it is boring. But it's the kind of boring that LGBTQ+ people have often felt excluded from. Generations of us would have loved the opportunity to be so dull, or at least the choice when faced with the sometimes terrifying alternative – to be open. For a lot of gay people, coming out of the closet has meant coming out of suburbia too. So much so that the suburbs themselves often feel synonymous with the closet, a Narnia where there's always flag-waving but never Pride. But suburbia is not so straightforward and, despite the best efforts of its guardians and promoters, it never has been. It's a myriad of hidden worlds, fuelled by secrets and omissions. Those worlds are now more visible, those old no-go areas (either physical or cultural) bypassed no longer. And it's where the energy in much of our national conversation comes from, where cultures clash and subcultures are born and thrive. Just think of all the queer goths we've met across these pages. It's where life actually is, even if it often feels like it's elsewhere. Increasingly, it's where many LGBTQ+ people are choosing to be, too.

And yet, for all of that, LGBTQ+ visibility in the suburbs remains a curious thing. Sure, we have seen big advances since the 1990s, from an equalised age of consent to civil partnerships, equal marriage and adoption rights, all of which seem designed to fit us right in to those patterns of suburban life. And apps might have made hooking up or connecting with other queer people easier than ever. But to anyone not paying attention, we can still feel lonely or invisible here. Or all too visible, if meeting abuse on the streets or social media. And recent rulings about gender identity have undone decades of legal progress for trans and non-binary people, threatening their identities and enshrining a hostile climate in law, just as Section 28 did for all LGBTQ+ people for over two decades. Suburbia can often feel like a manifestation of those reactionary attitudes, projecting the privilege of straight nuclear families on to the rest of us. The secret reality that no Neighbourhood Watch will tell you is that all families and households are different, no matter how tightly some might cling to ideas of fitting in and of appearing 'normal'.

The most aspirational of suburban homes can feel more cookie-cutter than ever, too, sliding from the magnolia minimalism of the nineties to the tasteful grey plague of today, stripped of colour, renouncing all memory of the seventies excess of nylon sheets and swirly carpets. As we endure a period of perma-housing crisis, with the closure of pubs and shops altering the social fabric of our towns, along with the rise of home working, we see something else occurring: the urban trailblazers of the queer community returning to the suburbs, to a place once – still? – feared and derided. Now it feels a little less disconnected than it used to, in its homogenous, homo-hostile twentieth-century past. Meanwhile, those semis keep being redecorated and recast over and over, a form of transitioning that keeps pushing at the boundaries. For every Farrow & Ball paint job there's a maximalist palace and a ramshackle retreat. These old homes play host to new ways of living and working, new ideals and aspirations. On the outside, ornamental fish ponds, gnomes and crazy paving have given way to decking, astroturf and barbecue stations, stained-glass porches and Ring doorbells. Inside, more has changed than just the décor. These are the houses that have been the backdrop to the domestic dramas of the day, be they *Brookside*, *The Buddha of Suburbia* or *Big Boys*. And to ours too.

For many of us, the suburbs have been places of oppression, of not belonging, of boredom, of bogus notions of 'normality', and the thought of moving or returning there may fill us with dread – or bafflement. But we should hope and expect to be ourselves there, with all the constellations of diversity that implies, places where hedging decreases as each year goes by. Creating new families and connections, some of us demanding to be at the heart of things rather than the margins, others happy to live a quieter life under the radar in the cul-de-sacs and crescents. Or embracing both, the thrill of identities that can be fluid, both outside of the mainstream but also at the very centre too, in the restless tides of the worlds we live in. Making ourselves at home where once we were pushed out. Belonging.

DEEP WATER IN DULVERTON

Cara lets out a cry of shock. The river is ice cold and fast flowing. Her dad leaves her in the middle and wades backwards towards the shore. *Come towards me*, he says. Cara is four; she's had a couple of swimming lessons, but the nearest pool is a forty-minute drive away, so not ideal for her parents, and besides it's a Dulverton tradition to throw your kids into the river to see if they sink or swim. 'That was kind of normal,' Cara tells me. 'This was the feral childhood years of the '70s.' The River Barle winds its way through Exmoor and on to the Somerset market town of Dulverton. Where Cara lives is the shadow of a suburb, an echo of those bigger places connected to cities full of busy commuters, but here just some straggle on the edge of a small town, a municipal estate of plain cream-washed 1960s semis and bungalows landed on lumpy grassland. 'When I think of suburbs it's perhaps like a hinterland, or that space between the centre and the rural,' she explains, 'the other. We were in that middle bit.' By the time she has learned to swim her parents have split up, her dad ending up in Taunton, while Cara lives in the bungalow with her mum, a bungalow designed for pensioners in a place where she's sixty years younger than any of her neighbours. By the time she's a teenager she might be listening to The Cure in her bedroom, but knows all of Daniel O'Donnell's words because of what comes through the walls from next door.

Her parents are one of the first to get divorced in the area – 'everybody else just seemed to suffer in quite unhappy marriages'. Her dad is a farmer, and it's on the farm while doing the dutiful birds and bees talk that he comes out to her. *Not everyone is like that*, he explains. *I'm not like that. I like men.* 'That's how he told me,' recalls Cara. 'And it doesn't mean anything. He's my dad, and I love him. But to other people in rural Somerset in the '70s and '80s, it meant something very, very different to them.' Kids at school, for example, who hear from their parents that her dad is gay, and bully Cara because of it. They might not know what it means, but they know that it makes Cara different. And although she does feel different, that doesn't feel like a bad thing. After all, she sees her dad most days, and her parents are still friends. 'They're really caring,' she says. 'I had total wraparound love from both of them. I've looked at other friends' families, who were desperately unhappy. I was like, *Actually, this isn't a broken family situation.*' Her dad isn't the only gay farmer around – although, unlike him, the others tend to be married and closeted – and he has boyfriends and lovers. He sells the farm in 1982 and moves to a 1970s brick newbuild in Taunton, working as a motorcycle courier, but Cara still gets to spend lots of time with him. He would go off to the West Country's two gay clubs, in Bristol and Plymouth, and up to London to Heaven. There's even a tiny underground gay club in Taunton, frequently raided by the police, and Cara gets to know the clubbers well. 'I was raised by some incredible gay men,' she recalls. Not just her dad but Steve, his partner, who she thinks of as her stepdad, and their friends from that tiny gay club, all alongside her mother in the bungalow in Dulverton. 'It was chalk and cheese, to put it mildly,' she says. 'There was a kind of mask that I had to put on at school just to get me through it, to rise above the bullying.'

But soon even this beautiful new family is under threat. When Cara is eight, she goes with her dad to visit the hospital in Taunton to see Steve. 'They'd closed off a whole ward and he was the only one there,' she tells me, 'and they had screens around his bed and I could sit 20 feet or so away from him and I couldn't go any closer. And Dad, to get close to him, had to be fully haz-matted.' This is HIV care in 1983. It's the last time she sees him, because Steve becomes 'something like the fourth person to have HIV/AIDS on their death certificate in the UK'. Soon there are other gaps in her dad's tight-knit group of friends, men she'd got used to seeing who suddenly aren't there any more. 'And that was my life experience from the age of – well, Steve died in '83, '84 – say eight or nine,' she tells me.

A couple of years later, Cara is waiting anxiously at the front door of the bungalow, because today the 'AIDS: Don't Die of Ignorance' leaflets are being delivered. 'I was hoping it would get to me before I had to get the bus to school,' she says, 'and it did.' *I don't want them to see that you're waiting for this,* her mum says anxiously. Cara can sense the curtains twitching, all the grand-parents in the other bungalows watching her, watching each other. And she thinks, *You should read this leaflet, grandparents, because I doubt you know your grandson is gay – but I do.* 'There's such complex, deep lives behind those net curtains,' she says. 'Every little house is its own insular little island. There wasn't much coming together of people beyond neighbourly things, but talking about your interior life, or talking about the travails that your family had been through and the pain that they've seen, that kind of thing was never talked about.'

When Cara comes to do her A-levels, she chooses to study in Taunton, and so moves in with her dad in the red-brick suburb of Staplegrove. Compared to Dulverton it feels like New York, with pubs and shops that stay open beyond 4 p.m. Life is so dif-ferent from the bungalow. 'Every Saturday afternoon, we would watch the *Stop Making Sense* video really, really loud and dance around the room,' she recalls. 'My dad would do the hoovering to "Groove Is in the Heart".' They cram into his sporty MG and sing Pet Shop Boys, Erasure and Hazell Dean songs, or dance round the house. He's big into the early-nineties rave scene, so there are tales of his adventures in clubs or warehouses or fields to catch up on. And she also has to endure him watching endless sport on TV, going, *For fuck's sake, when is this cricket match gonna end?* But still their days are ruled by the kind of domesticity she was used to in Dulverton. 'Our life was really suburban,' she says. *Haven't you got to get to college now?* he'd nag her. *Why aren't you out the door?* He does the classic dad thing of driving her to gigs. *I'm coming to get you at half past ten,* he'd say. 'I mean, he never would,' she remembers, 'he was always late. But you know, he tried.' Living with him fuses together different sorts of lives, the ordinary with the avant garde. 'He was showing me wonderful things about the world and about humanity.'

And for Cara, it's a massive turnaround. Whereas at school her unusual domestic life was a cause for bullying, here it makes her the most interesting student at college. She describes it as 'like a debutante party just for myself'. The excitement is liberating. 'I told people there that I had a gay dad, and it made me really fucking cool. I dated the college heartthrob for three years. I would never have got on his radar if I hadn't had a gay dad.' She also finds a group of kids with similar tastes and clothes, the oddballs, and they become a gang. 'They all came around to my dad's and they all got on, and it suddenly felt really grown-up and mature. Like, *Oh my God, I'm such an adult.* It was absolutely brilliant.' Much of the liberation she feels is powered by her dad's eclectic group of friends. 'There was a lot of people there at the time that weren't called this then, but were gender-queer, non-binary. So they were very much part of that group that was bringing me up as well.' All along she sees that there are ways to live differently, despite being surrounded by all the eighties and nineties homophobia and misogyny. But because of the world her dad has shown her, she knows she doesn't have to stay in Dulverton and marry the boy next door. So she heads off to Brighton, to university, and feels the suburbs falling away.

'I didn't necessarily put a label on my sexuality, though most of my relationships were with men,' she explains, 'and I guess I kind of got over that affliction.' She laughs. 'For a long time I called myself straight, though I did sleep with a lot of women and I did have relationships with women.' After all, she was taught that you love who you love. 'There's some reverse privilege in that, because I didn't actually have to come out to my mum or my dad.' She never feels different or other. 'I took some girlfriends home to meet my mum, and she just didn't blink an eye and she didn't ask me, *Does that mean you're a lesbian now? It's just, This is the person I'm with now.*' She does sometimes call herself queer, but has a difficult time reconciling that word with her father's painful experience of it. Cara is currently in a relationship with a trans man. 'My partner and I have talked a lot about the word "queer", and they say, *You're so queer, Cara, you're so queer!* But when I was introduced to the word "queer", it was by my dad. If you are called queer, you will be put in prison and it could mean life or death for you. So I kind of struggle with that word, though I'm getting better.' Reclaiming it brings back the trauma of the generation who pioneered Pride marches, ever ready to flee if things kicked off.

She's at university, about to take her final second-year exam, when she gets the call to return home. *AIDS motherfucker* has been spray-painted on her father's garage door. The social worker is out of their depth. 'It was kind of leaked that there's a man in this community with HIV/AIDS,' she recalls. Cara has noticed his health going downhill over the period of a year. 'In the back of my mind, I was thinking, *I wonder if it is that*, and lo and behold, it did turn out to be that.' But later she discovers something else. Her father also has Creutzfeldt-Jakob disease. He has been vegetarian most of his life, so how he ends up with mad cow disease remains a mystery. 'There's the joke there that my dad was just like a complete label whore who wanted just to collect what was really in fashion at the time,' she says. For the last couple of months of her father's life, Cara, back from university, shares caring duties with one of his mates. Three of the neighbours routinely ignore her and her father. 'They were really suspicious of a gay man with a daughter and thinking abuse might be happening, with all the prejudice of the time.' Yet one remains kind and friendly throughout it all, smiling and saying hello and having a bit of chat when they see Cara. In hospital, the palliative care nursing given to him is totally different from what Steve had to endure a decade before. But Cara is initially worried when she discovers that the sister of a girl from school is to be one of his nurses. 'And she was great,' she says, with relief, 'and she actually said to me, *We were always so in awe of the life that we knew that you had, or suspected that you had growing up, but we didn't know what to say to you.* It's like, *Fuck, I wish I'd known that! I wish I'd known that, because I felt something very, very different.*'

Along from her dad's house, past the parade of shops and the Spar, is the crematorium, all in the same '70s red brick. *Oh my goodness, that's a posh house*, people would say. *Oh no, it's the cremmy.* On the day of his funeral, the collision between the different sorts of people in his life would surely have delighted him. 'There was the small-c conservative family, and then all these people turning up with smiley-face T-shirts, that kind of thing. Just a whole tribe of gay men of different types, and transgender people in there as well. It was such a mix.' Cara learned from an early age about code-switching, keeping the different worlds separate and holding secrets close, things that she discovered much earlier than her peers. Here at the funeral those barriers are blurring, the codes cracked. She's been that bored teenager, hanging round bus stops or friends' houses till late. 'All of those usual tropes of growing up in the suburbs,' she says. 'But when you shut the door of my house, a very different set-up.'

People are still amazed by the life she lived when she was growing up. 'It's totally normal to me,' she says, 'because I lived it.' And she has managed to negotiate the curious codes of both her mum's and dad's houses. 'The social rules of suburbia, you know them through osmosis, you know them through socialising. And they trap you and then you get stuck. And I could see friends of mine at school so desperately unhappy. I was really lucky I had that when I was with my dad. I had this pressure valve, or I had this sense of freedom. I had this sense of there's a world out there, and you can go and get it. It's really possible. I've got one step closer to it by just getting to Taunton.' All these years later here she still is, swimming against the current, just like her dad taught her, two generations of LGBTQ+ people making suburbia their home – because, of course, it is their home.

ACKNOWLEDGEMENTS

This book has relied hugely on the generosity and time of all the interviewees. I'm so proud to share their extraordinary stories, and I feel honoured that they put their trust in me to be able to tell them. It's been brilliant meeting other people who saw a gap in LGBTQ+ social history and realised that their experiences could help illuminate an otherwise opaque part of our experience. Some of the interviews didn't make it into the book, and I'd like to thank those people too, because everyone I spoke to helped inform the writing, either directly or indirectly.

It would not have been possible without the help of the Bishopsgate Institute, whose archive of LGBTQ+ publications was invaluable, and whose staff were enormously helpful and knowledgeable. I'd also especially like to show my appreciation to members of the Croydon Area Gay Society for their time and generosity of spirit. Many others also helped put me in touch with people to speak to, and particular gratitude is due to Leigh Bird, Bold Mellon, Ant Grindrod, Lorna Rees, Christine Townley and Megan Townley-Wakelin.

Much love to my friend and agent, Nicola Barr of Rye Literary, for helping me get this book off the ground. Fred Baty commissioned it for Faber and his kindness and enthusiasm really helped it at an early stage, and Fiona Crosby's insightful edits really helped shape it. Likewise, Jenni Davis's hawk-like copy-editing has wrung out some of the unintended ambiguities and let the intended ones resonate a little harder. I'd like to thank Josephine Salverda for the page design, Sarah Stoll in production, Pete Adlington for the cover design, and Jess Kim and Lauren Nicoll for their campaign. Big thanks too to Sam Brown and team, Mary Cannam, Catherine Daly, Rachel Darling, Sarah Davison-Aitkins, Paddy Fox, Katie Hall, Fiona Smith, Hayley Sothinathan and Sara Talbot. I'd also like to thank the bookshops, libraries, archives, festivals and arts organisations who have supported my books, had me along for a talk or a walk, and allowed me to make a bit of an idiot of myself. And much love to all the LGBTQ+ organisations, libraries, booksellers and writers who have helped make a book like this feel at home in the world.

To all the friends who have supported me throughout the writing of the book, and have put up with me being elusive, much love and dancing: Mike Althorpe, Susan and Dennis Le Baigue, Helen Barrett, Mark Brummitt, Chris Butler, Dylan Rees Coshan, Alison Davies, Tom Dyckhoff, Jo Ellis, Mark Evans, Chris Gough, Lynsey Hanley, Colin Harvey, Alex Linsdell, Christian Manley, Peter Matthews, Nicky McIver, Andy Miller, Tina Miller, Mary Morris, Noel Murphy, Sylvia Novak, Anna Pallai, Donna Payne, Richard de Pesando, Jude Rogers, Emily Rose, Lesley Rose, Conrad Westmaas, Richard Woods and Thaddeus Zupančič.

During the writing, my brother Paul and my sister-in-law Fern died, and I hope their spirit of mischief and bloody-mindedness suffuses this book. Their daughters, Lily and Daisy, have been an astonishing inspiration throughout, as has Ben. My brother Ian continues to be a huge support, as do Ann and Jane Nightingale. Most of all, thank you to my partner, Adam Nightingale, for helping to navigate all those strange and wonderful bits of suburbia together, from the garden centre to the Dunelm café.

And finally, thank you for reading.

FURTHER READING

On my travels I've encountered many books that I'm sure would appeal to anyone interested in this subject, so here are some starting points.

ORAL HISTORY

Hall Carpenter Archives/Gay Men's Oral History Group, *Walking After Midnight: Gay Men's Life Stories* (Routledge, 1989)

Hall Carpenter Archives/Lesbian Oral History Project, *Inventing Ourselves: Lesbian Life Stories* (Routledge, 1989)

Bryan Magee, *One in Twenty: A Study of Homosexuality in Men and Women* (Secker & Warburg, 1966)

Suzanne Neild and Rosalind Pearson, *Women Like Us* (The Women's Press, 1992)

Kevin Porter and Jeffrey Weeks (eds), *Between the Acts: Lives of Homosexual Men 1885–1967* (Routledge, 1991)

Norena Shopland, *Forbidden Lives: LGBT Stories from Wales* (Seren, 2017)

Jane Traies (ed.), *Now You See Me: Lesbian Life Stories* (Tollington Press, 2018)

MEMOIR AND BIOGRAPHY

Quentin Crisp, *The Naked Civil Servant* (Flamingo, 1985)

Michael Gilson, *Behind the Privet Hedge: Richard Sudell, the Suburban Garden and the Beautification of Britain* (Reaktion, 2024)

Hugo Greenhalgh, *The Diaries of Mr Lucas: Notes from a Lost Gay Life* (Atlantic, 2024)

Jackie Kay, *Red Dust Road* (Picador, 2010)

Oscar Moore, *PWA: Looking AIDS in the Face* (Picador, 1996)

Tony Nicholson, *Shut That Door! The Definitive Biography of Larry Grayson* (Great Northern, 2017)

Peter Wildeblood, *Against the Law* (Penguin, 1957)

NARRATIVE HISTORY AND ESSAYS

Paul Baker, *Fabulosa! The Story of Polari, Britain's Secret Gay Language* (Reaktion, 2019)

Darryl W. Bullock, *Pride, Pop and Politics: Music, Theatre and LGBT Activism, 1970–2021* (Omnibus Press, 2022)

Christine Burns (ed.), *Trans Britain: Our Long Journey from the Shadows* (Unbound, 2018)

Matt Cook, *Queer Domesticities: Homosexuality and Home Life in Twentieth-Century London* (Palgrave Macmillan, 2014)

Matt Cook and Alison Oram, *Queer Beyond London* (Manchester University Press, 2022)

Hugh David, *On Queer Street: A Social History of British Homosexuality 1895–1995* (HarperCollins, 1997)

Martin Dines, *Gay Suburban Narratives in American and British Culture* (Palgrave Macmillan, 2010)

Dan Glass, *United Queerdom: From the Legends of the Gay Liberation Front to the Queers of Tomorrow* (Zed Books, 2020)

Rebecca Jennings, *Tomboys and Bachelor Girls: A Lesbian*

History of Post-War Britain 1945–71 (Manchester University Press, 2007)

Alkarim Jivani, *It's Not Unusual: A History of Lesbian and Gay Britain in the Twentieth Century* (Michael O'Mara, 1997)

Jason Okundaye, *Revolutionary Acts: Love & Brotherhood in Black Gay Britain* (Faber, 2024)

Jon Savage, *The Secret Public: How LGBTQ Resistance Shaped Popular Culture, 1955–1979* (Faber, 2024)

Peter Scott-Presland, *Amiable Warriors: A History of the Campaign for Homosexual Equality and Its Times*, Volume One (Paradise Press, 2015)

SUBURBAN HISTORY

Paul Barker, *The Freedoms of Suburbia* (Frances Lincoln, 2009)

Helena Barrett and John Phillips, *Suburban Style: The British Home, 1840–1960* (Little, Brown, 1993)

Tony Chapman and Jenny Hockey, *Ideal Homes? Social Change and Domestic Life* (Routledge, 1999)

Paul Oliver, Ian Davis and Ian Bentley, *Dunroamin: The Suburban Semi and Its Enemies* (Pimlico, 1981)

J. M. Richards, *The Castles on the Ground: The Anatomy of Suburbia* (John Murray, 1946)

A number of the contributors have also published books, including Jack Cornish (from the introduction) with his book on rambling, *The Lost Paths*; Cara Courage ('Deep Water in Dulverton'), who has edited books including *Trauma Informed Placemaking*, as well as several on *The Archers*; So Mayer ('Escape from Edgware'), who has published poetry, fiction and non-fiction, including *A Nazi Word for a Nazi Thing* and *Bad Language*; Karen McLeod

('The Woman Who Fell to Penge'), who has published a novel, *In Search of the Missing Eyelash*, and a memoir of life as cabin crew, *Lifting Off*; Rose Ruane ('The Eyes of Bearsden'), who has published two novels, *This Is Yesterday* and *Birding*; and Seena ('Love and Hate in Surbiton'), who publishes queer zines as Sina Sparrow.

NOTES

1 Kevin Porter and Jeffrey Weeks (eds), *Between the Acts: Lives of Homosexual Men 1885–1967* (Routledge, 1991), p. 25.

2 Quentin Crisp, *The Naked Civil Servant* (Fontana, 1977), p. 39.

3 Michael Gilson, *Behind the Privet Hedge* (Reaktion, 2024), p. 302.

4 Kevin Porter and Jeffrey Weeks (eds), *Between the Acts: Lives of Homosexual Men 1885–1967* (Routledge, 1991), p. 7.

5 Allan Horsfall, 'The Altrincham Lads', *Gay Life*, 5 October 1986, pp. 16–19.

6 Hall Carpenter Archives, Lesbian Oral History Group, *Inventing Ourselves: Lesbian Life Stories* (Routledge, 1989), p. 96.

7 Hall Carpenter Archives, Gay Men's Oral History Group, *Walking After Midnight: Gay Men's Life Stories* (Routledge, 1989), pp. 114–17.

8 *Guardian*, 24 June 2007.

9 Peter Scott-Presland, *Amiable Warriors: A History of the Campaign for Homosexual Equality and Its Times* (Paradise Press, 2015), p. 116.

10 Helene Curtis and Mimi Sanderson, *The Unsung Sixties: Memoirs of Social Innovation* (Whiting and Birch, 2004).

11 Peter Scott-Presland, *Amiable Warriors: A History of the Campaign for Homosexual Equality and Its Times* (Paradise Press, 2015), p. 84.

12 Alkarim Jivani, *It's Not Unusual: A History of Lesbian and Gay Britain in the Twentieth Century* (Michael O'Mara, 1997), p. 116.

13 Alkarim Jivani, *It's Not Unusual: A History of Lesbian and Gay Britain in the Twentieth Century* (Michael O'Mara, 1997), p. 120.

14 Hester Caulton in Rebecca Jennings, *Tomboys and Bachelor Girls: A Lesbian History of Post-War Britain 1945–71* (Manchester University Press, 2007), p. 55.

15 As of December 2024, thirty-eight of forty-nine recommendations have been implemented.

16 Kevin Porter and Jeffrey Weeks (eds), *Between the Acts: Lives of Homosexual Men 1885–1967* (Routledge, 1991), p. 65.

17 Kevin Porter and Jeffrey Weeks (eds), *Between the Acts: Lives of Homosexual Men 1885–1967* (Routledge, 1991), p. 70.

18 Bryan Magee, *One in Twenty: A Study of Homosexuality in Men and Women* (Secker & Warburg, 1966), p. 114.

19 Bryan Magee, *One in Twenty: A Study of Homosexuality in Men and Women* (Secker & Warburg, 1966), p. 175.

20 *Gay News*, no. 1, 1972, p. 6.

21 *Gay News*, no. 7, 1972, p. 8.

22 David Richardson, *Gay News*, issue 17, p. 2.

23 Antony Seib, *Thame Gazette*, 13 November 1973, p. 4.

24 Peter Scott-Presland, Obituary of Peter Katin, CHE Annual Report 2014–15, p. 12.

25 CAGS newsletter, May 2015, p. 1.

26 Peter Scott-Presland, *Amiable Warriors: A History of the Campaign for Homosexual Equality and Its Times* (Paradise Press, 2015), p. 443.

27 *Gay News*, 27 February–12 March 1975, no. 65. p. 1.

28 *Gay News*, 13–26 March 1975, no. 66, p. 9.

29 Checkpoint: CHE Croydon News, August 1979, p. 1.

30 Jackie Kay, *Red Dust Road* (Picador, 2010), p. 57.

31 Lisa Allardice, 'Poet Jackie Kay: "I could have been brought up by Tories!"', *Guardian*, 13 April 2024.

32 Checkpoint: CHE Croydon News, December 1980, p. 3.

33 Checkpoint: CHE Croydon News, May 1980, p. 2.

34 *Kent Gay Action*, issue 6, August 1982, p. 1.

35 Gay Men's Disabled Group Newsletter, Winter '83, p. 11.
36 GAGS Mag, Guildford Area Gay Society, no. 130, July–August 1993, p. 1.
37 GAGS Mag, Guildford Area Gay Society, no. 134, April–June 1994, p. 2.
38 Jane Traies, *Now You See Me* (Tollington, 2018), p. 29.
39 Geneva Abdul, '"It makes me less lonely": LGBTQ+ group thrives in England's straightest place', *Guardian*, 27 February 2025.